Access to Justice in Iran

Women, Perceptions, and Reality

This book offers a critical analysis of access to justice from international / Islamic perspectives to highlight various aspects of access to justice previously not discussed in the body of literature in the context of Iran. It provides a detailed picture of the workings of the Iranian legal system, together with a review of barriers that people face in their path to justice. This book explores legal empowerment and gender, and presents the findings of a survey study on the perceptions of Iranian women toward the justice system in their country. It is designed to focus on women's basic legal knowledge, their familiarity with legal procedure, their perceptions of cultural barriers, the issues that influence their preference for mechanisms of dispute solutions, and their level of satisfaction with their chosen courses of action. The book draws upon a broad range of primary and secondary data sources to offer pragmatic policy solutions.

Sahar (Zahra) Maranlou is an independent legal researcher who has written extensively in the fields of the Iranian legal system, women's rights, civil society, human rights, and Islamic law. She has consulted for a range of national and international organisations, including UNICEF and UNDP, and has provided Iranian organisations with her expert legal opinion in the areas of law and empowerment. She is a member of the steering committee for the Global Alliance of Justice Education. She is a visiting lecturer at the University of Brunel and has taught Islamic Law at the University of Warwick. Please visit her website, www.saharmaranlou.com, for additional information.

Access to Justice in Iran

Women, Perceptions, and Reality

SAHAR MARANLOU

CAMBRIDGE
UNIVERSITY PRESS

CAMBRIDGE
UNIVERSITY PRESS

32 Avenue of the Americas, New York, NY 10013-2473, USA

Cambridge University Press is part of the University of Cambridge.

It furthers the University's mission by disseminating knowledge in the pursuit of education, learning, and research at the highest international levels of excellence.

www.cambridge.org
Information on this title: www.cambridge.org/9781107072602

First published 2015

Printed in Great Britain by Clays Ltd, St Ives plc

A catalog record for this publication is available from the British Library.

Library of Congress Cataloging in Publication data
Maranlou, Sahar, 1974– author.
Access to justice in Iran : women, perceptions, and reality / Sahar Maranlou.
pages cm
Includes bibliographical references and index.
ISBN 978-1-107-07260-2 (hardback)
1. Women – Legal status, laws, etc. – Iran. 2. Women's rights – Iran. 3. Justice, Administration of – Iran. 4. Women (Islamic law) 5. Justice, Administration of (Islamic law) I. Title.
KMH517.5.M37 2014
342.5508′78–dc23 2014021768

ISBN 978-1-107-07260-2 Hardback

Contents

Acknowledgements

> I turn to right and left, in all the earth
> I see no signs of justice, sense or worth:
> A man does evil deeds, and all his days
> Are filled with luck and universal praise;
> Another's good in all he does – he dies
> A wretched, broken man whom all despise.
>
> Ferdowsi

This journey I have undertaken has been long, fascinating, and sometimes arduous, with obstacles and limitations littering its path. Along the way, numerous individuals have helped me and supported this process. First and foremost, I would like to thank my mentor, Professor Shaheen Sardar Ali, for her inspiration, direction, and support throughout the study. Significant recognition must go to all those individuals who gave their time to share their experience and expertise with me. I thank all of the participants who supported this research by completing questionnaires and participating in interviews. Without that group of women, researchers, scholars, officers, judges, and law professors, this research could not have taken place. Because of the sensitive political atmosphere, many of these individuals are not explicitly identified, yet they have provided a significant background to the study.

Most important, I am deeply indebted to my family, for their support and love. Particularly, I would like to dedicate this book to my husband Sasan, in grateful appreciation for his support and continued enthusiasm throughout this project, and also to my beautiful little girl, my star Tara.

Abbreviations

ABA	American Bar Association
ADB	Asian Development Bank
ADR	Alternative Dispute Resolution
CCA	United Nations Common Country Assessment
CEDAW	United Nations Convention on the Elimination of All Forms of Discrimination against Women
CEU	Central European University
ECHR	European Convention on Human Rights
GEM	Gender Empowerment Measure
GLPLI	Global Law Programs Learning Initiative
GPD	Gross Domestic Product
HDI	Human Development Index
ICCPR	International Covenant on Civil and Political Rights
IRI	Islamic Republic of Iran
NGOs	Non Governmental Organisations
OEO	Office of Economic Opportunities
OSJI	Open Society Justice Initiative
PPP	Purchasing Power Parity
RBA	Rights-Based Approach
UDHR	Universal Declaration of Human Rights
UN	United Nations
UNCAC	United Nations Convention against Corruption
UNDP	United Nations Development Program

UNESCO	United Nations Educational, Scientific and Cultural Organization
UK	United Kingdom
WB	World Bank

Introduction

This book is concerned with exploring access to justice in the Islamic Republic of Iran, with particular reference to the perceptions of women. The use of the term "access to justice" is as diverse as the literature, encompassing "accessibility of court processes for resolving disputes over mutual rights and responsibilities, availability of adequate legal representation in criminal trials, access to more informal legal processes such as small claims courts and administrative tribunals, availability of legal advice, public legal education" (Parker, 1999: 30). In particular, this book has broadened its focus from the procedural aspects of access such as cost barriers and substantive justice, to legal empowerment in order to enable disadvantaged groups to seek "justice" and challenge the multidimensional barriers to "access." This work is based around interviews with women in order to measure their perceptions of access to justice from a legal empowerment perspective in Iran.

The issue of legal empowerment enhancing access to justice has been one of interest in several research studies across the world (see, for example, Golub and McQuay, 2000; Palacio, 2006), so this study has international relevance. However, legal empowerment was employed as a model to bring together the concepts that focus on the subjective approaches in which I was interested, and exclude other top-down-oriented approaches such as the development of justice institutions' capacity, legitimisation, and policy formulation.

As this research focused on access to justice (claimed to be linked to the notion of the Western welfare state) in Iran (a Muslim country), this book draws from concepts of access to justice from both Western and Islamic perspectives. The comparative nature of the theoretical analysis discusses the gaps and similarities between Western and Islamic-related notions to inform the conceptual framework for this study. This enabled the concepts to be compared, thereby incorporating and reinforcing each other. As the conceptual framework grew, links between the meaning of justice and the setting of contexts in which justice needs to be realised became more apparent. These correlations led to a contextualised analysis of access to justice in Iran.

This study, therefore, focused on the concept and context of access to justice with particular reference to barriers in Iran. The research applied both qualitative and quantitative methods. The data gathering also was founded on triangulation methodology that included multiple data collection techniques. The research methodology mainly was derived from grounded theory, as it has been cited as the best methodology for feminist research (Bentzon et al., 1998).[1]

In addition, a parallel quantitative study was added that surveyed women's perceptions of access to justice. This combination of qualitative and quantitative data collection methods was aimed at enhancing confidence in findings (Oakley, 2000). This research therefore relied on quantities, and qualitative and

[1] Accordingly, the analysis begins through the examination of data in the initial phases of data collection (Strauss and Corbin, 1994) and theory can be "discovered" from data which has been collected and examined during the research (Glaser and Strauss, 1967).

descriptive data. The qualitative research included a combination of a questionnaire, and semi-structured and in-depth interviews. The methodology and survey study are described in Chapters 5 and 6.

Brief Aside: How I Became Interested

To understand why this book is about access to justice and women's perceptions in Iran, the reader might be interested in knowing how I originally became involved with this theme. My interest in access to justice and legal empowerment was formed by quite a few years' work experience and research. I began working as a journalist, writing legal and political columns in Iranian reformist newspapers after earning a law degree. After years of related work mainly with NGOs on empowerment and governance, I completed a postgraduate study on human rights as Justice Initiative Fellow at the Central European University. When I graduated from the CEU, I began to implement a project promoting access to justice based on the approach of legal empowerment through education. I also developed a module for clinical legal education, and in 2006 I founded the first university-based legal clinic in Iran. Later, I had the chance to initiate and coordinate several national projects to support legal aid and clinical legal education within several law schools.

While working in this area, I realised that it is the formal obstacles to access to justice, which comprise direct obstructions (such as lack of affordable legal representation, lack of adequate laws and regulations, delays in the justice system, weak enforcement of laws, lack of remedies provided by law, and lack of de facto protection) that are the most "publicised" barriers to access to justice. However, limited knowledge of rights and discriminatory social norms and cultural constructions are the main barriers to access to justice for disadvantaged groups and, in particular, for women; hence the need for research to investigate access to justice from a user's perspective.

Important Questions to Ask

Despite the absence of statistical data, there exists an argument that the Iranian justice system faces various challenges, such as a lack of transparency and accountability; a lack of gender sensitisation; a lack of access to legal information; failure to protect poor and marginalised groups, in particular women and minorities; lengthy delays and bureaucratic processes; lack of a legal aid system; inadequate, long, and discriminatory remedies; the large number of undecided cases in the public courts and courts of appeal; and a limited number of female judges (*Common Country Assessment*, 2003).

As we discuss later, the Iranian constitution quarantines access to justice within fair trial provisions similar to major international human rights conventions, yet it seems that the constitutional basis for equal justice has been broadly violated. Throughout this book we will see that existing legislative frameworks are not sufficient in many respects. The domestic laws do not explicitly enumerate the principles of equal access to justice. Moreover, despite the presence of constitutional provisions, ground realities reveal that the implementation of such laws and providing greater access to justice for disadvantaged groups needs to incorporate components of socioeconomic and political interventions. Also, as this book concludes, any reform of public policy will be more successful if based upon the understanding of barriers to access to justice, and theoretical and empirical methodologies. However, the knowledge of the Iranian legal community with regard to the area under discussion is rather poor. There are only a few small-scale empirical research studies about the accessibility of justice and also very few published articles on the subject. As a result, legal institutions are not familiar with the concept and scope of access to justice as such.

On the contrary, during the course of past decades, the international access to justice debate has grown into a collection of multinational, reform-oriented associations of legal workers, government reformers, and law and society scholars (Parker, 1999). As we discuss later, "access to justice orthodoxy"[2] focuses excessively on the state's legal institutions rather than people and, in particular, disadvantaged groups. However, it is uncertain whether the state-centred approach to reforming justice institutions pursued by most international organisations can share adequate benefits with disadvantaged groups in developing countries.

Therefore, this study endeavours to respond to the following questions: (1) What does access to justice mean both from international and so-called Islamic discourses? (2) How is access to justice defined in Iranian law, legal system, and practice? (3) What are the main barriers to justice from Iranian users' perspective? (4) How do Iranian women perceive access to justice? and (5) Do Iranian women have knowledge of their rights, the legal system, and the role and procedures of legal institutions?

Key Concepts

This book employs several frequently used terms that need to be defined and understood from the beginning. The meanings of key words and concepts such as "access to justice" and "legal empowerment" will be discussed throughout this study but need a brief explanation here. The term "access to justice" requires clarification, because it is used in different ways within the related literature. It has been used in sociolegal research in a variety of contexts, often without explicit explanation of its meaning. Also it has been noted that in the context of pluralistic societies, there is no singular meaning of access to justice (Cappelletti and Garth, 1978; Morris and White, 1973).

[2] The term "orthodoxy" has been used to describe a state-centred approach to access to justice. For a detailed discussion on the rule of law orthodoxy model, see Upham (2002) and Golub (2003).

It is interesting to note that the scholarly tensions regarding the definitional framework of access to justice are growing because of differences between those who advocate minimal rights to ensure some level of access and those who claim equality should be absolute (Moorhead and Pleasence, 2003). However, related studies demonstrate that there are two key factors in determining whether people have access to justice: the first is access to financial resources; the second refers to the ability of people to understand and use the justice system (Cappelletti and Garth, 1978). The definitional scope of access to justice, thus far, has covered different aspects such as legal assistance to disadvantaged groups, alternative dispute resolution mechanisms, and enhancement of public legal awareness to understand the legal system and legal empowerment.

This book uses a broad definition of access to justice, which examines the perspective of the justice user as its point of departure and studies the barriers the justice user faces in order to solve a legal problem. From a user perspective, women's access to justice refers to access to a fair and efficient legal process, either through judicial process, administration, alternative dispute resolution, or other informal mechanisms, and resulting in a just outcome. It must be noted that there are formal and informal barriers to women's access to justice. Formal obstacles include direct obstructions such as a lack of affordable legal representation, abuse of authority, lack of adequate laws and regulations, delays in the justice system, weak enforcement of laws, lack of remedies provided by law particularly in cases of violence against women, lack of de facto protection, and also the lack of legal aid. Discriminatory social norms and cultural constructions constitute informal barriers to women's access to justice. In other words, traditional gender biases preclude the ability of women to take legal actions. Cultural obstacles also have an effect on women's confidence in seeking justice, and the legal system, under the control of gender biases, fails to equally support women's rights.

Another key term that needs clarification here is legal empowerment. The concept of legal empowerment is still evolving and ill-defined. However, legal empowerment could be defined as encompassing the various processes by which disadvantaged groups become able to use the law and legal institutions to enforce their existing rights or demand new legal rights. These processes and approaches vary widely across contexts, yet share some common ideas to reform legislative, judicial, and dispute resolution bodies and public education about law and legal systems that empower disadvantaged populations.

Structure of This Book

The book is organised into two parts. Part I includes four chapters that present the conceptual framework and a contextualised analysis of the Iranian justice system. Chapter 1 provides the theoretical framework and analyses the existing hypothesis of access to justice in order to underline the gap between the contextual frameworks of Western- and Islamic-related discourses. This chapter, therefore, deals with the main objective of the study; that is, to assess whether internationally related models can be effective in providing access to justice in Iran. Chapter 2 moves from international and Islamic-related debates to the Iranian setting and provides a contextual analysis of access to justice. It provides a historical review of the justice system and examines some of the key dimensions of access to justice in Iran. Chapter 3 presents an analysis of the barriers from the users of justice's perspective in Iran. Chapter 4 discusses access of women to justice in Iran with particular reference to legal empowerment.

Part II includes two chapters, which look at measuring women's perceptions of access to justice in Iran. Chapter 5 discusses the methodology and reviews access to justice measurement models, and suggests an appropriate model to assess Iranian women's access to justice. Chapter 6 provides the findings from the survey study in order to assess women's perceptions of access to justice and analyse the data from the empirical research. The conclusion summarises the lessons that may be drawn from the research and offers some thoughts for future research in the area.

PART I

Access to justice is a complex phenomenon with various meanings across different legal systems and sociocultural settings. Access to justice is also associated with people's everyday lives, as their common problems such as employment, debt, housing, divorce, and so on, must be equally protected by law and effectively resolved through the legal system. The complex nature of access to justice underlines the importance of contextualising related concepts in a particular legal setting such as Iran. However, in order to examine access to justice in Iran, it is essential to first have a thorough understanding of the notion of justice from both international and Islamic perspectives as well as an understanding of the meaning and scope of access.

Part I focuses on the concept and contextual analysis of access to justice: its definition, its realisation, its barriers, and its enhancement by legal empowerment. Thus, each of the chapters examines one of these dimensions. Chapter 1 provides the basis for initiating a discussion about the definition of access to justice from a non-essentialist perspective. It attempts to expose some of the key components of the access to justice debate from Western and Islamic perspectives. The comparative nature of the theoretical framework, by following Western and Islamic literatures, seeks to highlight a significant difference: Western conceptions of access to justice are mainly based on the explanation of "access" and how the state needs to provide access for its citizens, whereas the Islamic-related conceptions are often based on a definition of "justice" and how it can be realised for individuals.

Chapter 2 draws up a contextualised framework of access to justice in Iran by reviewing constitutional and legislative provisions and the performance of the justice sector with particular reference to access to justice. The discussion of the development of the Iranian justice system attempts to understand how the concept of "access to judicial protection" has been formed in Iran. There are many reasons why the disadvantaged population and, in particular, women are often unable to use the law and the legal system to protect the rights and interests to which they are entitled. It may be because of discriminatory laws, an expensive legal process, or the deficiency of judicial proceedings. Chapter 3 provides a review of the barriers that Iranians who need access to justice may face, such as lengthy delays, the lack of a legal aid system, and insufficient adequate remedies. Adopting a qualitative analysis, the chapter outlines the examination of a contextual barrier from a user's perspective.

Chapter 4 seeks to engage in a discussion on women's access to justice and legal empowerment in Iran, where sociolegal norms coexist and play an essential part in women's lives. It thus examines gender-specific barriers to access to justice and also provides a conceptual analysis of empowerment. It especially claims that in the presence of diverse sociolegal barriers and multiple costs of justice, it is equally important to recognise the impact of the sociocultural dimensions of inaccessibility that women face in their path to justice.

1 Access to Justice Perspectives

A Conceptual Analysis

This chapter analyses the existing hypothesis of access to justice in order to highlight gaps and similarities between the contextual frameworks of Islamic and Western legal concepts and institutions.[1] The comparative nature of the present discussion emphasises the importance of providing a general overview of how the access to justice debate has been formulated in Western and Islamic legal systems. Therefore, the main purpose is to develop a comparative framework for conceptualising access to justice from an Islamic Law perspective. The objective of this chapter is to present the correlation between Islamic notions of access to justice and Western models.

Although the argument I present here compares Islamic and Western conceptions of access to justice, it does not advocate for developing an Islamic system of access to justice against the existing international models, as we discuss later. However, the comparison is important not only because this study is about a Muslim country but also, from a comparative perspective, because

[1] Islamic Law here refers to the Islamic normative system without any reference to a particular school of thought.

it is imperative to understand access to justice in terms of other cultural traditions and religious legal systems.

While access to justice is often treated as a "universal," "procedural," and "technical" matter, this book stresses understanding historical/political factors and the most important religious and cultural dynamics. In a plural context, such as Iran, justice, legal entitlements, and obstacles to legal access are distributed according to religious readings of law and legal procedures.

Moreover, a brief overview of examples of good practice of the different types of informal and traditional justice systems and their role to improve access to justice in various contexts explains the importance of understanding indigenous access to justice models.[2] Many examples, from sub-Saharan Africa to South Asia, Middle East to North America, value the rise of traditional justice and customary law in providing access to justice for poor and marginalised populations. Hybrid justice systems with their own strengths and weaknesses rooted in traditional justice are based on restorative justice.[3] As shown later in this text, Islamic ideas

[2] See for example Penal Reform International 2001, "Access to Justice in Sub-Saharan Africa: The Role of Traditional and Informal Justice Systems," Penal Reform International, London. Also see Traditional Justice: Practitioners' Perspectives' Working Paper Series, available at http://www.idlo.int/Publications/WP2rawls.pdf.

[3] Restorative justice theory aims to provide compensation to victims, enhancing the offender's obedience with the law, integrating offenders, and also reestablishing the relationship between offenders and society (Gromet and Darley, 2006). Most definitions given for restorative justice underline the view that the nature of the violation indicates the manner of healing. Restorative justice reflects the idea that crime causes harm to victims, the community, and the offender (Zehr, 1990); therefore the criminal justice system should facilitate in compensating for the harm caused by crime (Wright, 1996). However, the community, victim, and offender should also be involved as much as possible in response to the crime. There are three fundamentals to restorative justice definition and practice: "First, crime is viewed primarily as a conflict between individuals that results in injuries to victims,

of access to justice are also rooted mainly in notions of rights of individuals, obligations of the state, and reconciliations.[4]

Just as promising for hybrid justice is the global call to move beyond Western law and rights discourses. One interesting conception is to understand human rights "in the vernacular,"[5] meaning that human rights must be theorised and also legitimated based on the "practice of everyday life."[6] Thus, in a plural setting such as Iran, not only ideological norms are tied up with everyday life but also religion as a key normative framework is involved with the "vernacularisation" of human rights.

Also from an advocacy point of view, traditional and theological foundations of rights and responsibilities from religious perspectives can be used as analytical and procedural tools to improve access to justice in Muslim societies and especially Iran, as a constitutional Islamic Republic country. I have learned how religious notions can play a significant role in furthering human rights and good governance, in my earlier practice in working with Non-Governmental Organisations (NGOs). For instance, during law

communities and the offenders themselves, and only secondarily as a violation against the state. Second, the aim of the criminal justice process should be to create peace in communities by reconciling the parties and repairing the injuries caused by the dispute. Third, the criminal justice process should facilitate active participation by victims, offenders, and their communities in order to find solutions to the conflict" (Galaway and Hudson, 1996: 2).

4 It also needs to be added here that from Western theories of justice, restorative justice advocates a variety of practices including restitution, reconciliation, forgiveness, apology, acknowledgement of injury, community conferencing, and the re-integration of offenders into their communities (Menkel-Meadow, 2007; Strickland, 2004).The effectiveness of restorative justice, however, as a continuing debate shares success and failures learned; for instance, some argue that restorative justice has been successful in decreasing recidivism (Latimer et al., 2001).

5 See Goodale, 2006; Engle Merry, 2001, 2006.

6 Goodale, 2006: 14.

reform of Iranian NGOs, radical groups asserted that NGOs are used as tools by Western imperialism for soft revolutions in Muslim countries. At that time, I was working with the Iran NGO Initiative[7] and was responsible for research that resulted in law reform. In a national conference, I cited that the Prophet Muhammad himself was a member of an NGO[8] and gave examples of similar religious charities and endowments from Islamic Law (*waqf*)[9] perspectives. This brief citation was soon used as a means of trust-building with the government for law reform of Iranian NGOs. Another example is the concept "Islamic feminism," which is carried out from within a Muslim framework but is part of the global women's rights movement to challenge gender inequality. Islamic feminists constantly question women's status in Iran and provide an alternative concept of women's rights from Islamic perspectives.[10]

Dimensions of Analysis

The so-called international access to justice debate is founded on "key notions of legality and legitimacy, in particular, the

[7] Iran NGO Initiative, A Project of the Population Council Regional Office for the West Asia and North Africa.

[8] *Hilf al-Fudul* or حلف الفضول (often translated as Alliance of the Virtuous), a seventh-century alliance, was established by several Meccans including the Prophet Muhammad to respect the principles of justice. See Mahmood Ibrahim (1982), "Social and Economic Conditions in Pre-Islamic Mecca," *International Journal of Middle East Studies*, 14(3): 355. Also see Tariq Ramadan, *In the Footsteps of the Prophet* (Oxford: Oxford University Press, 2007).

[9] *Waqf* (endowment) is an Islamic Law mechanism for charitable purposes by which one makes a voluntary dedication of one's wealth for certain beneficiaries.

[10] For more detailed analyses of Iranian Islamic feminism, see Mir-Hosseini, 1996. Also see Afsaneh Najmabadi, "Feminism in an Islamic Republic: Years of Hardship, Years of Growth," in *Islam, Gender and Social Change*, Haddad and Esposito (ed.). Oxford: Oxford University Press, 1997.

rule of law and equality" (Moorhead and Pleasence, 2003: 1). This discourse is closely associated with the equal application of law as a response to existing inequalities. The broad range of inequalities, including poverty, unemployment, and deprivations, that arise from sex, ethnicity, religion, nationality, political views, social class, disability, as well as many more, is directly involved with our understanding of justice and what is meant by access to justice.

Given that an historic breakthrough took place in post-industrial Western countries, there are rational justifications to suppose that interconnected notions of access to justice can, in one way or another, be associated with the philosophical origins, legal concepts, and sociocultural contexts of what are identified as Western societies. However, the complex sociolegal notions of justice emphasise that any account of access to justice must be able to encompass the enormous variety of social settings, political atmospheres, ideological frameworks, and cultural contexts. This means that social and cultural contexts as a "culture of access" define the scope and sense of what is referred to as justice. Therefore, the conceptual analysis cannot be completely based on the so-called international discourse of access to justice but must also be able to take into account the sociolegal relativisms.

Also, the practical use of language with regard to access to justice needs to be examined. This is a preliminary question as to why other similar phrases such as access to court, access to legal justice, access to the machinery of justice, access to the enforcement of rights, and access to equal application of law, for example, have been isolated from introducing the international discourse of access to justice (Cappelletti and Garth, 1981: 316).

The related discussion should be able to address why the expression access to justice has been widely used to initiate the debate. Moreover, a comparative study of the concepts or related foundations of access to justice cannot be comprehensive if based on the hypothesis that there is one comprehensible idea of how justice can be equally accessible. The comparative study, however, must be open to the non-restricted analysis of the concepts of justice and how it can be realised in various social and legal contexts.

The discussion surrounding access to justice must, if possible, be able to respond to some fundamental questions about justice: what does justice mean and how is justice defined in the context of accessibility? Also it is equally important to characterise and contextualise injustice. The discussion of access to justice also needs to clarify whether specific attention must be paid to justice or access, that is, how can access to justice be maximised and equalised? It is imperative to understand whether institutions of justice need to be a centre of importance or people who are engaged with the concept of justice as part of their everyday life.

Therefore, one underlying question here pertains to the definition of justice. The discussion about the theories of justice seem to be rather unfitting in Western-related debates that focus on grounds of accessibility based on assumed substantive justice. That is, the Western notion of rule of law presumes the existence of a just rule as law and discusses how it can be realised for those who are affected within the framework of access to justice. However, for many non-Western legal systems, any discussion about access to justice must include a definitional analysis of justice as well.

In my understanding of the theories of justice, Western or non-Western, it is useful to construct various indexes of indicators to identify the scope and weight of "access." The social-theoretical premises that are involved in Western notions of access to justice have more often emphasised theories of justice to measure the quality of legal procedures, their outcomes, and also the issue of costly justice. As we see throughout this book, most international initiatives regarding access to justice often employ indicators to measure the fairness of accessibility of the justice systems at the national level. This explains the popularity of the rule of law model to measure access to justice. Nevertheless, any promising conceptions from non-Western perspectives should be able to recognise the complex and distinctive diverse factors correlated to the meaning and scope of justice and access that vary across societies, legal systems, and social and cultural contexts.

Access to Justice Orthodoxy

The most dominant paradigms of the debate surrounding so-called international access to justice are derived from the historical contexts of post-industrial Western countries. The emphasis on the importance of access to justice was instigated during the 1960s, in the age of the welfare state, to emphasise better social services.[11] Repeated studies identified three "waves" of development in access to justice, particularly with reference to the U.S. experience. The first wave, which began in 1965, included institutional reform to provide legal aid for the poor. The second wave in 1970 advocated greater representative actions (public interest law), and the third focused on dispute resolution mechanisms, mostly non-judicial alternatives and the effectiveness of court procedural reforms (Cappelletti and Garth, 1981: 4–20). Between 1950 and 1973, legal aid reforms were carried out in the United States, the UK, the Netherlands, Canada, Australia, and Sweden. Although the oldest legal aid development comprised the neighbourhood law centres in England (Zander, 1978), the most publicised reform introduced was the American "legal service" movement of President Johnson's "war on poverty" in the 1960s, which was a reflection of the Office of Economic Opportunities (OEO); the OEO radically changed the rate of legal services to

[11] The linkage between welfare states and access to justice is understood generally as follows: "In welfare states generally, rights on behalf of disadvantaged or unorganised groups such as the poor and consumers, and the like have proliferated recently, concern has arisen about the effectiveness and enforcement of those rights, and the political, and constitutional principle of equality has been applied in order to enhance access to courts and to order dispute-processing machinery" (Cappelletti and Garth, 1981: 5).

the poor. The 1970s' literature regarding legal aid based on the liberal vision for realising the notion of equality before the law was optimistic (Regan, 1999). However, some commentators, such as Johnson (1978), who documented the history of the OEO legal service program in the United States, questioned the quality of justice the American poor received:

> Are they [America's poor] to be entitled to equal justice only when their causes are minor or consonant with the philosophy of the ruling political party? Or will they be able to pursue any legal objective through any lawful means in keeping with the ideas of the legal profession? In the long run this question will be answered by the American public. The response most certainly will be the measure of the poor man's opportunity for justice in this nation and his right to seek better conditions through the orderly processes of the law. (Johnson, 1978: 284)

The third wave of development in access to justice extended legal representation to "diffuse interests," first in the United States with the establishment of public interest firms in the 1970s. The public interest law initiative was aimed at "providing mechanisms, both governmental and private, to protect the diffuse interests of consumers, environmentalists, and other traditionally unrepresented or underrepresented groups" (Cappelletti and Garth, 1981: 11) in North America and Europe. The importance of providing protection against group injuries emerged in post-industrial Western countries as a key legal reform.[12] The

[12] Cappelletti provides a detailed explanation: "More and more frequently the complexity of modern societies generates situations in which a single human action can be beneficial or prejudicial to large numbers of people, thus making entirely inadequate the traditional scheme of litigation as merely a two-party affair. For example, false information divulged by large corporations may cause injury to all who buy shares in that corporation; an antitrust violation may damage all who are effected by the unfair competition; the infringement by an employer of a collective labor agreement violates the rights of all

reasons behind these group suits clearly were related to costs, as group suits decreased the cost of legal action for multiple claims. This is true despite the fact that awards would be granted to individuals for whom pursuing an individual claim would not be cost-effective, particularly when small sums are involved (Miller, 1998). Similar justification for advocating the sociolegal significance of public interest firms during the 1970s in the United States has been shared for the development of public interest litigation in South Asia (Hossain, Malik, and Musa, 1997). The phrase "public law litigation" was used by Professor Abram Chayes of the Harvard Law School in 1976 to refer to the practice of lawyers seeking to motivate social change through court-ordered verdicts that reform legal rules, enforce existing laws, and articulate public norms in the United States (Chayes, 1976). Public interest litigation, more highly established in the United States, endorsed the representation of the collective interest to a large extent, and was later introduced mainly in Europe and by some Asian civil law countries.

During the 1970s, the alternative dispute resolution (ADR) movement was initiated to avoid the delay and cost of formal litigation in the United States.[13] The court dispute resolution mechanisms comprise mainly mediation and conciliation. In the last two decades, ADR mechanisms developed into a more formalised procedure: "arbitration has already lost all the advantages of an

his employees; the imposition of an unconstitutional tax or the illegal discontinuance of a social benefit may be detrimental to large communities of citisens; the discharge of waste into a lake or river harms all who want to enjoy its clean waters; defective or unhealthy packing may cause damage to all consumers of these goods. The possibility of such mass injuries represents a characteristic feature of our epoch" (Cappelletti and Weisner, 1979: 519).

[13] "Third wave of access to justice movement followed in the 1970s 'with a shift in focus to dispute-processing institutions in general, rather than simply on institution of legal representation; less formal alternatives to courts and court procedures have merged in bold relief as part of this new reform trend'" (Cappelletti and Garth, 1981: 11).

'alternative' practice, and is now as complex and dependent on legal expertise as litigation" (Brooker, 1999: 1–36). It has been argued that the new trend in dispute resolution is a reaction to the failure of various legal systems to provide equal access to justice. The key characteristic of this movement is an emphasis on human rights values, social justice, and an interdisciplinary approach to the legal system: "It is the result of a synthesis of a number of new disciplines within law and legal practice that have been rapidly gaining visibility, acceptance, and popularity in the last decade and a half. These disciplines represent a number of emerging, new, or alternative forms of law practice, dispute resolution, and criminal justice. The converging main 'vectors' of this movement are 1) collaborative law, 2) creative problem solving, 3) holistic justice, 4) preventive law, 5) problem solving courts, 6) procedural justice, 7) restorative justice, 8) therapeutic jurisprudence and 9) transformative mediation" (Daicoff, 2006: 113–14).

As discussed in detail earlier, Western advocacy for access to justice from the 1960s has covered a wide range of issues, yet most of the related discussions are concerned with providing affordable legal assistance to disadvantaged groups. These debates focus on the procedures and outcomes of legal aid and raise critical questions regarding government funding of legal assistance. In addition, other approaches such as public interest litigations and alternative dispute resolution mechanisms often seek to enable people to overcome the cost barriers to using the legal system. The conventional approach to access to justice, implemented during the 1980s and 1990s, widely focused on procedural access rather than substantive justice. The neoliberalism approach to access to justice has advocated more often for efficiency and spending less in social services. Nevertheless, a new trend to call for a better understanding of access to justice based on user perspectives in various sociolegal setting has emerged during recent years. It has been noted that the lack of quantitative information to examine the needs and perceptions of individuals has been considered the main barrier to understanding whether legal policies have had any positive effect on the community (Genn and Beinart, 1999).

A Definitional Analysis

In the post–United Nations human rights standards, the definitional framework of access to justice has narrowed to key principles of the fair trial provision. This conventional definition, associated with a minimal understanding of equal administration of justice, has mainly emphasised the right to equal treatment before the tribunal. These provisions include the right to an effective remedy by competent national tribunals,[14] the principle of equality before the law, the presumption of innocence, freedom from arbitrary arrest, and the right to a fair and independent tribunal established by law.[15] Regional human rights instruments such as the European Convention on Human Rights,[16] the African Charter on Human Rights and People's Rights,[17] and the American Convention on Human Rights[18] have articulated more specific aspects of "access to fair trial" including the right to a fair

[14] Article 8 of the 1948 Universal Declaration of Human Rights (UDHR): "Everyone has the right to an effective remedy by the competent national tribunals for acts violating the fundamental rights granted him by the constitution or by law."

[15] The International Covenant on Civil and Political Rights protects the principle of equality before the law, the presumption of innocence, freedom from arbitrary arrest and the right to a fair and independent tribunal established by law.

[16] The Convention for the Protection of Human Rights and Fundamental Freedoms (commonly referred to as the European Convention on Human Rights [ECHR]) was adopted in 1950 and came into force in 1953.

[17] African [Banjul] Charter on Human and Peoples' Rights, adopted 27 June 1981, OAU Doc. CAB/LEG/67/3 rev. 5, 21 I.L.M. 58 (1982), entered into force 21 October 1986.

[18] American Convention on Human Rights, O.A.S. Treaty Series No. 36, 1144 U.N.T.S. 123, entered into force 18 July 1978.

and public hearing within a reasonable time[19] and the right to judicial protection.[20]

Article 6 of the European Convention on Human Rights (ECHR) guarantees the right to a fair trial in both civil and criminal proceedings.[21] In criminal cases, the right to legal assistance is explicitly set out in Article 6 (3) (C). In the "*McLibel case*," the European Court of Human Rights referred to the provision of legal aid that should be accessible in all criminal proceedings and also, exceptionally, in civil proceedings: "the question whether the

[19] Article 6 (1) of the European Convention on Human Rights (ECHR) declares: "In the determination of his civil rights and obligations or of any criminal charge against him, everyone is entitled to a fair and public hearing within a reasonable time by an independent and impartial tribunal established by law."

[20] Article 25 of the American Convention: "(1) Everyone has the right to simple and prompt recourse, or any other effective resource, to a competent court of tribunal for protection against acts that violate his fundamental rights recognised by the constitution or laws of the state concerned or by the Convention, though such violation may have been committed by persons acting in the course of their official duties." Also see the African Charter on Human Rights and People's Rights: "Every individual shall have the right to have his cause heard. This comprises a) The right to an appeal to competent national organs against acts of violating his fundamental rights to recognised and guaranteed by conventions, laws, regulations and customs in force, b) The right to be presumed innocent until proved guilty by a competent court or tribunal, c) The right to defence, including the right to be defended by counsel of his choice and d) The right to be tried within a reasonable time by an impartial court or tribunal."

[21] Regarding the scope of legal aid, see *Golder v. United Kingdom*, Application No. 4451/70, Judgment of 21 February 1975; *Airey v. Ireland*, Application No. 6289/73, Judgment of 9 October 1979; *Artico v. Italy*, Application No. 6694/74, Judgment of 13 May 1980; *Jordan v. United Kingdom*, Application No. 24746/94, Judgment of 4 May 2001; *Bubbins v. United Kingdom*, Application No. 50196/99, Judgment of 17 March 2005; *Biondo v. Italy*, Application No. 8821/70, Judgment of 28 February 2002.

provision of legal aid was necessary for a fair hearing had to be determined on the basis of the particular facts and circumstances of each case and depended inter alia upon the importance of what was at stake for the applicant in the proceedings, the complexity of the relevant law and procedure and the applicant's capacity to represent him or herself effectively" (*Steel and Morris v. UK*, 15 February 2005).

The provision of legal aid in criminal proceedings as required by Article 6.2 of the convention and also, exceptionally, in civil proceedings, should be "practical and effective" and not "theoretical or illusory" (Alston, 1999: 187–214). For cases in which free legal aid is required, Article 6 (3) (c) requires that the assistance of the lawyer be effective, and formal appointment alone is not sufficient. Legal representation should be accessible for hearings concerning the deprivation of liberty required by Article 5 (4) of the ECHR. Other hearings may also be entitled to free legal aid, including the relative of someone who died in the custody of the state required by Article 2 (the right to life).

Another, more specific, convention is the Hague Convention on International Access to Justice, concluded on 25 October 1980 and entered into force on 1 May 1988. The Access to Justice Convention is seen as an enhancement to the Hague Convention of 15 November 1965 on the Service Abroad of Judicial and Extrajudicial Documents in Civil or Commercial Matters and the Hague Convention of 18 March 1970 on the Taking of Evidence Abroad in Civil or Commercial Matters. This Convention aims to ensure that status as an alien or the absence of residence in a state is not a basis for unequal access to justice in that state. The Access to Justice Convention tries to provide nondiscriminatory legal aid as well as legal advice, security for costs, copies of entries and decisions, and physical detention and safe conduct. In particular, regarding legal aid provision, the Convention establishes the entitlement to legal aid of nationals of any contracting state and persons habitually resident in any contracting state, for court proceedings in civil and commercial matters, under the same conditions as if they were themselves nationals of and habitually resident in that state (Article 1), and the entitlement of all such persons, when pursuing their proceedings in any other contracting states, to free service of documents, letters of request, and social enquiry reports, and to legal aid to secure the recognition and enforcement of the decision obtained (Article 13).

The definitional analysis, as outlined, leads to an assumption that international human rights standards have formulated access to equal treatment before tribunals as an equivalent conception with access to justice. It is clear that some components of access to justice are associated with access to equal treatment, which is to be found in the so-called principles of fair trial. It is, however, neither broad nor flexible enough to capture various paradigms, to realise justice for people and to maximise their access to what they believe to be justice.

In order to provide a definitional analysis of access to justice, it is important also to answer the question asked earlier about the use of the term "access to justice" instead of other similar phrases. The definitional discussion should be able to address why the phrase "access to justice" has been used to introduce the debate. In the historical context, major use of the phrase access to justice occurred during the Florence project funded by the Ford Foundation.[22] In October 1979, a conference was held at the European University Institute to discuss the prospects for further action after the Florence Project. As stated by the project leader, Mauro Cappelletti, "the conference participants determined what issues were most silent from their vantage points, what insights or conclusion seemed more or less valid to them and how generally to assess what we termed the 'access to justice' movement" (Cappelletti and Garth, 1981: 3).

Therefore, the phrase access to justice acquired a broader meaning beyond access to court and legal representations by the

[22] The Italian National Council of Research and the European University Institute also were included as donors.

Florence Project. However, it appears that the practice of using the phrase has resulted in a very distinct concept of justice and what is meant by access. It is equally pertinent to understand the ability of the Florence Project to confine access to justice to the state-centred in terms of its notion and framework.

Islamic Conceptualisation

Although it is common to confine the access to justice movement to the notion of the Western welfare state, various conceptions of access to justice can be found in correlated theories and practices within the contexts of non-Western societies. The Islamic conceptions of access to justice underline the importance of inner meanings and the definitional scope of justice, as well as its external aspects (procedural or formal justice), which can be compared to internationally debated access to justice within the context of the rule of law.

The essentially religious nature of Islamic conceptions of access to justice and their focus on individuals shows how it is fundamentally different from Western debate, which is instead state-centred with emphasis on institutions of access. If this is true, as I argue, how is it possible to compare Islamic theories of justice to correlated notions of access? It is necessary to establish a clear understanding of classical Islamic thoughts of justice before we can appreciate how it defines accessibility in contemporary Muslim communities.[23]

Justice as a complex concept plays a prominent role in current Islamic debate since so many conflicting ideas of justice have emerged in the history of Islamic thoughts from its inception to modern times. The enormous body of classical literature on

[23] The introductory definition of justice in Islamic Law offered here is by no means comprehensive or inclusive. For a more detailed analysis of justice in Islamic thoughts, see, for example, Khadduri (1984); Smirnov 1996). Also see Rosen (2000).

Islamic conceptions of justice presents a combination of prevalent principles as well as battlefields of disagreement; therefore, Islamic conceptualisation of justice remains a contested debate in the absence of any specific analysis with a general recognition. The analytical argument about justice in Islamic studies, however, does share a number of key similarities with related discourses in Western philosophical tradition, including comparable debates regarding the definition of justice.

Islamic conceptions of justice derive from the *Quran*,[24] the *Hadith*,[25] and also the interpretations of the early Muslim philosophers. The Quranic term for justice is *adl*, which means to be fair, balanced, and neutral. The Quran says: "be just even if it should be to near kinsman."[26] Understanding justice as fairness or giving every man what is his due[27] appears in the Quran as the following: "humanity were a single nation at the beginning; God sent forth prophets to deliver both tidings glad and warnings,

[24] The Quran is the primary source of law in Islam and is believed to be the word of God revealed over a period of approximately twenty-three years. It includes 114 chapters and 6,666 verses.

[25] The Hadith refers to the reports of the Prophet Muhammad's statements and actions.

[26] Quran 6:152.

[27] The most promising aspect of the concept of justice, which was articulated in ancient literature, is that "justice is the set and constant purpose to give every man his due" (see *Plato*, ed. Allan Bloom (1968). Aristotle (384 BC–322 BC) supported the same definition: "what is Justice? To give every man his due" and developed his theory of distributive justice based on proportionality. Konow (2003) argues that there are four theoretical categories in which to place justice theories. Three of them are associated with distributive justice and the fourth reviews the context dependency of justice principles. The three theoretical categories comprise equality and needs perspectives, utilitarianism and welfare economics, and equity perspectives. Mainly egalitarian thinkers such as Rawls (1971) have placed their theories of justice within the first theoretical group, which emphasises the importance of equality and the needs of those who are least advantaged in society.

and He sent down with them Scriptures based on Truth, in order to judge disputes between the people."[28] And of course Allah is *ahkam al-hakimin*, best of the judges (95:8). The Quran also defines justice as a basis for compromise: "If two parties among the faithful are at war against each other, make peace between them; ... make peace between them in fairness and with justice; for God surely loves the people who are truly equitable."[29]

Justice is a tool for sustainability: "and the Firmament (sky) has he raised high, and he has set up the balance of justice in order that you may not transgress balance. So establish weight with justice and fall not short in the balance."[30] Various Quranic commentators have explained the meaning of balance (*al-mizan*) in this verse ("The Beneficent," *al-Rahman*). "In fact, many Islamic works on ethics have appeared over the ages with the title of *mizan al-amal* or balance of 'human actions.' Others have interpreted the term to mean the discernment that allows to establish balance in all aspects of life and have identified it with the Quran itself, one of whose names is *al-Furqan*, or discernment" (Nasr, 1999: 128). In other words, *al-mizan* or balance as another meaning of justice[31] is a governing principle of the circle of life. In this understanding, justice is not only a supreme virtue but also an obligation.[32]

According to the verse: "we sent our messengers with clear signs and sent down with them the book and the measure in order to establish justice among the people,"[33] the principle of justice must be measured and realised by the standards set by revelation. As one commentor has cited, in the Quran there is no reference of the

28 Quran 2:213.

29 Quran 49:9.

30 Quran 55:7–9.

31 "And the measuring out (*wazn*) on that day will be just" (Quran 7:8).

32 "God commands justice and fair dealing" (Quran 16:90). Also see "O you who believe, be upright for God, and (be) bearers of witness with justice" (Quran 5:8).

33 Quran 57:25.

measures to indicate what the constituent elements of justice are or how justice can be realised on earth (Khadduri, 1984: 10–11). The Quran, however, explains justice in different contexts and sets up specific examples of how justice can be implemented. Some of these include the requirement of just treatment of orphans,[34] fair trade,[35] personal virtue,[36] and fair judgement.[37] In many of these Quranic examples, justice is an indicator of human responsibility for its action. "A person who is just therefore engages in acts that are framed by awareness, born of the pursuit of reason over passion, of the harm that may be done to the community of believers by acting otherwise" (Rosen, 2000: 154).

The focus on humankind responsibility and intention (*batin*), therefore, defines injustice. The Quranic expression for injustice is *zulm*, which is derived from the Arabic *z.l.m.* which means oppression, doing wrong, darkness, and inequity. In short, the meaning of zulm is "in the opinion of many of the authoritative lexicographers, that of putting in a wrong place. In the sphere of ethics, it seems to mean primarily to act in such a way as to transgress the proper limit and encroach upon the right of some other person … Briefly and generally speaking *zulm* is to do with injustice in the sense of going beyond one's own bounds and doing what one has no right to do" (Izutsu, 1966: 164–5).

The definition of injustice draws a very interesting distinction between Western and Islamic conceptualisations of justice. Classical Western philosophy negatively defines injustice as the opposite of justice: "if the unjust is unfair, the justice is fair" (Aristotle). A cursory look at the Quranic definition of

[34] "And approach not the property of the orphan except in the fairest way, until he [or she] attains the age of full strength, and give measurement and weight with justice" (Quran 6:152; also see 89:17, 93:9, and 107:2).

[35] The entire chapter 83 of the Quran, "*Surah al-Mutaffifeen*," deals with fair trade and fraud issues.

[36] "Be just, for it is closest to God-consciousness" (Quran 5:8).

[37] "If you judge, judge between them with justice" (Quran 5:42).

justice initiates the question about injustice in Islamic classical literature, as defining unfairness can present core ideas associated with the notion of justice and describe its dominant controversial expectations. The Quran uses the term zulm to describe oppression and doing wrong; "And what reason do you have not to fight in the cause of Allah, to rescue the helpless oppressed old men, women, and children who are crying: 'Our Lord! Lead us to freedom out of this land whose people are oppressors, and raise for us a protector by your Grace and send us a successor from your presence!" (4:75). In the Quranic description, a just society is a land free from all forms of oppression; thus, the Islamic political ethic approves of violence only to remove injustice (zulm). It has been reported that the Prophet said a society can persevere with unbelief (*kufr*) but not with injustice (zulm).[38] The Quran indicates explicitly that God does not oppress (9:70, 10:44, 29:40, and 30:9); therefore, injustice or oppression occurs only through human intervention, and the only path to justice is the divine order because God does not oppress. "To be removed from injustice, one must be similar to God, or in the god-full state. Justice is god-fullness, oppression is God-lesson" (Wadud, 1995).

The Islamic theologian and mystic, Ghazali (d. 1111), explained the theory of ethical justice as the "pathway" to the attainment of ultimate and eternal heavenly happiness (Khadduri, 1984: 120–1). This divine or ideal justice that is "known through revelation is an expression of God's perfection" and practical or human justice "arrived at through reason is imperfect" (ibid., 103). Other classical Islamic philosophers such as Kindi,[39]

[38] Bahar-ul-Anvar, Vol. 76 (Farsi translation) 1365, Tehran: Eslamiyeh, p. 321.

[39] Abu Yusuf Ya'qub ibn Ishaq Al-Kindi (AD 800–870), known as "the Philosopher of the Arabs," worked with a group of translators who rendered works of Aristotle and Greek mathematicians and scientists into Arabic. He also wrote on different philosophical topics, mathematics, and the sciences.

Farabi,[40] Ibn Sina,[41] and Ibn Rushd,[42] similar to Socrates and Aristotle, developed their theories of "ideal justice" as an absolute and logical negation of "injustice." According to Khadduri (1984), Farabi has explained justice as the highest of human virtues in the Virtuous City,[43] where the Imam "holds the scale of justice" and controls the sharing of the "good things" and the prevention of the bad (pp. 86–7). Ibn Sina, the Iranian philosopher, outlined a legal foundation for the establishment of justice in the virtuous city, similar to a social contract between the Imam (head of state) and citizens, "through consensus and tacit agreement" (ibid., 89). However, the virtuous city is the only arrangement where divine and practical justice can reach an agreement "founded upon wisdom, courage, temperance and justice" (ibid., 98).

The doctrine of *istishab* is another concept of justice, one that approves the linkage between the natural justice and social values that are embodied in cultural practices and customs. Istishab promotes the idea that Islam does not seek to change, reform, or replace all of the laws and traditions within society. Istishab or the presumption of continuity technically means that a situation known to exist continues to exist until its opposite is proven. It denotes "a rational proof which may be employed in the absence

[40] Abu Nasr Mohammad Ibn al-Farakh al-Farabi (AD 870–950) is known as Mallim-e-Sani, which often is translated as "second master" or "second teacher."

[41] Ibn Sina or Avicenna (AD 980–1037). His philosophical work is mostly about the nature of God, Being, and the concept of reality and reasoning.

[42] Abu'l-Walid Ibn Rushd, better known as Averroes (AD 1126–1198), has contributed to philosophy in many forms, such as detailed commentaries on Aristotle and writing about no incompatibility between religion and philosophy.

[43] The virtuous city (al-madina al-fadila) is a hierarchical ideal society in which the responsibility of the ruler is to educate the people to act in a manner that will achieve their ultimate happiness.

of other indications; specifically, those facts, or rules of law and reason, whose existence or non-existence had been proven in the past, and which are presumed to remain so for lack of evidence to establish any change" (Kamali, 1991: 259). Istishab is divided into different categories, allowing for a range of examples. Under the presumption of original absence (*istishab al-'adam al-asli*), for example, a person accused of a crime is presumed to be innocent until the contrary is proved (the presumption of innocence).

The doctrine of Istishab creates a substantive basis for permissibility and conformity within the rules of natural justice and the customs and conscience of decent individuals. Therefore, natural justice and equity validate social practices and customs that are not regulated by *Sharia*,[44] so where the Quran uses the term *'adl wa ihsan'* for justice, it, inter alia, includes natural justice and the fundamental values of justice that appeal to the good conscience of decent individuals. Similarly, the Prophet only replaced those social customs that were unjust and repressive (Turabi, 1980; Kamali, 1991).

It is evident, then, that istishab is not only a method of juristic deduction or a means of implementing an existing indication (*dalil*); it also provides a strong basis on which to value free liability of people unless the rule of law has determined otherwise. Moreover, the doctrine of istishab maintains what is meant as a just outcome for individuals by giving natural justice priority over procedural justice. This is thus one of the main differences between Western and Islamic perspectives of access to justice.

The Islamic conceptualisation of access to justice begins with the right to justice. The right to justice is based on the Quranic verses. "And do not let ill-will towards any folk incite you so that you swerve from dealing justly. Be just; that is nearest to heedfulness";[45] "Do not let your hatred of a people incite you to

[44] The religious normative system of Islam; see An-Na'im (2008).

[45] Quran 5:8.

aggression";[46] and "You who believe stand steadfast before God as witness for [truth and] fair play."[47] The question here is how can justice be defined from Islamic perspectives so it provides a religious foundation to promote access to justice in Muslim countries.

One possible framework would be viewing justice as a right (*haqq*), which can also explain the legal associations of justice. Majid Khadduri lists the right of justice among five other rights held by men according to Islam: rights to personal safety, respect of personal reputation, equality, and brotherhood (1946: 77–8).

In Islamic legal theory, the capacity to possess rights begins with birth and ends with death: even a child in the womb will enjoy civil rights provided that it comes into the world alive.[48] Although all human beings are entitled to civil rights (*ita u-l huqu*), no one can employ these rights unless they possess the legal capacity to do so (*istifa al-huquq*).[49] Therefore, Islamic legal terminology such as *ita u-l huquq* or *istifa al-huquq* is used in reference to rehabilitation and reinstatement, justice, and consequently might be defined as "establishing the right (*haqq*) in its due place" (Smirnov, 1996: 337–50). Also, it has been argued that "given what is due" in order to "guarantee" (*istifa*) this *huquq* set is not only and not just an act of moral righteousness; it is first and foremost implemented to secure the ontological stability of the thing in question, that is to say, its being truly established in the flow of change. This justice or "giving what is due" and "establishing the true" (haqq) turns out to be the "preservation and maintenance" of this needed-in-order-to-exist assemblage of rights (ibid., 345–6).

A more specific suggestion to describe justice as being given what is due is made by Izutsu (1966) in a structure of the rights

[46] Quran 5:3.

[47] Quran 4:135.

[48] Article 957, Iranian Civil Code.

[49] Article 958, Iranian Civil Code.

obligation set as it is "at the same time an ontologically necessary assemblage of traits that characterise the given existing thing, the given link of the power and rule-structure." This proposition defines justice (*'adala*) as the right of individuals, therefore "political justice is the right (*haqq*) of an individual to participate in political power and rule. Social justice is the right (*haqq*) to have equal opportunity, to avoid exploitation, to receive a true evaluation of one's labour and to satisfy the natural and social needs of each individual in harmony (*fi al-it'dal*) without injury to the rights, public affairs or common values of others. Judicial (*qada iyya*) justice is the right (*haqq*) of an individual to have a clear idea of the rules and laws that regulate his relations with other individuals and with society, as well as his right to equality with his opponent under these rules and laws" (ibid., 337–50).

The justice as right theory, as discussed above, shares the common analysis that the possession of rights enhances the dignity of rights-holders (Feinberg, 1970). The same idea also has been extended to Islamic political theory in particular from the *Shia*[50] perspective. Imam Ali,[51] in his letter to Malik ibn Al-Ashtar, the governor of Egypt, wrote: "all this is a necessary factor of your rule because I have often heard the Holy Prophet (s) saying, 'the nation, where the rights of the depressed, destitute and suppressed are not guarded and where the mighty and powerful persons are not forced to accede these rights, cannot achieve salvation.'"[52]

50 The school of Shia is the official religion of Iran, which refers to those who believe that, following the death of the Prophet, the Imamate (the political and religious leadership of the Muslim community) should have gone to 'Ali – the cousin and son-in-law of the prophet – and his descendants.

51 'Ali is the cousin and son-in-law of the prophet who is regarded as the first Imam and the rightful successor of the prophet by the Shia school of thought.

52 Nahjul Balagha, *Peak of Eloquence, Sermons, Letters and Sayings of Imam Ali ibn Abu Talib*, trans. Sayed Ali Resa (Elmhurst, NY: Tahrike Tarsile Qur'an, Inc., 1996).

The preceding discussion highlights one of the central concepts in Islamic political thought – that the legitimacy of the state is reinforced by providing a situation in which citizens can claim their rights and seek justice. This concept was emphasised by Ayatollah Mohaghegh Damad in the interview that I conducted to ask his opinion about access to justice from an Islamic perspective. He said, "If the Islamic state fails to uphold 'the citizen's ability to claim rights or barriers right-holders path to justice, its legitimacy will be questioned and challenged."[53] In fact, the legitimacy of the Islamic state derives from its action, upholding the Sharia or how the state's power acts, not how the state's power is established (contrary to the concept of legitimacy in Western democracies). Therefore, one of the indicators of the fairness of the Islamic state is that citizens have access with no barriers to the judicial and political authorities.[54] However, the adoption of national constitutions in the transitional Muslim countries transformed the legitimacy or political justice from the succession of the Imam to the legality of laws. In this process, the justice-related issues, as legal orders, transferred from a sacred to a secular premise (Khadduri, 1984).

Another important dimension of the conceptualisation of access to justice is procedural justice,[55] or the legal dimension

[53] Interviewed on 12 May 2010, Tehran.

[54] Ibid.

[55] Rawls (1971) in *A Theory of Justice* distinguishes three ideas of procedural justice: (1) perfect procedural justice combines an independent criterion for what makes a fair outcome of the procedure, and also a procedure that assures that the fair outcome will be achieved; (2) imperfect procedural justice focuses on an independent criterion for a fair outcome. "The desired outcome is that the defendant should be declared guilty if and only if he has committed the offence with which he is charged. The trial procedure is framed to search for and to establish the truth in this regard. But it seems impossible to design the legal rules so that they always lead to the correct result" (85). Finally, (3) pure procedural justice refers to a situation where there is

of formal justice that is associated with the key notions of equal treatment and equality before the law. According to Rawls (1971), justice can be achieved only through the equal application of law. Rawls claims that moral judgements that are based on experience, logic, and "the moral sense" must affect and be affected by the formal theory of justice, and also that legal guidelines should be made public and clear so that those addressed by them are able to fulfil them. His example of the procedure for dividing a cake gives a simple picture of procedural justice: the person who slices the cake picks last (1971: 85).

The basic connection of what is called formal justice theory is that procedural justice is an exterior feature of the law. "Procedural justice is the external aspect of the law by virtue of which substantive justice is realised. This aspect of justice, often called formal justice, is manifested in the degree of regularity, meticulousness, and impartiality in the application of the Law. As a procedural form of justice it may not seem as significant as substantive justice, but in reality it is no less important and its processes are intricate and highly complicated" (Khadduri, 1984: 144). Accordingly, formal justice is consistent with a definite procedure for establishing the facts required for the submission of the legal command (Rawls, 1971).

A very important aspect of procedural justice relates to fair trial provision. The Universal Islamic Declaration of Human

no independent criterion for the right result; instead, there is a correct or fair procedure. "Pure procedural justice means that in their rational deliberations the parties do not view themselves as required to apply, or as bound by, any antecedent given principles of right and justice. Put another way, they recognise no standpoint external to their own point of view as rational representatives from which they are constrained by prior and independent principles of justice" (Rawls, 1993: 73). Rawls argues that his rules involve pure procedural justice so if the rule is applied, the outcome will be just. However, justice is done through application of the rules, and any procedure of the rules will be just, no matter what the outcome.

Rights[56] provides that every person has the right to a fair trial. Article 19 of the declaration reads as follows: "a) All individuals are equal before the law, without distinction between ruler and ruled, b) The right to resort to justice is guaranteed to everyone, c) Liability is in essence personal, d) There shall be no crime or punishment except as provided for in the *Sharia*, e) A defendant is innocent until his guilt is proven in a fair trial in which he shall be given all the guarantees of defense." Article 20 continues: "It is not permitted without legitimate reason to arrest an individual, restrict his freedom, to exile or to punish him. It is not permitted to subject him to physical or psychological torture or to any form of humiliation, cruelty or indignity. Nor is it permitted to subject an individual to medical or scientific experimentation without his consent or at the risk of his health or of his life. Nor is it permitted to promulgate emergency laws that would provide executive authority for such actions."

All of the Islamic jurisprudential schools, similar to international and regional human rights standards as reviewed earlier, recognise fair trial principles that include: (1) preclusion of crime or punishment without law;[57] (2) the presumption of innocence;[58] (3) prevention of retroactive application of law; (4) the rights to life, liberty, and security of person for all individuals; (5) the right of equal access to a fair and open hearing and trial by a neutral court and an impartial judge; (6) the right to protection against arbitrary arrest and detention; (7) the right to due process of law;

[56] The Cairo Declaration on Human Rights in Islam (CDHRI) was adopted on 5 August 1990 by representatives of fifty-four Muslim countries to serve as guidance for the member states in the matters of human rights.

[57] The Quran contains different verses regarding the principle of legality and the principle of non-retroactivity, such as: "We never punish until we have sent a messenger" (17:15).

[58] The next chapter explains the presumption of innocence under the Islamic Law embodied in the Iranian legal system.

(8) prompt judicial proceedings; (9) cross-examination of the case; and (10) the right of appeal.

These key principles of fair trial are based on the specific provisions of the Quran and the *Sunnah*.[59] The right to life and liberty, for instance, is one of the basic principles of Islamic Law as declared by the Prophet: "Your lives, your property, and your honour are a burden upon you until you meet your Lord on the Day of Resurrection." This *Hadith* is interpreted to mean that there is a legal duty to protect life, property, and honour. Thus, in *hudud* (those who are punishable by a pre-established punishment found in the Quran), circumstantial evidence is avoided, and in the *qesas*, crimes (of retaliation), circumstantial evidence is favourable to the accused.

Another practical example of procedural justice from the Islamic perspective is the formulation of councils of Complaints (*Mazalim*), a tradition that brings individual complaints to the government personally. Mazalim literally means "wrongful exactions"[60] but in practice it was commonly used to refer to the discretionary jurisdiction of governors to settle grievances without directly basing themselves on the *shari'ah*.[61]

According to Khadduri, "in the experience of Islam, the equity that came into existence took the form of councils of Complaints (*Mazalim*) and sundry special courts designed to improve procedural justice as well as to provide a set of positive laws to deal with questions for which there existed no applicable rules in the *Sharia* ... they came into existence in the third/ninth century" (1984: 156).

[59] *Sunnah* refers to the Prophet Mohammed's words and deeds.

[60] Jorgen S. Nielsen, *Secular Justice in an Islamic State: Mazalim Under the Bahri Mamluks*, 662/1264–789/1387 (Istanbul, 1985); Nielsen, "Mazalim and Dara- al-Adl Under the Early Mamluks," *Muslim World* 66 (1976): 114–15.

[61] There is a vast amount of literature about the *mazalim* court and justice in the Islamic Law history. See for example Darling (2007); Irwin (2002); and Khalid (1976).

I shall end this section by emphasising that conceptions of justice are the substance of any possible conceptions of "access to justice" from an Islamic perspective. It appears that Islamic conceptions of access to justice have the potential to move beyond access to legal justice or judicial mechanisms of justice. It is intertwined also with the social, political justice and in particular procedural justice and how these concepts can be realised for individuals as their right (haqq) in their path to justice. Another significant aspect of Islamic conceptions of access to justice is access to alternative dispute resolution to underline social justice and to avoid the delay and cost of formal litigation. Since the argument I am putting forward about Islamic conceptions of access to justice is premised also on similar Western model notions, the following section presents alternative dispute resolutions from the Islamic perspective.

Alternative Dispute Resolution

As discussed earlier, alternative dispute resolutions, or ADRs, refer to a wide range of dispute resolution mechanisms to settle legal problems without resorting to litigation. ADR is often viewed as an intervention between parties to encourage reconciliation, compromise, and understanding. In many jurisdictions, ADR processes have been increasingly incorporated within courts and tribunals to provide greater access to justice. In my view, ADR mechanisms can be seen as an incorporative and responsive area for access to justice particularly for poor and disadvantaged people in Muslim societies. Therefore, in order to extend the Islamic conception of access to justice from a consensus-compromise perspective, some of the correlated notions of alternative dispute resolution from Islamic Law perspective will be reviewed.

It is important to note that Islamic Law recognises adjudication and reconciliation-based dispute resolution processes. Adjudication is used as a rule in hudud offences, because their punishments are fixed in the primary sources of Sharia (Quran

Table 1. Islamic Dispute Resolutions

Court-Based Dispute Resolution	Reconciliation-Based Dispute Resolution
Adjudication	Mediation
Formal process	Nonformal process
Fact-oriented reasoning	Perspective-oriented reasoning
Coercive power of the judge	Noncoercive power of the mediator/ arbitrator
Judge knowledge-based resolution process	Parties agreement-based resolution process
Excluding	Compromising
Need for legal scholarship	No need for legal scholarship
Binding verdict	Nonbinding opinion

and Sunnah). Also, the Islamic legal system has introduced a wide array of reconciliation-based dispute resolution mechanisms which in modern terms are referred to as Alternative Dispute Resolutions (ADR).

Table 1 illustrates the major distinctions between court-based and reconciliation-based dispute resolution in Islamic Law.[62]

One of the major distinctions between Islamic court-based and reconciliation-based dispute resolution relates to methodology and process of reasoning. In the adjudication system, the court refers to Islamic sources of law including the Quran and Sunnah, as primary sources of Sharia and reasoning by analogy *(qiyas)* in Sunni tradition or reason *(aql)* in *Shia* theology and consensus *(ijma)* as secondary sources of Sharia. The reasoning methodology is called *Usul al-fiqh*, which determines the substantive regulations or practical jurisprudence *(fiqh)*.

In contrast, in reconciliation-based dispute resolution, the mediator/arbitrator might refer to Islamic Law, in particular the Quran and Sunnah, to encourage parties to reconcile, but the primary source for settlement is the application of reason *(aql)* to

62 The differences highlighted previously are based on my own comparison between court and reconciliation dispute resolutions and are by no means exhaustive.

the dispute for parties to compromise. Also, it needs to be cited that the judge (*Qadi*) within the Islamic legal system balances the "rights" owed to God with the rights of individuals based on Islamic law, but the mediator balances the rights of individuals based on their own interest and consent.

Islamic legal tradition did include use of alternative dispute resolution mechanisms. During the Ottoman Empire, all judges were facilitating *sulh* (meaning peace/compromise/dispute resolution) between parties (Iqbal, 2001: 1035–7). In our time, most Muslim countries practice dispute settlement mechanisms based on Quran and Sunnah, as primary sources of Sharia. In the Islamic Republic of Iran, as an example of a Muslim-*Shia* country, the legal system does acknowledge Islamic reconciliation-based dispute resolution mechanisms through dispute settlement councils, arbitration, family mediation, and compromised settlement.[63] In Saudi Arabia, as an example of a Muslim-Sunni society, the legal system principally settles most civil cases in reconciliation, following the Quranic verse "*sulh* is best."[64]

The faith-based approach to dispute resolution rooted in the Quran verses promotes compromised resolution and reconciliation: "you who believe! Be decent for Allah, bearers of witness with justice, and let not hatred of a people provoke you not to act equitably; act equitably, that is nearer to faithfulness, and be careful of (your obligation to) Allah; without doubt Allah is Aware of what you do."[65] The Quran also says, "Walk on the earth in modesty, and when the ignorant address them, they

[63] According to Article 752 of Iranian civil code, "A settlement of account is possible either in the case of the adjustment of an existing dispute, or for avoidance of a possible dispute, or in the case of a transaction and the like." There is no legal limitation for parties to construct a legally accepted settlement unless it is to have "capacity for the transaction" and "an interest in the subject of the settlement."

[64] Quran 4:128.

[65] Quran 5:8.

say: Peace."[66] Also, "These hasten to good things and they are leading in (attaining) them."[67]

One of the primary Quranic values regarding dispute resolution is that of forgiveness (*Afv*), which encourages Muslims to resort to forgiveness. "Allah promises those who avoid the great sins, and whenever they are angry they forgive a highest reward."[68] Some scholars argue that the Quran encourages forgiveness in three different ways: first is forgetting a wrong done; second, ignoring an offensive act or person; and the third one refers to Allah's divine forgiveness (Gopin, 2005). Other Quranic core principles including *adl* (justice), *sulh* (negotiated settlement), *musalaha* (reconciliation), *Hakam* (arbitration), *Hikmah* (wisdom), *Ihsan* (beneficence), and *salam* (peace) construct the Islamic framework for dispute resolution.[69]

In addition, Islamic human rights values can be considered as a related source for reconciliation-based dispute resolution. The Islamic scholar, Majid Khadduri, has illustrated the five most important principles of human rights in Islam: (1) dignity and brotherhood; (2) equality among members of the community, without distinction on the basis of race, colour, or class; (3) respect for the honour, reputation, and family of each individual; (4) the right of each individual to be presumed innocent until proven guilty; and (5) individual freedom (1984: 236–7). The linkages between the role of individual, honour, and brotherhood to Islamic dispute resolution should be examined, as Islamic dispute settlement

[66] Quran 25:63.

[67] Quran 23:61.

[68] Quran 42:37.

[69] The principles of Adl, Ihsan, and Hikmah also have been referred to as core values of the Islamic peacemaking framework: "Islam yields a set of peace building values that if consistently and systematically applied can transcend and govern all types and levels of conflict, values such as justice (adl) beneficence (Ihsan) and wisdom (Hikmah) which constitute core principles of peacemaking strategies and framework." See Abu-Nimer, 2000–2001.

practices include structuring the individual's consent, motivated by honour and brotherhood, to settle the dispute. Also, there is a need to appreciate the Islamic style of communication, negotiation, mediation, forgiveness, and code of honour (and its opposite meaning, shame) in analysing Islamic dispute resolution.

In addition, the Quran values peace as a fundamental component of the well-being of human beings. One of the Quranic terms for the peaceful settlement of disputes is *silm* and its derivatives, such as salam, which means peace, security, and acceptance. The alternative expression, which the Quran uses to advocate the compromised settlement of disputes, is sulh, meaning peace and reconciliation. The Quran values sulh, stating: "compromise is better."'[70] In Islamic law, sulh is a self-governing arrangement and may be affected in exchange for wealth or in exchange for benefits. In accordance with the principles of Islamic Law, "the purpose of *sulh* is to end conflict and hostility among believers so that they may conduct their relationships in peace and amity.... In Islamic law, *sulh* is a form of contract (*'akd*), legally binding on both the individual and community levels" (Khadduri, 1984: 845–6). Like the private sulh between two believers, "the purpose of public *sulh* is to suspend fighting between two parties and establish peace, called *muwada'a* (peace or gentle relationship), for a specific period of time" (ibid.).

Many Muslim countries have provisions within their laws regarding sulh. Note, for example, the Iranian Civil Code that stated sulh or compromised settlement is legally enforceable except in that which relates to an unlawful matter (Article 754). According to Article 752 of the Iranian Civil Code, "a settlement of account is possible either in the case of the adjustment of an existing dispute, or for avoidance of a possible dispute, or in the case of a transaction and the like." There is no legal limitation for parties to construct a legally accepted settlement unless there

[70] Quran 3:128.

exists a "capacity for the transaction" and "an interest in the subject of the settlement."[71]

Another important dimension of ADR in Islamic Law is mediation, a negotiated dispute resolution mechanism in which a neutral intervener facilitates between disputing parties to agree on a joint settlement. In the words of the Quran: "If a couple fears separation, you shall appoint an arbitrator from his family and an arbitrator from her family; if they decide to reconcile, GOD will help them get together."[72] In Shia tradition as well as Sunni (with the exception of *Maliki* law), arbitrators have no power to decide that a marriage shall be terminated. Their function ends once they have made their attempt at reconciliation. The principle of family mediation, known as *hakam*, has been taught within the family law statutes of most Muslim countries.

An example of this is the Iranian Family Protection Act, which emphasises reconciliation based on Sharia. The responsibility of the mediator/arbitrator is to settle the family dispute. According to the Act, the Family Court is bound to ask divorcing parties to appoint a mediator. The mediator should primarily attempt to reconcile the parties, but if the parties fail, the mediator must submit their opinion to the court. These findings will be shared with the parties within a specified period and implemented, except where the parties raise an objection. In the case of objection, the court will examine the matter and make a judgement.

Arbitration is another type of ADR mechanism recognised by Islamic Law. As stated in the Quran: "Allah command you to render back your trusts to those to whom they are due; And when ye judge Between man and man, That ye judge with justice: verily how excellent is the teaching which he gives you"[73] [4:35]. Although there is no exact definition of *tahkìm* or arbitration in the early history of Islam, the Treaty of Medina of AD 622 called

71 Iranian Civil Code, Article 753.

72 Quran 4:35.

73 Ibid.

for the arbitration of any disputes. This concept of reconciliation can also be found in the traditions of the Prophet Muhammad in the reconstruction of the *Kaaba*. This involved a dispute over placing the Black Stone (*Hajr al-Aswad*) into the building between the tribes of the *Quraysh* who wanted to have the honour of placing the stone. The Prophet asked each of the tribes to introduce a representative. He then placed the stone in a cloth, asking all representatives to hold it and raise it together, thus resolving the matter to the satisfaction of all parties. The Prophet had also taken action as an arbitrator over several disputes. In another incident, reported in Sahih a-Bukhari, the Prophet had conciliated between litigants on a dispute over debt. He was reported to have cut the claim of a creditor in half in order to reach a rapid settlement.[74]

In relation to the Shia tradition, Imam Hassan[75] defines arbitration in accordance with the Shia School as a voluntary procedure whereby a neutral qualified jurist in a case is chosen by opposing parties to settle the dispute according to Islamic law (Halili, 2006: 181–207). This definition is in line with the Sunni School, which defines arbitration as an agreement by the disputants to appoint a qualified person to settle their dispute by reference to Islamic law (ibid.).

For example, I may refer to the Iranian International Commercial Arbitration Act, which includes nine sections and thirty six articles, was enacted on 17 September 1997 by the Iranian Parliament, and was affirmed by the Guardian Council in October 1997. In accordance with this act, arbitration "means the settlement of disputes between litigants out of court by mutually agreed natural or legal persons and/or appointed ones."[76]

[74] Muhammad Muhsin Khan, *Sahih al-Bukhari*, vol. 3 (Riyadh: Darussalam, 1997).

[75] The second Imam according to the *Shia* school of thought.

[76] Iranian International Commercial Arbitration Act, Article 1.a.

An interesting area of the ADR process within Islamic Law is *Fatwa*, which is issued by a recognised religious authority in Islam and can be referred to as one of the Islamic dispute resolution mechanisms. Fatwa is a nonbinding mechanism, comparable in modern terms with an expert opinion. However, because of the high respect and high standing afforded a Mufti in Islamic society, the parties who have preferred to seek Fatwa over their dispute will comply with scholarly opinion on a matter of Islamic law.

Also, *Muhtasib*, or an ombudsman, in early Islamic history, was a learned jurist who functioned as a public inspector, complaint receiver, and enforcer. The notion of Muhtasib is derived from the duty of promoting good (*ma'ruf*) and preventing wrongdoing (*munkar*) in Islamic law. This concept can be compared in a modern context with community advocates who settle disputes at a community level.

Although ADRs have been promoted as an alternative to the frustrating processes of adjudication since the early 1970s, critics describe ADR as a system of second-class justice that has none of the procedural safeguards of the formal justice system.[77] In addition, some feel ADR creates a division between the rich and the poor, and fosters formal adjudication for the wealthy and alternative forms for the poor and marginalised groups. Criticisms also focus on the perceived limitations of informal resolution procedures to enable broader social change, especially in discrimination cases.[78] Because of the confidential nature of conciliation settlements, discriminatory acts are hidden from public scrutiny.

In the context of Muslim societies too, the idea of ADR could function against the interests of marginalised groups, especially women. This is particularly so when discrimination against women is inherent in local norms or traditional dispute resolution

[77] Clarke and Davies (1992). Also see Krishnan and Galanter (2004).

[78] Cobb and Rifkin (1991).

mechanisms.[79] Mediation, for example, can be problematic in cases of violence against women where unequal power relationships between the parties are involved.[80]

It is also important to note that alternative mechanisms cannot replace the adjudication by the courts nor reduce the need to improve the justice system, particularly in Muslim societies. The formal justice system is the required intervention in many circumstances, such as criminal justice, social order, and where a court ruling on a case may result in positive law reform. Therefore any intervention by ADR programs, in particular those dealing with cases involving women, not only must be fully voluntary but also must ensure protection from further discrimination and aim at empowering disadvantaged groups.

Conclusion

The discussion regarding access to justice is, in a sense, about how justice can be defined and realised for people, in particular those who are poor and disadvantaged. Justice therefore is the substance of procedures and outcomes of a path to justice when people must resolve problems that have potential legal aspects and also potential legal solutions. In this sense, access to justice is not only about access to the legal system and the fact that every person should receive a just and fair treatment within the legal system" (Muralidhar, 2004a: 1). It is also about access to substantive justice, access to a just social and political context that permits a person to seek simultaneous legal redress.

The conceptual analysis of access to justice as discussed earlier comes close to a view claimed by Rawls (1971) in using the concept-conception distinction, which stressed that the concept of

[79] USAID Office of Democracy and Governance (1998), *Alternative Dispute Resolution Practitioners' Guide*.

[80] See for example UN Handbook for Legislation on Violence Against Women.

justice can be understood to function as a regulative idea for conceptions of justice. Western legal positivism and legal realism, for instance, developed conceptions of justice to articulate how a just rule can be realised for those who are affected by the law (rule of law). The comparative nature of the present discussion emphasised the importance of providing a general overview of how the access to justice debate has been formulated in Islamic thought. Western legal positivism and legal realism developed concepts of justice to represent how a rule (that is supposed to be just) can be realised for average people – those who are affected by the law. In other words, law and justice are synonymous in the Western debate on access to justice. Thus the term "access to justice" often refers to access to the legal system to obtain legal redress for a legal problem. The term "legal" here appears to identify as "justice" in addressing many problems encountered in people's everyday lives.

In contrast, Islamic conceptions of access to justice are, for the most part, rooted in establishing justice rather than maximising accessibility of justice by the state. However, as already noted, Western welfare state plans for access to justice are predominantly state-centred, placing greater emphasis on strengthening the structure and function of judicial institutions. Another difference between Islamic and Western conceptions of access to justice relates to the nature of justice and how it moves far beyond legal justice. A different distinction lies in the meaning of access. In most models of access to justice offered by Western scholars, access has a physical (objective) dimension, such as long delay, cost, and legal representation. These models also often focus on top-down approaches to overcome barriers to access to justice. On the contrary, the notion and scope of access from an Islamic perspective would appear to be subjective, as it highlights the role of an individual to have access as their right.

Therefore, analysing the concept-conception of access to justice in order to underline the gap between the contextual framework of Western and Islamic related discourses is primarily concerned with understanding the concept of justice. Also, it requires an appreciation of what context must exist in order for justice to be realised and how the concept of justice is meant to be accessible for "ordinary" people. Since context defines access, my conclusion therefore is that multiple and multifaceted approaches from Islamic Law perspectives can be incorporated into contextualising various conceptions of access to justice. The Indonesian understanding of access to justice, for instance, varies from the Iranian or Pakistani definition of access to justice.[81]

This understanding also fits into legal pluralism that challenges mainstream legal discourse. In other words, legal pluralism is based on "corporations" of different subgroups.[82] From a historical point of view, legal pluralism was a response to European legal positivist philosophy that is more centralist.[83] Law therefore should be seen in the context of society and culture, where it exists in the form of customs and rules that have their own ways of inducing compliance.[84]

In the final analysis, however, while I agree that conceptualising access to justice from the Islamic Law perspective should be based on a multifaceted context-dependent approach, I also assume that Islamic conceptions of access to justice are mainly dominated by four key paradigms: the first is concerned with the rights-obligations theory as discussed previously in the review of Islamic conceptions of justice; the second dimension is about how justice as a right or truth (haqq) can be established (procedural justice and fair trail principles); the third component is associated with how a rights-holder can possess justice as a right or haqq

[81] I owe this remark to Professor Abdullahi Ahmed An-Na'im (interviewed on 20 October 2010, Coventry).

[82] Smith (1969).

[83] See for instance Galanter's and Griffiths's comments on naming the mainstream legal discourse as a "legal centralist" or "formalist" model of law (Galanter, 1981; Griffiths, 1986).

[84] Falkmoore (1973).

(access); and the fourth notion pertains to compromising between the rights of conflicting parties, which in many modern legal systems are referred to as alternative dispute resolutions (ADRs).

This chapter thus reviews some of the literature relating to the field of access to justice. The literature reviewed points to the fact that Western models of access to justice are predominantly state-centred with particular emphasis on institutions of access. In contrast, Islamic conceptions of access to justice focus particularly on the definition of justice and its realisation for people.

The next chapter provides a contextual analysis of access to justice in Iran by providing a historical perspective of how the justice system has been developed and examines related dimensions, such as performance of the justice system and legal protection.

2 The System of Justice in Iran

Access to justice is recognised by the Constitution of the Islamic Republic of Iran within the fair trial provisions, yet, there is a growing concern that "justice for all" does not apply to every Iranian and in all cases. There is unequal access to justice among people in many societies, characterised by gaps between the socio-economic status of citizens, level of education, gender, religion, and so on. However, Iran is a country where the fundamental commitment of the Islamic Revolution toward more broadly establishing equal justice has been violated.[1]

[1] The form of government of Iran is that of an Islamic Republic, endorsed by the people of Iran on the basis of their long-standing belief in the sovereignty of truth and Qur'anic justice, in the referendum of 29 and 30 March 1979, through the affirmative vote of a majority of 98.2 percent of eligible voters, held after the victorious Islamic Revolution led by Imam Khumayni (Article 1 of the constitution), and also, according to Article 2 of the constitution, the Islamic Republic is a system based on belief in: the exalted dignity and value of man, and his freedom coupled with responsibility before God; which includes equity, justice, political, economic, social, and cultural independence, and national solidarity.

Qualifying Remarks

Several qualifying remarks should be made at the outset of this chapter. The first relates to the source of this study. It is important to note that any assessment of access to justice in Iran is constrained by the limited coverage of official data. While ample statistics are available for certain factors, such as legal aid provided by the Bar Association for instance, little data have been collected or published about other components of the access to justice paradigm, such as legal awareness; legal protection; or the effectiveness, transparency, and accountability of the administration of justice. On the subject of women's access to justice, in particular, various studies have been conducted on the legal protection of women's rights and interests,[2] but there is no research that includes quantitative and qualitative data on the sensitisation of the judiciary toward gender. Also, virtually no official data exist on women's access to justice in the context of domestic violence. More research is needed regarding the factors that are detrimental to women's access to justice, such as cultural barriers. Therefore, the primary source of data for this chapter is a comparative literature review. The review includes an exploration of legal documents (including laws and case summaries where available), historical documents, anthropological texts, and the findings from related research studies.[3] The review presented in

[2] A vast literature (which varies from fiction to feminist critics, family relation to politics, etc.) has been written about women in Iran to criticise sociolegal inequalities and emphasis on gender disparities. A subject bibliography has listed 871 materials written in Farsi from 1979 to 2000 on women of Iran (Mojab and Hojabri, 2000). There are also numerous scholarly entries on law, rights, power relations, and Iranian women. See for example Mir-Hosseini (1996: 149–69). Also see her book *Marriage on Trial: A Comparative Study of Islamic Family Law in Iran and Morocco* (2000); Hoodfar (1999); Ebady (2000); Haeri (1992); Kar (2001); Kian-Thiebaut (2002). Also see Paidar (1995); Afkhami (1994).

[3] Iranian archival collections include a wide variety of primary source material such as books, documents, reports, newspapers, laws,

this study, however, should not be regarded as comprehensive, but rather as a hypothesis requiring further study and analysis on many levels.

The second qualifying remark is that this study is limited to the sphere of civil and criminal justice. Terms such as "justice

correspondence, diaries, as well as photographs, sound recordings, films, videotapes, electronic data and artifacts. Regarding the official archives facilities, there are three major institutions: (1) National Library and Archives of Islamic Republic of Iran (NLAI) is the nation's recordkeeper and also functions as a research and service institution chaired by the president. The National Library of Iran was established in 1937. In 1999, the Islamic Revolution Cultural Documentation Organisation and Tehran Book Processing Center merged into the National Library. In 2002, the National Archives joined, so NLAI was created. In addition to organisation of sources (cataloguing, book classification) the National Library is also responsible for restoring old periodicals (including the *Vaghaye Ettefaghieh*, *Dowlat Alayhe Iran*, *Iran va Iran-e-Soltani*, *Anjoman-e-Tabriz*, *Akhtar*, *Hablol Mateen*, *Hekmat*, *Sorayya*, *Shokoufeh van Danesh*, and the *Tarbiat* newspapers), developing bibliographies (such as the Iranian History Bibliography, the Azerbaijan Bibliography), and also developing the Encyclopaedia of Library and Information Science (two volumes have been published in 2002 and 2006); (2) Islamic Revolution Document Center (IRDC) was founded in 1981 to collect documents about the history of the Iranian Islamic Revolution, similar movements in Muslim societies, and also Islamic history. The Center holds thousands of manuscripts, photographs, sound recordings, and films. The Center also has published numerous books (such as *Sedition Theory*, *Iranian Hostage Taking*, *The Islamic Revolution and Lebanese Shiites*, *Color Revolutions*, and *Iran's Islamic Revolution*); (3) Iran Official Journal is an executive branch of the Ministry of Justice responsible for publishing all of Iran's legislations (acts of the parliament, government circulars, decisions of the Supreme Court, decisions of the Expediency Council, and decisions of the Court of Administrative Justice) and also publishing new entries and changes in the commercial register. The Official Journal of Iran was published for the first in 1910 by the parliament, but since 1959 it has been under the administration of the Ministry of Justice to be published daily.

system" or "judicial" as used herein should be understood to refer to the mechanisms used for resolving legal disputes. They form part of the formal, official state system of courts of law. This study applies a holistic approach in examining access to justice in the Islamic Republic of Iran and presents a general overview of the main dimensions of access to justice: (1) access to court; (2) access to legal remedies and the enforcement of rights; and (3) access to legal representation. This chapter thus reviews a general framework with regard to access to justice in Iran, while the following chapter will examine some common barriers to access to justice.

The third qualifying remark is related to development and access to justice. Any assessment of access to justice cannot be complete unless a brief overview of the country's human development indicators is provided. The links between access to justice and development have confirmed that, in most cases, the marginalised groups perceive themselves as "divorced" from the protection of justice institutions.[4] This divorce illustrates a gap between "law in the books" and "law-in-action."[5] The poorest populations are at a significant institutional disadvantage in terms of their access to justice. To help illustrate how developed Iran is in this

Most of the judicial complexes have already begun to automate the court processes and monitoring case activities by using the Case Management System (CMS), a computer program designed to provide a complete set of functionality for courts to cover online data entry, scheduling, analytics, reporting, workflow management, and system administration. It has also strengthened the accessibility of the justice system by enabling citizens to interface electronically with judicial bodies and services. In addition, most judicial institutions, such as the police and the prison system, manage their information and provide archival sources and statistical reports. Some of these reports are available to the public through the organisation's website, library, or archival center, but in most cases official approval is required to gain access to the information.

[4] For data on law and development, see Seidman (1978), and Trubek and Galanter (1974). Also see Cooter (1996).

[5] See Buscaglia (1996).

regard, the discussion that follows briefly reviews key human development indicators before examining access to justice. The 70 million inhabitants[6] of Iran have an average quality of life that is within the high-level development category as quantified by the human development index (HDI).[7] Iran has a very young population, with 25 percent of the population below the age group of 15–25 and nearly 70 percent between 15 and 64 years of age.[8] This is because two key demographic changes occurred during the last quarter of a century. It began with an increase in the birth rate during the 1980s, followed by a large decrease during the 1990s. An assessment of national human development indicators discloses broad inter-provincial inequalities, rural-urban gaps, and disparate income distribution among the population.[9] About 20 percent of the population currently lives below the poverty line;[10] a significant proportion are unemployed.[11] However, Iran has achieved notable successes in the fields of healthcare, life expectancy, and education in recent years. Iranian women, in particular, are becoming more educated than men. Recent reports show that nearly 70 percent of the university intake is female.[12]

Moreover, there should be a distinction between the legal process and the outcome of a legal proceeding. Access to the justice system, any kind of formal legal services or what might be called legal proceedings, does not always result in a just outcome for a

[6] The 2006–2007 (SH 1385) National Census; the Office for National Statistics.

[7] The human development index (HDI) for Iran (Islamic Republic of) is 0.702, which gives the country a rank of 70th out of 169 countries based on updated 2010 statistics cited in the Human Development Report conducted by the United Nations Development Programs (UNDP, 2010).

[8] See note 67.

[9] Ibid.

[10] 18 percent according to the UN (2007 estimate).

[11] 11.8 percent according to the Iranian government (2009 estimate).

[12] UNESCO Science Report 2010. Also see Vakil (2011), p.111.

person who is taking legal action to overcome a legal problem. In Iran, just as elsewhere, there is no common understanding of justice, since it is not an objective concept. The same is true of the meaning of a "just outcome," which obviously depends on the context. It is also commonly accepted that the legal remedies provided by the customary laws are not just.[13] The survey study in Chapter 6 supports these lines of argument.

The last observation that needs to be considered pertains to the meaning and scope of access to justice. In other words, what does access to justice mean within the context of the Islamic Republic of Iran? Is it about establishing "justice"? Does it mean equal legal protection? What about administration of justice? What is the main focus, then – justice or access? How can "access" be defined when the public seems to perceive that justice is one of the most violated promises? Why does examining access to justice in a Muslim country such as Iran seem to involve extending its scope from the conventional definition of "access to justice"?[14]

At the time of this study, justice and access to justice were subject to considerable revision as to their meaning and extent of coverage, particularly with reference to Iran. It was important to decide whether to apply the "path to justice" approach to analyse access to justice within the context of Iran. This approach defines justice as both fairness of process and fairness of outcome in addressing justiciable issues. Justiciable issues are those

[13] There is a vast amount of literature that indicates Iranian customary laws are not providing equal protection of justice for all. See the work of Mehrangiz Kar (1999, 2000). Another book by Kar (2001), *Women's Participation in Politics: Obstacles and Possibilities*, studies unequal legal protections regarding political rights. Also see the writing of Iranian women activists collected by the "One Million Signatures Campaign" which aims to collect one million signatures to demand changes to discriminatory laws against women. Available online at http://we-change.org/english/.

[14] See the definitional analysis of access to justice in Chapter 1.

problems for which there is a potential legal remedy within a civil and/or criminal justice framework (Buck et al., 2005: 302).[15]

It should be noted that most of the recent studies adopt this model to examine access to justice within the context of Western societies (see for example Genn and Beinart, 1999; Genn et al., 2001). However, the path to justice model does not appear to be an adequate theoretical framework for a country like Iran. This is so not because the path to justice model adopts a reductionist approach that understands the complex nature of access to justice to be the sum of the ability to seek justice for a justiciable issue, but because the main presumption of this model is the existence of a legal remedy that legitimises the idea of justiciable issues. In other words, path to justice presumes that equal legal remedies exist based on the normative protection of rights by international and constitutional law, as well as a legal framework, customary norms, and jurisprudence. Nevertheless, in a country like Iran, one key concern regarding access to justice is the lack of adequate remedies that are protected by both legal and customary frameworks (CCA, 2003).

Now that these qualifications have been introduced, the discussion can proceed: first, a brief presentation of the Iranian legal system and the state of national justice institutions; then, a historical background coupled with an analysis of the performance of the justice system. This background provides the preliminary dimensions necessary to structure a contextual framework of access to justice in Iran. The focus is on both formal justice systems and legal processes.

The Legal System

This section synthesises the main characteristics of the Iranian legal system and development of the justice system in order to

[15] A detailed discussion of the path to justice model will be presented in Chapter 5.

emphasise how, historically, the concept of "access to judicial protection" has been formed in Iran. By analysing both historical and descriptive aspects of judicial protection, this section suggests that the development of justice institutions has reinforced access to mechanisms of justice and so access to justice in Iran.

In Iran, the formal justice system is tied to the legal values inherited from the Shia theology, the French and Belgian laws that were used as models for legislation before the Islamic Revolution of 1979. The preamble of the Islamic Republic Constitution enshrines Sharia as the supreme law, which refers to the "twelve Imams" *fiqh*[16] or the *Jafari* school of thought. The Jafari school of thought derives from the name of the Sixth Imam, Ja'far, known as al-Sadiq.[17] Article 12 of the Iranian Constitution establishes the Shia Jafari School of Law as the official school of Islamic Law (*madhab*) of the Iranian government. The combination of Islam as the state religion and the general legal principles of the country makes Iran a mixed type of constitutional theocracy. In fact, "the Islamic Republic of Iran is commonly considered to be a fundamentalist theocracy, with governing principles and practices that bear very little resemblance to prevailing principles of western constitutionalism. In practice, however, its system of government features many elements of modern constitutionalism" (Hirschl, 2008: 78). The law is rooted in both secular and religious sources such as (1) codified legislation, (2) judicial procedure, (3) custom, (4) doctrine, as well as Islamic law sources as we discuss later.

[16] Science of Jurisprudence.

[17] Imam, Ja'far lived from 83H to 148H. He was born and died in the city of Madina, where he was able to teach during the Abbasid caliphs. His teachings were collected in 400 *usul* (foundations), which were written by his students and encompass Hadith, Islamic philosophy, theology, commentary of the Quran, literature, and ethics. After a period of time, some scholars categorised these 400 usul in four books, which are the main sources of Hadith for the Shia. They are: *Usul al-Kafi* by al-Kulayni (d.329H), *Man La Yahduruh al-Faqih* by al-Saduq (d.381H), and *al-Tahdib* and *al-Istibsar* by al-Tusi (d.460H).

The first source, codified legislation or what is called *Qanun*,[18] can be divided into three main categories beginning with the constitutional law, which sets the limits of jurisdiction of the three branches of government. The Parliament does not have the authority to alter or change the Constitution and must always adhere to its Articles. The second category is called common laws, which are ratified by the Islamic Parliament as a result of general consultations. International treaties become a part of the common law, when the government or the Parliament ratifies them.[19] The third category, which refers to legislation, regulation, and government circulars, is exercised, following determination and deliberation, by the executive branch with regard to its approval, with respect to the implementation of the common laws (Jafari-Langroudi, 1997). The judicial procedure or jurisprudence is the second source of the law. The jurisprudence of the Supreme Court has the force of law and all courts are obliged to follow it. The third source refers to custom or *Urf*, which means whatever is regarded as normal and routine by the common people.[20] Whenever the law is insufficient, contradictory, silent, or vague about an issue, the judge will try to issue a judgement through reference to custom. The same rule applies to doctrine or the opinions of legal scholars as the fourth source of the law.

According to the Constitution, all civil, criminal, financial, economic, administrative, cultural, military, political, and other laws and regulations must be based on Islamic criteria (Article 4). Article 146 of the Constitution binds the Judge who "endeavours to judge each case on the basis of the codified law. In case of the absence of any such law, s/he has to deliver his judgment on the basis of

[18] The word '*Qanun*' derives from the Latin word "canon," ultimately from the Greek "kanon" (akin to the English "cane"), which means a rule or a standard.

[19] Iranian Civil Code, Article 9.

[20] Articles 132 and 220 of the Civil Code have indicated customs as source of law.

authoritative Islamic sources and authentic *Fatwa*." The Islamic sources include Quran, Sunnah, consensus, and reason.[21] In the Shia theology, Sunnah refers to the deeds, sayings, and approvals of the Prophet and the twelve Imams who Shia believes are chosen by the Prophet to lead the Muslim community (*Ummah*). According to the Shia, if an Islamic commandment cannot be found within the primary sources (Quran and Sunnah), then reason or *Aql* should be given leave to deduce a proper response from the primary sources. The doctrine of *Ijtihad* is applied in deducing laws from primary sources. In fact, the legal jurisprudence in the Jafari school of thought in based on Ijtihad, which means deduction of *Ahkam* (the Islamic commandments) from the sources and through the principles of the Sharia.

Historical Perspective

In order to understand how the concept of "access to judicial protection" has been formed in Iran, this section provides a brief review of the historical development of the justice system. In this context, the early development of Iranian access to justice can be found in connection with "access to court" whereby the claims of an individual whose rights and interests were breached by others or the state could be heard. This historical examination of how the justice system has developed also depicts the significant role of economic growth and political development in Iran. The Western access to justice debate defines "in its ordinary usage, the term access to justice as (is) a synonym of judicial protection accordingly the term would normally refer to the right to seek a remedy before a court of law or tribunal which is constituted by law" (Francioni, 2007: 3). Therefore, from the historical perspective, Iran's experience in terms of access to justice has been

[21] In the Sunni school of thought, the Quran and the Sunnah are considered as primary sources of Islamic law, as are *Ijma* (consensus) and *qiyas* (reasoning by analogy) as secondary sources for legal judgement.

shaped largely by the development of judicial institutions and legal orders rather than the rule of legal idealism.

Pre-Islamic Era

The ancient Iranian justice system was part of the Persian Empire, with the courts controlled by the king, thereby making him the country's senior judge (Ahmadi, 1959; 40–5). The sources of law were the king's issued orders, local customs, and religious rules. Court proceedings changed extensively during the reigns of Darrius (522–486 BC) and Cyrus (590–580 BC). As a result of these changes, the courts had a specific period of time in which to conduct hearings. The personality and past record of the accused were taken into consideration at the time of sentencing, and if a sentence was issued unjustly, the presiding judges were punished (Will Durant, 1935: 531). Similar to most ancient justice systems, the burden of proof was on the plaintiff (Amin, 2003: 90); however, cultural norms enjoined judges to encourage reconciliation between the parties. During the Sassanid Empire (224–651 BC), the justice system was in the hands of the Zoroastrian priests who were authorised by the State to carry out the judgement as well as register the four personal records (birth, marriage, divorce, death).[22] The court consisted of a judge, a counsel, and an observer, and there were preliminary and appeals courts (Amin, 2003: 85). In Sassanid theory, the ideal society was one that could maintain stability and justice, and the necessary instrument for this was a strong monarch (Daniel, 2001: 57).

Textual examination of sacred books and the early literature of ancient Persia extrapolates that access to justice was seen as fairness of the court procedure and also fairness of the court outcome. The "just judgement" was the main constituent of how justice could be accessed. However, a just judgement was a

[22] Zoroastrianism is a religion based on the teachings of Zoroaster founded some time before the sixth century BCE in Iran.

context-dependent concept, as there was no realisation of the rule of law. The judges had to apply the principle of justice when the sentences were given. Zoroastrianism strongly advised the judges to follow the principle of justice and fairness; otherwise they would face the promise of punishment in the Hereafter. Chapter 91 of the book of *Arda Viraf,*[23] which discusses an unfair judge, states: "then I saw the soul of a man who slew his own child and even ate the brains. And I asked so: what sin was committed by this body, whose soul suffers such a brutal punishment? Srosh (the angel) and Adar the angel, responded: 'this is the soul of that sentencing judge whose decision was founded on the lie and unfairness between those seeking for justice; he didn't treat the litigants and defendants justly; but through a hunger of wealth, he shouted at those seeking for justice with anger and harshness."

Justice also is one of the main elements of the Persian national epic Shāhnāmé.[24] The theme of the unjust ruler and how a nation can act in response to an unjust order plays an essential role in this national epic. The story of Zahhak, for instance, is one of the narratives that explores this theme. Zahhak is Shāhnāmé's first evil king who was cursed with a snake growing out of each shoulder, to which he must feed one human brain per night; this meant he must kill two people a day in order to keep the snakes fed. The reaction of the nation in response to an unjust ruler was revolution. This idea of the just ruler[25] was the test of the ruler's legitimacy: "there can be no clear notion of justice without reference to a legal framework. In such a case justice may be perceived to exist only in relation to the existing social expectations.

[23] The book of Arda Viraf as a Zoroastrian religious text describes the dream-journey of a devout Zoroastrian through the next world.

[24] Shāhnāmé or "The Book of Kings" (Persian: شاهنامه) is a poetic piece written by the Abolqasem Ferdowsi (c. 935–1020). Shāhnāmé tells the historical past from the Persian Empire until the Islamic conquest of Persia in the seventh century CE.

[25] In the Islamic terminology known as Malek-e Adel.

The evidence shows that the just ruler corresponding to the ideal concept was one who ran the country well, maintained peace and security within as well as without his realm, employed able officials and governors (and punished them for injustice, i.e., actions not permitted by the ruler himself), and thus promoted peace and prosperity"(Katouzian, 1997: 62).

Islamic Era

The Islamic conquest of Persia led to the end of the Sassanid Empire in AC 644. The Islamisation process took place within the sociolegal structure of Iranian society. The primary emphasis was on the legal structure seeing that control of the clergy in the judicial system was profound. During the Safavid period (1500–1722), the *Ithnā'ashari* (Twelver) school of Shia became the official religion of Iran. In the Safavid state, "the administration of justice was a complicated affair" (Savory, 1974: 201). The judiciary was divided into secular and religious courts under *Sadr* (head of the religious court for the administration of canon law). The Sharia courts were in the hands of a number of other religious officials such as the *qaz'l al-guzat*[26] and the *shafih al-islam.*[27] As a result there was a considerable degree of conflict of jurisdiction" (ibid.). At this time, a new secular judicial institution, *divanbagi*, was created to draw together all these strands under one overarching body and also to address the four criminal acts, which included murder, rape, assaults leading to injury, and stealing (Ravandi, 1989: 222). The divanbagi was also the highest court of appeal. All civil cases were settled by the religious courts under Shia jurisprudence. For nearly two hundred years, from the Safavid period (1722) to the Constitutional movement (1907), the Iranian legal system was based on Shia jurisprudence and also was anchored in unwritten laws and orders.

[26] The highest judge.

[27] The friend of Islam.

The Constitutional Revolutionary Movement[28] resulted in the first gathering of parliament who had the right to make a constitution, thus becoming a Constitutional Assembly on October 1906. One of the main demands on the people during the constitutional movement was the establishment of the House of Justice (*adalat khaneh*) in 1905. The period 1906–1911 witnessed the transformation of the Iranian Judiciary when a number of provisional civil and criminal courts were set up and principles related to the structure of the judiciary were codified.[29] During the rule of Reza Shah, the structure of the judiciary changed once again and several laws were also adopted, such as the Civil Code (1928), Penal Code (1925), Commercial Code (1939), and the Code of Civil Procedure (1939).[30] During the period of Mohammad – Reza Shah, the organisations affiliated with the judiciary were expanded.[31]

A major transformation regarding access to justice was in establishing the House of Justice and Arbitration Council.[32] These institutions applied an alternative dispute resolution scheme such as mediation, arbitration, conciliation, and encouraging parties toward compromise and reconciliation. All the council members were elected by the local community from among capable

[28] Mashrutiyyat (Persian: مشروطیت).

[29] Hassan Moshir- ol- Doleh (Pirnia), Justice Minister, drafted the Principles of the Judiciary Structure Act. According to Article 1 and 4 of this law, courts were divided into two main categories: general and special courts. The general courts included the reconciliation court, preliminary court, and appeal court, and special courts consisted of trade court, military court, special criminal court, and the disciplinary court of judges. See Zerang (2002) *Development of the Legal System in Iran*. Tehran: Islamic Revolution Documentation Center.

[30] The schools of law, recruitment of foreign professors, and exchange were set up. See ibid., at p. 371.

[31] The organisational establishment of the Juvenile Court in 1959, also the Family Support Court based the first article of the Family Support Act 1967 to hear all disputes arising from marital and family issues.

[32] House Act passed in 1965 and the Arbitration Council Act in 1966.

educated candidates over thirty-five years old, with a good reputation for honesty and decency, and without any actual criminal convictions. Since the Council members often had no judicial education, the Council took advice from former judges, lawyers, or legal advisors.

The structure of the Iranian justice system underwent major change and reform after the 1979 Islamic Revolution. The Constitution of the 1979 Islamic Revolution declares that the Judiciary is an independent power whose purpose is to protect the rights of individuals and to implement justice.[33] The Head of Judiciary, appointed by the Leader,[34] is responsible for all matters concerning the judiciary, administration, and execution of the judicial system.[35]

The Constitution of the Islamic Republic states that the laws and legal system should be based on "Islamic justice" and operated by "just judges with meticulous knowledge of the Islamic

[33] According to Article 156 of the Constitution, "the Judiciary responsibilities include: (1) investigating and passing judgement on grievances, violations of rights, and complaints; resolving litigation; settling disputes; and taking all necessary decisions and measures in probate matters as the law may determine; (2) restoring public rights and promoting justice and legitimate freedoms; (3) supervising the proper enforcement of laws; (4) uncovering crimes; prosecuting, punishing, and chastising criminals; and enacting the penalties and provisions of the Islamic penal code; and (5) taking suitable measures to prevent the occurrence of crime and to reform criminals."

[34] Leader of the Revolution (Maghame Rahbari) is the highest ranking political and religious authority in the Islamic Republic of Iran.

[35] Article 157 of the Constitution also calls for specific mandate of the Head of Judiciary for such cases as establishing the organisational structure necessary for the administration of justice, commensurate with the responsibilities mentioned under Article 156; drafting judiciary bills appropriate for the Islamic Republic; employing just and worthy judges, as well as their dismissal, appointment, transfer, and assignment to particular duties; promotions, and carrying out similar administrative duties, in accordance with the law.

laws" and so this "ideological conformity, must be free from every kind of unhealthy relation and connection (this is in accordance with this Quran verse that says; 'when you judge among the people, judge with justice.'"[36]

The judiciary system of the Islamic Republic of Iran includes general and special judicial establishments, and affiliate organisations.[37] The current structure of the Iranian court system includes: the Supreme Court,[38] the Court of Administrative Justice,[39] the Courts of Appeal,[40] the Public Courts,[41] the Revolutionary Courts,[42]

[36] The preamble of the Constitution.

[37] As put forth in Article 1 of the Establishment of General and Revolutionary Courts: "for the purpose of dealing with resolving all claims and direct referrals to the judges, and creating a consistent judicial authority, courts with general jurisdictions are established." The Supreme Court has the authority to deal with monitoring, the correct implementation of the law in courts, creating common judicial precedence (Article 161 of the Constitution) each branch consists of two judges.

[38] The highest judicial authority is responsible for: supervising implementation of laws by the courts and making judicial precedents (Article 161 of the constitution), verifying violations committed by the president (Article 110), and verifying the requests for revision of major judgements of the common courts Revolutionary court and Military Court 1 and to solve the difference of opinions over the matter of jurisdiction and transfer of cases to the courts.

[39] This court has to investigate complaints by privates against actions by public institutions and organs (Article 173 of the constitution).

[40] The Second Instance Court that is competent for reviewing cases decided by public and revolutionary courts.

[41] These courts have jurisdiction to deal with first instance tribunals and are divided into two categories, dealing with civil cases and criminal offences respectively.

[42] The Revolutionary Courts have jurisdiction over various offences, including: crimes against national security, narcotic drugs, terrorism, state-related embezzlement, bribery and profiteering, all acts that undermine the system of the Islamic Republic of Iran. Settled cases at the Revolutionary courts can be forwarded to the courts of Appeal.

the Military Courts,[43] the Office of the Public Prosecutor,[44] and the Court of Administrative Justice, which was established to deal with "complaints by citizens against the officials, units or government's regulations and administration of justice."[45]

The Ministry of Justice also developed different methods of redress and compensation. Means of adjudication have been regulated by quasi-judicial and administrative bodies such as the Dispute Resolution Councils. The Dispute Resolution Councils were established under Article 189 of the Third National Economic, Social and Cultural Development Plan (NESCD) aiming at reconciliation in order to minimise long delays in settling cases.[46] They are responsible for the settlement of minor civil and criminal cases through mediation before their referral to the courts. Article 7 of the Implementation Regulation of Articles 189 of the Third National Economic, Social and Cultural Development Plan gives them jurisdiction to hear all matters relating to civil affairs and penal cases.[47] However, the Dispute Resolution Councils seem to

[43] They have jurisdiction to investigate crimes committed in connection with military or security duties by members of the armed forces, the police, and the Islamic Revolution Guards Corps. The office of the military prosecutor and the military courts are also part of the judiciary and are subject to the same principles that regulate the Judiciary (Article 172 of the constitution).

[44] The offices of prosecutor general are responsible for all pretrial investigations and referrals to the courts of those cases where there is strong evidence of a crime.

[45] Article 1 of the Court of Administrative Justice also states that in application of Article 173 of the Constitution.

[46] See Articles 1 and 4 of the Implementation Regulation of Articles 189 of the Third Five-Year Economic, Social and Cultural Development Plan, 2002.

[47] This Article reads as follows: All claims about moveable properties, debts, benefits and harms arising out of a crime, constructive trust where the claim is not over ten million rials, disputes about eviction from immovable properties, eviction of residential places and disputes

have a serious problem involving inefficiency and inadequacy. The statistics show that almost five million cases were brought to the Arbitration Councils during 2008 but only 20 percent of them led to reconciliation.[48]

There are also various organisations affiliated with the justice system, including the National Inspection Organization, the Organization for Prisons, the Document and Land Registration Organization,[49] and the Forensic Medicine Organization. In 2000, the Iranian Judiciary launched the first five-year Judicial Reform plan to improve the policymaking capacity concerning criminal justice and protecting the rule of law. The Commission on Making Criminal Policy and Reforming the Penal Laws has been established

about easement rights, such as right passage, right of carriage, disturbance and also denial of rights and forcible entry, in cases where the ownership of the property is not disputed, enforcement of the conditions and commitments related to trades and agreements, within the limits of jurisdiction in financial disputes, taking inventories of estates of the deceased, and keeping them under lock and key, securing and protection of evidences, financial disputes with the consent of the parties concerned with no limits. Also in penal matters: securing the protection of evidence of crime and preventing the accused from escaping in evident crimes committed in public, by immediately reporting the case to the nearest judicial or police authorities, dealing with crimes where their legal punishments are less than 91 days, imprisonment or *tazir* punishment, which are related to traffic offences. The hearings in the Conflict Resolution Council are not bound by the Code of Procedure, the hearings are free, and is all disputes attempts are first made to achieve reconciliation (Article 10–14) the verdicts can be appealed against in the local general court and are executed by the Office of the Execution of Judicial Sentences. (Article 18–19).

48 The figure given by the Minister of Justice during the Judicial Council meeting on January 2010. Available online at http://www.tabnak.ir/fa/news/29583.

49 Registration of properties for the purpose of ascertaining the ownership of properties and protection of property-holders' rights and registration of the documents to give them official credence are listed as the main duties of the Document and Land Registration Organization.

with reference to judicial reform. The proposed policies comprise involving the public in the settlement of disputes; strengthening community-based mechanisms for the settlement of disputes including conciliation courts, prompt access to justice, and seeking the public's satisfaction with the judicial system, based on the justice-oriented values of Islam and Islamic dynamic jurisprudence (fiqh). The second Plan (2004–2008) addresses the restructuring of the Judiciary, improving court procedures, revising substantive and procedural laws and regulations, modifying the criminal policy in Iran, and providing protection forf victims of crime, for example.

Theoretically, the promise to assure all citizens equal access to justice under all of the previously mentioned organisations and systems seems easier to fulfill, but the reality is different. In practice, the idea of equal access to justice appeared to be something in books that even most members of the legal profession were not aware of, let alone poor and disadvantaged groups. It was argued that many Iranians fall very short of being provided with equal access to justice. In order to identify some major themes of inaccessibility, the next section will provide an overview of the performance of the Iranian justice system.

Performance of the Justice Sector

An increasing number of national scholars have examined the importance of judicial reform and development in Iran and argued that the problem of inaccessibility is combined with the inadequate performance of the justice sector.[50] However, any

[50] See Afsharnia and Mobin (2009). Also see Saaidi and Behrooz (2003). Several instances are reported in the local press about how lack of adequate performance of the judiciary prevents people's right to access to justice. For a ready reference see Farsi News, "Inadequate Judicial Process and the Need for Reform," which is a collection of religious arguments for justice sector reform. Available online at http://khabarfarsi.com/ext/1373886, accessed 12 July 2010.

assessment of the performance of the Iranian judicial system seems to be a difficult task. This is mainly due to the complex and multidimensional issues that are involved in analysing the performance of Iranian justice sectors. Diverse social norms, cultural values, the religious system as a legal source, legal structure, and also radical contemporary shifts in the power structure have made any feasible evaluation of the performance of the Iranian justice sector extremely complicated.

It becomes even more complicated when considering the public's perception of the justice system. In particular, relying on legitimacy theory, the public perception of justice is very difficult to read in Iran. The individual's perceptions of justice are based more on the public opinion of injustice. The group value theory (Lind and Tyler, 1988) supports the above-mentioned reading in that perception of justice is affected by the collectivities to which one belongs. It has been argued that we can understand more of the perceptions of individuals if we take into consideration the group values (Hegtvedt and Johnson, 2000). This hypothesis focuses on the collective context as a major constituent of legitimacy (ibid., 302–3). This theory is totally comprehensible in an Iranian context. The public perception of injustice constitutes the individual's understanding of how justice can be defined. The empirical data in Chapter 6 confirm that most of the respondents perceive "justice" with reference to the public understanding of "injustice." Most of the examples provided by the respondents regarding justice were in some way related to an illustration of injustice for a specific social group such as women.

Another source of the problems associated with the difficulty of evaluating the justice system's performance is the link between procedural and distributive justice.[51] In terms of the correlation between these two theories of justice, Chapter 5 examines the role of procedural justice in forming public perception of distributive

[51] The previous chapter presented a detailed discussion of the definition of procedural and distributive justice.

justice. It must be noted that most of the individual perceptions that were examined during my field research are based on perceptions of procedural justice, which even influence perceptions of distributive justice. Long delays or how a judge addresses the parties, for instance, were often quoted as examples of there being no justice. The link between perceptions of procedural justice and perceptions of distributive justice has been highlighted by several research studies (see Markovsky and Hegtvedt, 1995; Lind and Tyler, 1988).

The independence of the judiciary, fairness, effectiveness, and accessibility are often used as the main indicators in the evaluation of access to justice. Some scholars, particularly in the Latin American context, argue that evaluation of the performance of a judicial system must consider that system's level of independence, efficiency, and accessibility (e.g., Prillaman, 2000).

In light of these discussions, the next section analyses some common indicators used in examining the performance of the judiciary by looking at wider issues in the context of access to justice in Iran.

Judicial Independence

It seems difficult to summarise related definitions of judicial independence.[52] However, based on classical "separation of powers theory,"[53] two major elements constitute independence of the judiciary. The first is related to institutional autonomy whereby the judicial system must function independently from external political influence, in particular the legislative and the executive. The second is linked to the principles of impartiality[54] and political

[52] Much of the relevant literature is summarised in Larkins (1996).

[53] The creator of the idea of the separation of powers, Montesquieu (1689–1755), elaborated his theory in discussions about the English Constitution. See Krause (2000).

[54] Nicholson (1993).

insularity. Therefore, individual judges have to be able to make independent decisions in particular cases; in addition, judges cannot be subjected to threats for reaching decisions that are unpopular with the prevailing political power. These two aspects of judicial independence have been described by the related literature as external and internal independence (Russell and O'Brien, 2001: 11).

Judicial independence might appear to be a comprehensible concept as stated by Theodore Becker: "we all know what it means" (Becker, 1970: 1). Yet its implications and manifestations seem to be open to further argument. This debate develops into a more controversial argument when examining judicial independence during a time of political transition or any kind of democratisation process. This is particularly true in the case of contemporary political transitions in Iran. It is unfortunate that related academic research cannot be referenced because the scope and role of judicial independence and development of the institutional autonomy during contemporary Iranian democratisation processes has not been methodically examined.[55]

The Constitution of the 1979 Islamic Revolution guarantees that the Judiciary is an independent power, which protects the rights of individuals and implements justice. Article 164 of the Constitution reads as follows: "[Independence] a judge cannot be removed, whether temporarily or permanently, from the post he occupies except by trial and proof of his guilt, or in consequence of a violation entailing his dismissal. A judge cannot be transferred or redesignated without his consent, except in cases when the interest of society necessitates it, that too, with the decision of the head of the judiciary branch after consultation with the chief

[55] Even in the international context, "the little attention that has been paid to judicial independence during democratization is truly unfortunate, as the development of a more accurate understanding of this ideal would certainly benefit scholars and be of concrete use to those nations undergoing transitions from authoritarian rule" (Larkins, 1996: 607).

of the Supreme Court and the Prosecutor General. The periodic transfer and rotation of judges will be in accordance with general regulations to be laid down by law." However, as the following examples illustrate, it seems that judicial independence was often lacking and judges were often vulnerable to free external interference both during and after any form of political transition in Iran. Indeed, most of the extreme cases relating to denied access to justice originated from a lack of judicial independence as an essential component for controlling the abuse of political power.

The best example is the post-revolutionary judicial performance that is repeatedly highlighted as the most serious violation of the fair trial provision. The report "Law and Human Rights in the Islamic Republic of Iran" by Amnesty International (February 1980) has examined the performance of the Islamic Revolutionary Tribunals[56] within the seven-month period following the Revolution of 1979. The practice of the Islamic Revolutionary Tribunals was based on a broad jurisdiction of the courts; effective presumption of guilt; no facilities for defence; many trials being held in camera; and also with no possibility of appeal (Amnesty International, 1980: 41). The report concluded that "the guarantees necessary for a fair trial are effectively lacking in cases heard by the Revolutionary Tribunals."[57]

[56] The Islamic Revolutionary Court is a special court established after the Revolution of February 1979 to deal with anti-revolutionary and counterrevolutionary offences.

[57] The grounds for the conclusion were included: "1) the rights to know in detail and exactly the charges against one, 2) the right to be presumed innocent until found guilty by a competent and impartial tribunal in accordance with the law, 3) the right to a fair and public trial, 4) the right to present evidence and to call witnesses in one's own defence, 5) the right to examine, or have examined the witnesses against one and to obtain the attendance and examination of witnesses for the defence under the same conditions as witness for the prosecution, 6) the right to communicate with counsel or a representative of one's own choosing, 7) the right to adequate time and facilities for the preparation of the defence case, 8) the right to be afforded legal aid and

A more recent example of how judicial independence has been influenced by political transition and the democratisation process relates to what is called "political insularity" (Fiss, 1993: 59–60). In this context, political insularity means that the judiciary or judges should not be used as tools to advance either the political agenda or political objectives.[58] The performance of the judiciary after the presidential election on 12 June 2009 has been seen as political pressure to confront the opposition. For example, during the protests following the presidential election, several conservative members of parliament drafted a bill in which the judiciary was asked to reduce the time between sentencing and the executions of those who were sentenced as *Mohareb*.[59] Later, seven of the deputies withdrew signatures; Supreme Leader Ali Khamenei was quoted as demanding that suspects be treated according to current laws. Iran's judiciary chief Ayatollah Sadeq Larijani stated that while "some in Iran's ruling hard-line establishment are pushing the judiciary to step beyond the law in the crackdown on Iran's defiant opposition, he will not give in to political pressure to speed up the execution of opposition activists."[60]

representation without payment by the defendant in any case where he or she does not have sufficient means to pay for it, 9) the right to a decision based on the true merits of the case as established by the evidence, 10) the right to have the decision rendered in public, 11) the right of appeal, 12) the right to petition for review of the case." See Amnesty International (1980), "Law and Human Rights in the Islamic Republic of Iran," p. 58, accessed 12 March 2010, http://www.iranrights.org/english/document-338.php.

58 It also means the judges should not be punished or removed for reaching decisions (see Rosenn, 1987).

59 It's an Islamic offence that means waging war against God. The punishment for people convicted as mohareb is execution under Iran's Sharia legal code.

60 Ali Akbar Dareini, "Iranian Rejects Politicizing Executions," Associated Press, 1 February 2010. Available online at http://articles.boston.com/2011–06–24/news/29699767_1_esfandiar-rahim-mashaei-hard-line-clerics-iranian-leadership, accessed 18 April 2011.

Larijani maintained that political motives should not influence the investigations: "some people ... expect the judiciary to do more than implement the law," and stated, in comments posted on the judiciary's website, "this is a political expectation that goes against the *Sharia* (Islamic law) and the law" (ibid.).

With a review of this position by the Head of the Judiciary, a question arises: are hardliners co-opting the notion of "judicial independence" or is this indicative of some level of consciousness of the norm? The clash actually was part of a power struggle between those hardliners who supported Ahmadinejad and the judiciary. In fact, the judiciary has hit back at the president, on several occasions, accusing him of violating the separation of powers. For instance, in October 2012, the judiciary rejected a request by Ahmadinejad to visit Tehran's Evin prison. In response, Ahmadinejad and his entourage accused the judiciary of being used by his political opponents to imprison people close to him. However, opposition activists believe that since the judiciary is functioning under the direct leadership of the Supreme Leader, the justice system cannot be independent. "There are no clear boundaries between the judiciary, Revolutionary Guards, the Basij, police and the intelligence services. And therefore, hidden and open interference and interventions is seen."[61]

The above-mentioned examples illustrate the link between judicial independence, the democratisation process, and access to justice in Iran and how the lack of independence of the judicial power functions as a barrier to access to justice. In the following section, I will not attempt to explore theoretical and implementation problems related to judicial independence during the Iranian democratisation process, even though it is an extremely significant notion in examining the performance of the judiciary.

[61] Mehdi Khalaji, "Judicial System and Rule of Law," BBC Persian, 16 August 2009. Also see Meharngiz Kar, "The Future of Iran, Judicial Reform,Who Are the Judges in the Islamic Republic of Iran?" Working paper, LEGATUM Institute, May 2012.

I will review instead some key concepts with particular reference to the performance of the Iranian justice sector before analysing the barriers to access to justice.

Efficiency and Accessibility

In addition to judicial independence, accessibility and efficiency seem to be key indicators related to examining judicial performance. Although the next chapter analyses some major issues, with particular reference to accessibility as a barrier to access to justice, some elaboration is required here.

The main feature of efficiency is the ability of a judicial system to resolve disputes without unreasonable delays. There are different theories to explain why a justice system is not efficient. In the case of Iran, the inefficiency of the justice system is primarily based on the development theory. According to this hypothesis, the judiciary and, in particular, the courts work more efficiently in countries with higher levels of economic development and also a more educated population (North, 1981). The level of economic development has a direct impact on the level of operational efficiency issues, as does the lack of a human resource development program that includes limited access to updated judicial tools and textbooks, limited training opportunities for judges and administrative staff, an inadequate number of qualified competent judges or lawyers, the inadequate assessment of the needs of the judiciary, and a limited understanding of international human rights norms.

Another assumption that can explain the inefficiency of the Iranian justice system is that the performance of the courts is very much related to procedural formalism. For example, the lack of efficient procedures, a lack of legal information, excessively bureaucratic attitudes and behaviour all influence the justice system's efficiency. On the subject of efficient court procedures, there is also the "incentive" theory that claims courts work inadequately when the judges, lawyers, and litigants have poor motivation: lawyers are paid to delay proceedings, judges do not care about delays, and litigants seek to avoid judgement (Messick, 1999). In fact, inefficiency refers to circumstances where there is "the presence of 'uncontrolled variations' [in delays], those that arise from systemic distortions that are not inherent in the process itself and that can be identified and eliminated – but are not" (Prillaman, 2000: 18).

Independence of Lawyers

The independence of lawyers has been a subject of interest for scholars in the fields of social sciences and rule of law (Glendon, 1995; Halliday and Karpik, 1997). The very concept of the "independence of lawyers" is often viewed as a notion linked to "judicial independence." However, it has been argued that

> the analogy between the independence of judiciary and the independence of the Bar might be seductive and misleading. It is typical that in debates about the independence of the Bar the organisational elements are in the foreground (e.g. independence from the normative or administrative intervention of the public authorities), while all other aspects that characterise the independence of justice tend to be forgotten. Furthermore, it is questionable to what extent this analogy might be applicable, because the institutional position of the judiciary and the institutional position of the Bar are rather different.[62]

Another emerging expression in addition to "independence of lawyers" is the "independence of the Bar(s)" that is used predominantly in the language of the meetings organised by the

[62] Uzelac (2002), "The independence of the Bars and their relationship with the public authorities." Paper presented at 28ème Colloquy on European Law on "The Independence of Lawyers," 25–26 February 2002, Bayonne. Available online at http://alanuzelac.from.hr/pubs/B17bayonne.pdf, accessed 20 January 2010.

International Bar Association as well as the Council of Europe in cooperation with various Bar Associations.[63]

In the context of Iran, the 1954 Law concerning the independence of the Bar Association gave full independence to the Bar Associations. Before the 1979 revolution, there existed only the Central Bar Association in Tehran, the Tabriz Bar Association, and the Shiraz Bar Association, but in the wake of the revolution, more than twenty bars in major provinces have been established. The Central Bar Association has responsibility for the central province and six other provinces and is governed by an eighteen-member board of directors. Every two years the Central Bar Association holds elections to choose the board of directors.

However, the election is under the control of the judiciary. In 2010, the official website of the Iranian Bar Association reported that thirty-six candidates running for the board of directors at the Central Bar Association had been disqualified.[64] This constituted a major increase in the disqualification rate compared with previous elections. In 2008, two-thirds of the candidates were disqualified, while in 2010, the administrative body disqualified nearly half of the candidates.[65] The simple equation is that the more autonomous a Bar is in its decision making, the greater the possibility of its being independent from external mechanisms of control. Therefore, associations of lawyers should not be controlled by the public authorities. Lawyers have the right to form "self-governing" professional associations to "protect their professional integrity," which are able to "exercise its functions without external interference."[66]

[63] See reports from the Bar Association meetings in Budapest (1997), Prague (1999), and Dubrovnik (2001) in which this term was used.

[64] See Iranian Bar Association's Official website at www.iranbar.com.

[65] Ibid.

[66] The UN Basic Principles on the Role of Lawyers adopted by the Eighth United Nations Congress on the Prevention of Crime and the Treatment of Offenders, held in Havana (Cuba) from 27 August to 27 September 1990.

In discussions about the independence of lawyers, it should be further noted that as a member of the United Nations, Iran is bound by the "Basic Principles on the Role of Lawyers," accepted by the UN General Assembly in 1990 (Principles),[67] according to which lawyers must be allowed to carry out their work "without intimidation, hindrance, harassment or improper interference."[68] Moreover, the Basic Principles on the Role of Lawyers declares that

> Lawyers like other citizens are entitled to freedom of expression, belief, association and assembly. In particular, they shall have the right to take part in public discussion of matters concerning the law, the administration of justice and the promotion and protection of human rights and to join or form local, national or international organisations and attend their meetings, without suffering professional restrictions by reason of their lawful action or their membership in a lawful organisation. In exercising these rights, lawyers shall always conduct themselves in accordance with the law and the recognised standards and ethics of the legal profession.[69]

A general rule to be stated here is that the Iranian government must fulfill internationally protected rights of lawyers by the International Covenant on Civil and Political Rights (ICCPR), to which Iran is a state party. Article 19 of the ICCPR includes "the right to take part in public discussion of matters concerning the law, the administration of justice and the promotion and protection of human rights." However, several lawyers have, over a period of time, been sentenced to prison terms,[70] or are awaiting

67 Ibid.

68 Ibid.

69 Principle No. 23.

70 Nasrin Sotoudeh, a human rights lawyer, was sentenced to eleven years in jail and also was banned for twenty years from working as a lawyer and from leaving the country on January 2011. On October 2010, Mohammad Seifzadeh was sentenced to nine years in prison and to a ten-year ban on practicing law after his release.

trial and at risk of prosecution for their human rights work.[71] Several others have fled the country.[72] It is important to note that despite the Standing Invitation issued by Iran to all UN human rights mechanisms in 2002, the UN Special Rapporteur on the Independence of Lawyers and Judges has not been permitted to visit the country.

In a situation where lawyers may be forced to pay the price of their own freedom for defending people who are in need, justice and access denied prove to be particular obstacles for many human rights defenders. "We can certainly expect that every lawyer who says too much or accepts undesirable clients can expect to wake up in the morning and find that his license has been revoked. Intellectuals will be punished for their thoughts, and will not be able to retain suitable counsel because all of the lawyers with the courage to work on their cases have been or will be disbarred. Blacklisted politicians will search for independent and courageous lawyers, but will not be able to find them. Even more heart-wrenching is the situation of people who confront serious judicial proceedings but will have no refuge."[73]

In practical terms, the role of lawyers is to assist people to seek legal redress to their problems. By so doing, they are viewed as "the main guarantors of those human rights for the rest of the population" (Zeitune, 2004: 3). Lawyers, therefore, are essential to the right to a fair trial and also equal access to justice. Furthermore, legal assistance is effective only if carried out independently. Thus

71 Two human rights lawyers, Abdolfattah Soltaniand and Mohammad Ali Dadkhah, were claimed to be at risk of prosecution for their human rights work. For more detailed background, see Amnesty International joint statement (10 October 2010), "IRAN: Lawyers' defence work repaid with loss of freedom," accessed 12 January 2010, http://www.amnesty.org/en/library/asset/MDE13/093/2010/en/d4a07c06–70a0–4409–8c57-ec7142771309/mde130932010en.html.

72 Ibid.

73 Bahman Keshavarz, former chair of the Bar Association, daily *Etemad*, 2 July 2009.

the right of lawyers to exercise their profession freely, the right of defence, the right to communicate with their clients, and the right to have access to all the relevant information in their possession need to be protected. Otherwise, the right to a fair trial and access to justice are critically endangered.

Legal Protection of Access to Justice

Justice is one of the major foundational principles of the Iranian constitution. The Islamic Republic is a system based on belief in "the exalted dignity and value of man, and his freedom coupled with responsibility before God; in which equity, justice, political, economic, social, and cultural independence, and national solidarity are secured."[74] The constitution characterises the government of the Islamic Republic of Iran by describing the state's goals. The long list of state goals also includes "abolition of all forms of undesirable discrimination and the provision of equitable opportunities

[74] According to Article 2: The Islamic Republic is a system based on belief in: 1) the One God (as stated in the phrase 'There is no god except Allah'), His exclusive sovereignty and right to legislate, and the necessity of submission to His commands; 2) Divine revelation and its fundamental role in setting forth the laws; 3) the return to God in the Hereafter, and the constructive role of this belief in the course of man's ascent towards God; 4) the justice of God in creation and legislation; 5) continuous leadership and perpetual guidance, and its fundamental role in ensuring the uninterrupted process of the revolution of Islam; 6) the exalted dignity and value of man, and his freedom coupled with responsibility before God; in which equity, justice, political, economic, social, and cultural independence, and national solidarity are secured by recourse to: a) continuous leadership of the holy persons, possessing necessary qualifications, exercised on the basis of the Quran and the Sunnah, upon all of whom be peace; b) sciences and arts and the most advanced results of human experience, together with the effort to advance them further; c) negation of all forms of oppression, both the infliction of and the submission to it, and of dominance, both its imposition and its acceptance."

for all, in both the material and intellectual spheres; securing the multifarious rights of all citizens, both women and men, and providing legal protection for all, as well as the equality of all before the law."[75] These goals have been emphasised in Chapter III of the constitution, which guarantees the rights of the people by emphasising the principle of nondiscrimination,[76] and also equality before law.[77]

The Constitution of the Islamic Republic of Iran defines access to justice in a manner similar to major international human rights conventions, as mentioned elsewhere. Therefore, access to justice is a positive obligation for the Iranian state, which is linked as a rule to civil and political rights rather than economic rights (akin to many European jurisdictions). As described in an earlier chapter, the relevant articles of international and regional human rights such as the Universal Declaration of Human Rights,[78] the International Covenant on Civil and Political Rights,[79] the European Convention on Human Rights and others also define access to justice within fair trial provisions.

The fair trial provisions must be observed from the moment of arrest, particularly in a criminal charge. The prohibition on arbitrary arrest and detention is guaranteed by the constitution. Article 32 provides that "no one may be arrested except by the order and in accordance with the procedure laid down by law." Also, "all affronts to the dignity and repute of persons arrested,

75 Article 3 of the Constitution.

76 Article 19: All people of Iran, whatever the ethnic group or tribe to which they belong, enjoy equal rights; colour, race, language, and the like, do not bestow any privilege.

77 Article 20: All citizens of the country, both men and women, equally enjoy the protection of the law and enjoy all human, political, economic, social, and cultural rights, in conformity with Islamic criteria.

78 Adopted and proclaimed by General Assembly Resolution 217 A (III) of 10 December 1948.

79 Adopted by General Assembly Resolution 2200A (XXI) of 16 December 1966 and entered into force on 23 March 1976.

detained, imprisoned, or banished in accordance with the law, whatever form they may take, are forbidden and liable to punishment."[80] The right to humane treatment is a positive obligation that ensures minimum standards relating to the environment of detention and detainees' rights while deprived of liberty. Moreover, the arrested person must be informed of the reasons for arrest.[81]

Article 38 of the constitution prohibits "all forms of torture for the purpose of extracting confession or acquiring information." The "compulsion of individuals to testify, confess, or take an oath is not permissible; and any testimony, confession, or oath obtained under duress is devoid of value and credence." This article does not provide a legal definition of torture; also the penal code does not include torture as a definite criminal offence. However, Iranian parliament passed a bill in line with Article 38 of the constitution, known as the anti-torture law, in May 2004, and it was approved by the Guardian Council on the grounds that it was not found to be in conflict with Islamic law or the constitution. The bill construes the term "torture" to mean any act by which severe pain or suffering is inflicted.[82] The examples of "inhuman or degrading treatment" stated in the bill include all physical or mental acts by which severe pain or suffering is inflicted. Although the parliament and the Guardian Council passed the anti-torture law, Iran is not a member state of the 1984 Convention against Torture because the Guardian Council has refused to commit the country to the Convention against Torture and Other Cruel, Inhuman or

[80] Article 39.

[81] Article 32 of the Constitution reads as follows "in case of arrest, charges with the reasons for accusation must, without delay, be communicated and explained to the accused in writing, and a provisional dossier must be forwarded to the competent judicial authorities within a maximum of twenty-four hours so that the preliminaries to the trial can be completed as swiftly as possible. The violation of this article will be liable to punishment in accordance with the law."

[82] Article 1(6) of the anti-torture law.

Degrading Treatment on the basis that it conflicted with Islamic rules and principles.

The fundamental component of the benefit of the right to a fair trial is that any legal or criminal proceedings are to be carried out by an independent, impartial, and competent court established by law (Article 34).[83] The constitutional provision also states that "the passing and execution of a sentence must be only by a competent court and in accordance with law" (Article 36). Another key constituent of the right to adequate criminal and civil proceedings is the right to legal counsel as declared by Article 35 of the Constitution, where "both parties to a lawsuit have the right in all courts of law to select an attorney, and if they are unable to do so, arrangements must be made to provide them with legal counsel." The next chapter presents a detailed discussion of the right to legal counsel. However, it must also be noted that the Iranian constitutional provision does not apply to the right to be provided with counsel during pretrial detention. It is reported that approximately 25 percent of prisoners held in state prison facilities are pretrial detainees. Several human rights groups such as Amnesty International and Human Rights Watch condemned the Iranian government for disregarding international standards of fairness specifically for security detainees (Amnesty International Report, 2010; Human Rights Watch, 2011).

In August 2009, the UN special rapporteur on torture and other cruel, inhuman, or degrading treatment or punishment, the special rapporteur on the situation of human rights defenders, and the vice chairperson of the working group on arbitrary detention expressed "serious concern" about the situation of detainees in Iran.[84] Needless to say, the right to legal counsel is particularly

[83] Article 34 of the constitution: "It is the indisputable right of every citizen to seek justice by recourse to competent courts. All citizens have right of access to such courts, and no one can be barred from courts to which he has a legal right of recourse."

[84] See "Human Rights Report" (2009), accessed 7 January 2011, http://www.state.gov/g/drl/rls/hrrpt/2009/nea/136068.htm.

important in the case of pretrial detention, but it has been confirmed to be the one that is most often violated.[85] "It is at the discretion of the judges to prevent or limit the presence of lawyers at the investigation stage of certain cases such as those that involve national security" (CCA, 2003).

Article 165 of the constitution[86] guarantees the right to a public hearing as one of the key aspects of the fair trial.[87] Nevertheless, the constitutional provision of the right to a public hearing permits several exceptions to the general rule. The public may be excluded for grounds of morals, public orders and when the interest of the private parties so requires. Article 188 of the Code of Criminal Procedure explains that the public will be excluded in cases involving sexual offences, cases against approved ethics, cases involving the private lives of the parties such as family matters, or when there is a request from the parties of civil cases. And, last, the public may be banned from a trial where publicity is against national security or against the religious emotions of the public.

Under Article 188(1), public hearing means that the hearing should be conducted publicly (and include the press and the

[85] Instances are reported by the international human rights organisations regarding denial of basic fair trial rights, in particular the right to counsel to security detainees. For a ready reference, see the case of journalist Bahman Ahmadi-Amoee who was arrested on June 2009. It was reported that his access to legal counsel was prevented by the authorities.

[86] Article 165 provides that "Trials are to be held openly and members of the public may attend without any restriction unless the court determines that an open trial would be detrimental to public morality or public order, or if in case of private disputes, both the parties request not to hold open hearing."

[87] Article 168 [Political and Press Offences]: "Political and press offenses will be tried openly and in the presence of a jury, in courts of justice. The manner of the selection of the jury, its powers, and the definition of political offenses, will be determined by law in accordance with the Islamic criteria."

public) and the court is obliged to provide adequate facilities for attendance by interested members of the public. Judgement, however, can be made public, but must not be published unless it is a final decision. It seems that the exceptions to the public hearing are broad and can provide a general ground to limit the rule. The exemption based on approved ethics or what is described by the law as *akhlagh hasane*, for instance, grants a common position to prohibit publicity. Crimes in general are against the approved moral principles and so almost all criminal hearings should exclude the public.

According to Article 37 of the constitution, "innocence is to be presumed, and no one is to be held guilty of a charge unless his or her guilt has been established by a competent court." The presumption of innocence, inter alia, means that the burden of proof lies with the prosecution, and the accused has the benefit of the doubt. Also Article 197 of the Civil Procedure Code declares that the defendant has the benefit of the doubt and the burden of proof is on the plaintiff. Islamic jurisprudence recognises the presumption of innocence under the concept of *Bar'at* (أصل البراءة). This is a principle of liberty that is used in "the context of doubt" to provide an exemption of applicability of the primary sources of law (the Quran and the Sunnah). In accordance with this presumption, every person is supposed to act righteously until the contrary is proved. The Prophet said, "The burden of proof is on who makes the claim, whereas the oath is on him who denies" (Kamel and Bassiouni, 1982: 149).

The use of *Bar'at* is consistent with Article 167 of the constitution, which obliges the judge to endeavour to judge each case on the basis of the codified law. In case of the absence of any such law, the judgement will be delivered on the basis of Islamic sources and *fatawa*. The constitutional provisions of the fair trial also consist of an obligation to a reasoned verdict by the court of justice.[88]

[88] Article 166 provides that "the verdicts of courts must be well reasoned out and documented with reference to the articles and principles of the law in accordance with which they are delivered."

Last but not least is the constitutional guarantee for the right to compensation for miscarriage of justice. According to Article 171: "whenever an individual suffers moral or material loss as the result of a default or error of the judge with respect to the subject matter of a case or the verdict delivered, or the application of a rule in a particular case, the defaulting judge must stand surety for the reparation of that loss in accordance with the Islamic criteria, if it be a case of default. Otherwise, losses will be compensated for by the State. In all such cases, the repute and good standing of the accused will be restored."

This Article, although promising, has not yet been enforced. A major obstacle behind implementation of the law is a lack of awareness of such a constitutional right among the public. More importantly, there are no generic mechanisms for enforcing the law. "To understand why the law has been grossly neglected, we have to ask how it is possible for an individual to take a legal action against a judge, when there is no such legal mechanism to implement the law."[89]

Conclusion

This chapter set out to explore some key related issues of access to justice in Iran. It draws on research, which shows that there is a complex interaction of factors that might contribute to provide fair access to justice. The discussion of the legal framework helped to understand how the plurality of the legal system and customary practices determine access to justice in Iran. The analysis in this chapter shows that the development of the justice sector has a significant part to play in explaining the extent of accessibility of justice for people.

[89] Abdolfattah Soltani a prominent human rights lawyer in an interview with the Iranian Student News Agency (ISNA), accessed 15 June 2013, at http://www.isna.ir/fa/print/8306-04695/-نگاه-حقوقدانان-به-فصل-یازدهم-قانون-اساسي-عبدالف.

One important conclusion drawn is that the reform to provide fair and equal access to justice is associated with development and empowerment since being poor and marginalised relates to being disadvantaged in terms of choices, basic resources, legal information, and a voice in seeking justice. A link between the theoretical debates of access to justice as discussed in the first chapter, with particular reference to justice theories, fair trial provisions, and also the grounded reality of access to justice in Iran can thus be formed.

The contextualised analysis of access to justice highlights three points. The first is that when assessing the performance of the justice system with regard to access to justice, one should ensure that the independence of the judiciary factors are taken into account to provide us with as complete a picture as possible of the dimensions that constitute fair and unbiased access to justice. The second point is that law can only be effective if it is accessible and can be effectively implemented. The discussion on legal protection leads us to the conclusion that, despite the presence of constitutional provisions realities on the ground, securing the right to a fair trial in constitutional law alone is not sufficient to provide access to justice. It is therefore very important to create a normative protection of rights regarding access to justice not only by constitutional law but also via the legal framework, customary norms, jurisprudence, and international law. It is also significant to examine the possibility of using law in conjunction with political forces to guarantee the right to a fair trial. The third and last point relates to "effectiveness" and "accessibility" which are often used as key indicators to evaluate access to justice. It is therefore likely to be a complex interaction of these factors that contributes to the evaluation of access to justice in Iran.

3 Barriers in the Path to Justice

Access to justice at its most basic level shares similar concepts with access to the legal system; consequently, making courts and legal processes more accessible provides better access to justice (Bhabha, 2007). In this context, Iranians who need access to justice face numerous obstacles, including failure to protect poor and marginalised groups, long delays, the lack of a legal aid system, as well as insufficient adequate and equal remedies (CCA, 2003). Iran, however, is not only a country where there is a gap between the rhetoric and reality. In fact, that unequal justice could function against the primary values of the fair trial provisions. Those with more socioeconomic resources seem to benefit from faster access to justice and also greater protection of the law than those with fewer resources. This chapter therefore focuses on exploring some of the key barriers to access to justice from a user perspective.

Having outlined the overall contextual framework of access to justice, more specifically, this chapter describes some of the more recent national reforms and initiatives with particular reference to access to justice. The analysis here is largely qualitative; it involves the review of documentation and the examination of the constitution and a number of statutes, as well as some some of the relevant research findings about barriers to access to justice in Iran.

Classification of Barriers

In the related literature, there is no common definition of a barrier to justice; however, the cases or grounds which resulted in inaccessibility are considered as the barriers to access to justice (see Cappelletti, 1979; Genn and Paterson, 2001; Gramatikov and Porter, 2010). Despite different contexts, most of the barriers described are common to many communities, such as cost or long delays, but some are specific to a particular social group, such as distance for those who live in rural areas.

The barriers that Iranians might face when they are seeking a legal remedy to a legal problem are more or less contextual. Even though all barriers share the same notion of inaccessibility, based on their sources, they can be classified into different groups. There are different ways of arranging these barriers; however, the following classification applies with particular reference to Iran.

The first category of barriers is in relation to the legal protection of rights. One major reason behind a lack of legal protection is that Iran is not a state party of some international human rights standards, and even if Iran is a party to the international human rights conventions there is a lack of fulfilment of these rights. Iran is a member state of many international human rights treaties, including the Charter of the United Nations and Statute of the International Court of Justice,[1] Universal Declaration of Human Rights, International Covenant on Civil and Political Rights, International Covenant on Economic,

[1] The Charter of the United Nations was signed on 26 June 1945 and came into force on 24 October 1945. The Statute of the International Court of Justice is annexed to the Charter of the United Nations.

Social and Cultural Rights,[2] International Convention on the Elimination of All Forms of Racial Discrimination,[3] International Convention on the Suppression and Punishment of the Crime of Apartheid,[4] International Convention against Apartheid in Sports,[5] Convention on the Rights of the Child,[6] Convention Relating to the Status of Refugees,[7] Convention on the Prevention and Punishment of the Crime of Genocide,[8] Supplementary Convention on the Abolition of Slavery, the Slave Trade, and Institutions and Practices Similar to Slavery,[9] and finally, the Worst Forms of Child Labour Convention.[10] However Iran has significant reservations with regard to a number of them. Also Iran is not party to the Convention on the Elimination of All Forms of Discrimination against Women (CEDAW), Convention against Torture and other Cruel, Inhuman or Degrading Treatment or

[2] Adopted by General Assembly resolution 2200A (XXI) of 16 December 1966 and entered into force: 3 January 1976.

[3] Adopted by General Assembly resolution 2106 (XX) of 21 December 1965 and entered into force: 4 January 1969 in accordance with Article 19.

[4] Adopted by General Assembly on 30 November 1973 and entered into force:18 July 1976, in accordance with Article XV(1).

[5] Adopted by General Assembly on 10 December 1985 and entered into force: 3 April 1988, in accordance with Article 18 (1).

[6] Adopted by General Assembly on 20 November 1989 and entered into force: 2 September 1990 in accordance with Article 49.

[7] Adopted by the United Nations Conference of Plenipotentiaries on the Status of Refugees and Stateless Persons convened under General Assembly resolution 429 (V) of 14 December 1950 and entered into force: 22 April 1954, in accordance with Article 43.

[8] Adopted by General Assembly resolution 2200A (XXI) of 16 December 1966 and entered into force: 3 January 1976.

[9] Adopted by Economic and Social Council Resolution 608 (XXI) of 30 April 1956 and adopted at Geneva on 7 September 1956. Entered into force: 30 April 1957 in accordance with Article 13.

[10] Adopted by the General Conference of the International Labour Organization on 17 June 1999 and entered into force: 19 November 2000, in accordance with Article 10.

Punishment,[11] and some weapons treaties. Moreover, some laws at the national level contradict international human rights standards, as discussed earlier. Constitutional and legal discrimination against certain social groups and minorities provides important grounds for creating legal barriers in accessing justice (for example, the nonrecognition of certain religious groups such as *Bahai*).[12]

Another major barrier pertains to the economic aspects of access to justice. These barriers create a broad scope of inaccessibility such as social exclusion for disadvantaged groups, institutional discrimination, lack of physical access, lack of faith in formal institutions, and also a lack of awareness of rights and legal needs. An additional barrier that relates to the economic aspect of access to justice addresses the lack of access to legal assistance. Unaffordable legal counsel and an insufficient legal aid service both prevent people from taking legal action. The following sections present more detailed discussion regarding the cost of justice and legal assistance.

Barriers to access to justice can be caused by a lack of enforcement by the police. The lack of public confidence in the

[11] Adopted by the General Assembly of the United Nations on 10 December 1984 (resolution 39/46) and entered into force: 26 June 1987.

[12] It must be noted that this book does not examine related issues regarding access to justice for religious or ethnic minorities because this study focuses on women as a target group and in particular examines their perceptions of access to justice. Although women are not a homogenous category, the survey study does not include "religion" as a variable for barriers to access. This study relies on official data which show that the majority of Tehran populations are Shia Muslims. The respondents were also selected mainly from among women who participated in Shia Muslim community religious ceremonies. In addition, respondents did not comment on religious minorities during the in-depth interviews. I do believe, however, that it is extremely important to conduct an empirical study to examine the extent of barriers to access to justice for those who are a "minority" (religious and ethical) in Iran.

police can be found by examining the cultural expression of the police operation. For example, as a Farsi proverb puts it,"police is a friend of the burglar." Police practice has also been known to be discriminatory, not only because their attitude toward victims of crime is insensitive but also because of the unequal treatment of poor and disadvantaged groups.[13] Police misconduct due to widespread corruption and the power struggle, particularly in the control of external factors, fails to protect poor and disadvantaged groups,[14] not to mention the fact that investigation procedures are known to be inefficient and badly coordinated. Although recently there has been considerable training for Iranian police in order to increase the efficiency of the administration, the operational ethic still seems to be poor.[15]

[13] Local media have reported several cases to highlight police negative attitude toward victims of crime. For instance, police officials have blamed victims of gang rapes in two most recent cases. "If they had proper clothing and if the sound of their music was not so loud, the rapist would not have imagined it as a depraved get together" Colonel Hossein Yardoosti, local police chief, said. See BBC News, accessed 15 June 2011, http://www.bbc.co.uk/news/world-middle-east-13777308.

[14] Police corruption is a common and acknowledged problem in Iran. Ali Khamenei, the Supreme Leader, states that the police force's main responsibility is to fight corruption. "The essential requirement for a crackdown on corruption is to have no corruption in the body which fights corruption." He was condemning police corruption in a meeting with the Interior Minister and law enforcement officers in Tehran on Sunday, 25 April 2010. Other Iranian high-ranking police commanders have confirmed the public concern over police corruption (see MehrNews, accessed 12 August 2010, available online at http://www.mehrnews.com/fa/newsdetail.aspx?NewsID=1070819). In May 2011, Iran's police chief commented that about 1,500 police officers had been fired because of their misconduct of corruption during 2010 (see AftabNews, accessed 12 August 2010, available online at http://www.aftabnews.ir/vdcjtaevxuqe8iz.fsfu.html).

[15] A recent training event, for instance, was about the protection of witnesses and victims of crime. The event was part of a cycle of training workshops for police officers organised by the United Nations

With regard to various types of barriers, it must be noted that this chapter does not comprise an overview of gender-specific barriers to access to justice such as cultural issues or lack of legal knowledge. Chapter 4 evaluates gender-specific barriers, along with issues such as gender insensitivity in the justice system, lack of economic independence, legal discrimination, and fear of social exclusion, for example.

Also, this chapter does not review the access to justice barriers that are caused by the prison system because it is indeed an extensive debate. However, it is important to note that one of the most important challenges faced by the Iranian prison system (the State Prisons and Security and Corrective Measure Organization) is that it is overburdened, with a large number of prisoners who have been apprehended for drug offences. According to the Prisons Organization, 173,871 people were incarcerated in 2009–2010.[16] This number amounts to about 223 prisoners per 100,000 of the population, as a result placing Iran among the ten countries of the world with the highest incarceration rates. The high percentage of male prisoners (more than 95 percent of prisoners) represents the higher percentage of the adult male population. Pretrial detainees make up 24.7 percent of the prison population and the rest have already been convicted.[17] The State Prisons and Security and Corrective Measure Organization includes 253 establishments throughout the country.[18]

Office on Drugs and Crime in the Islamic Republic of Iran (UNODC). UNDOC Press Release, accessed 10 July 2011, available online at http://www.unodc.org/islamicrepublicofiran/en/unodc-iri-ini.html.

[16] The State Prisons and Security and Corrective Measure Organization statistical report, March 2010, accessed 17 May 2011, available online at http://www.prisons.ir/index.php?Module=SMMPrisonStat&SMMOp=IranPrStatView&SMM_CMD=&IranPrStatYear=1388&IranPrStatFollow=All&IranPrStatMonth=12.

[17] Ibid.

[18] See Farsi News, accessed 29 September 2011, available at http://www.farsnews.com/printable.php?nn=13900704000742.

During the last few years, the Iranian Judiciary and the Prisons Organization have employed a number of different approaches to policy to try to overcome these challenges. These include a law reform policy and revising prison and penal legislation, limiting use of pretrial detention, alternatives to imprisonment, and rehabilitation mechanisms. There have also been a number of training programs (the empowerment approach) regarding prison administration, professionalism, and a code of conduct. However, the main practice pursued by the Prisons Organization is with regard to reducing the number of the accused detained while awaiting trial, since overcrowding is the main challenge. Prison conditions have improved but are still poor. The path to justice for Iranian prisoners appears to be difficult, as access to legal information is inadequate and legal assistance mechanisms for the prisoners, while they do exist, are insufficient.

A different dimension of inaccessibility involves the lack of legal empowerment. This element of inaccessibility, on an individual level, relates to internalised insecurity, cultural norms of exclusion, and public discrimination. The lack of legal empowerment largely correlates to a lack of legal awareness, both of which will be explored by this research in the next chapter.

Cost

In many litigation systems, the cost of justice commonly has been considered the main reason why people avoid seeking justice. In fact, the cost of litigation has been characterised as a key barrier to access to justice in Western societies in recent decades (Cappeletti and Garth, 1978; Silver, 2002; Williams, 1994; Woolf, 1996). In the same way, the cost of litigation in developing countries is considered to be one of the main barriers to justice (Commission on Legal Empowerment of the Poor, 2008). The literature also suggests that most research studies identify the analytical distinction between the different costs that a person has to consider in order to solve a legal problem, presenting categories such as transaction costs, transfer costs, total spending, and total litigation costs (Miller, 2002; Silver, 2002).

In Iran, as elsewhere, public legal culture believes that justice is extremely expensive.[19] Much is said about the cost of litigation and the way in which it can exclude the poor from justice; however, no data exists that shows how much it actually costs to take a legal action through the court system, especially given the complexity of sociolegal grounds and the number of times one has to attend court or other related legal procedures. Also, there is no research data regarding the emotional costs incurred or how Iranians perceive the costs of accessing justice.

Therefore, at this initial stage of reflection, I would suggest that the costs of justice come in a variety of forms: litigation fees, fines, time, transportation, and emotional and sociocultural costs. In this classification, one practical category divides costs into out-of-pocket expenses (such as court fees, fares for travelling to court, witness fees, etc.) and non-monetary costs (time spent, emotional costs, and sociocultural costs). The differentiation criteria here will be based on Iranian market values and also the sociolegal circumstances. Time spent and long delay costs, for instance, should be regarded as non-monetary costs. In the same way, the social and cultural costs will be defined as non-monetary costs. Last but not least, this research will focus on the private costs of justice that are sustained by the individuals who have to take legal action for the resolution of disputes.[20] In order to explain discrete cost categories, the costs of justice will be examined from the perspective of barriers to justice.

Out-of-Pocket Expenses

Most studies on the costs of justice focus on the out-of-pocket expenses; some of the related empirical studies will be reviewed

[19] The data from the empirical research support this line of argument.
[20] Public cost.

briefly before proceeding with an evaluation of monetary costs in Iran. In a large-scale research on justiciable events in England and Wales, Genn and Beinart (1999) divide the costs of paths to justice into legal costs and other costs. In a similar piece of research on justiciable events in Scotland, Genn and Paterson (2001) confirmed that respondents who did have a justiciable problem, but did not seek professional advice, were fearful of legal costs; "respondents to survey interviews and qualitative interviews expressed a pervasive feeling that obtaining legal advice was hugely expensive and that for many kinds of problems obtaining such advice was simply not an option" (Genn and Paterson, 2001: 98).

At the most elementary level, one may consider transportation fees an important category within out-of-pocket expenses, particularly for residents in remote areas. Recent figures show that there are about 2,071 public courts, 353 courts of appeal, and 80 revolutionary courts across the country. In Tehran, the number of public courts is 287, with 56 courts of appeal and 5 revolutionary courts. In Isfahan, another major city, there are 128 public courts, 18 courts of appeal, and 9 revolutionary courts. In Kohgilūyé o Boyer-Ahmad, one of the poorest provinces, there is no revolutionary court, just 4 courts of appeal, and 21 public courts. Therefore, approximately 1,500 public courts are located in more than twenty-four provinces excluding Tehran and Isfahan. Also, there is not a single revolutionary court in more than fifteen provinces.[21] Most courts are based in district headquarters towns, located far from the residents of many small towns and villages; as a result, many inhabitants of rural communities find it financially prohibitive to access the courts, particularly for cases that can take several visits to provincial capitals to resolve. Although many of the public courts are also based in small towns, transportation can still be a barrier to access for those living some distance from the public courts. Most of the courts of appeal or special courts are

[21] The 1385 (2006) national Statistical Yearbook.

based in Tehran, quite an expensive city for those who are from small towns and villages.

Also it must be noted that there is no explicit definition of the litigation costs in Iranian customary laws. However, Article 502 of the Civil Procedure Code presents examples of litigation costs including the court fee, payments made to obtain expert assistance, and reimbursement. There is also wide agreement that the term "litigation cost"[22] in the context of civil litigation refers to "the costs that plaintiff has to pay to in order to take legal action" (Sdrzadh Afshar, 1993).

This definition focuses on the court fee and excludes other legal costs such as the lawyer's fee. In civil litigation, the court fee is basically a certain percentage of the total amount requested. In a monetary civil litigation amounting to ten million rials, for example, the court fee is 1.5 percent of the ten million rials requested. However, this percentage is slightly higher for appeal courts and the Supreme Court. Criminal litigation incurs significantly smaller fees in comparison to civil litigation.

In conjunction with access to justice for the poor and the litigation costs, the law of *Esar* is applicable to provide exemption from court fees for indigent litigants. The 1934 law of *Esar* applied the Quranic principle of exemption from *`usr* and *haraj* (hardship, difficulty), based on verses from the Quran, such as "He has laid on you no impediment in your religion"[23] and "God desires ease (*yusr*) for you, and desires not hardship (*'usr*) for you."[24] The law contains forty articles, including the definition of *mosar* or application for exemption based on Esar, which means either lack of financial resources or not having access to financial resources during the litigation. The law also describes the procedural aspects to establish an Esar case which is based on the testimony of four witnesses. Although the final decision regarding fees is left to

[22] *Hazinehaye dadresi.*

[23] Quran, 12:78.

[24] Quran, 2:185.

the courts, the Shia legal tradition prefers to accept usr (having difficulty) rather than *yusr* (not having difficulty) in Esar cases.

It appears that the doctrine of Esar is one of the major legal innovations introduced by Sharia to make litigation more affordable for poor and disadvantaged groups. This Quran-based doctrine exempts poor people not only from the court costs but also from civil remedies such as compensation. This leads to an understanding that litigation costs are not the key barrier to access to justice in Iran as they are in many litigation systems in Western society. This claim is based on three factors: (1) civil litigation costs seem to be affordable with a national GDP per capita (PPP)[25] $12,900 (2009 est.); (2) the criminal litigation cost is not considered as much of a "barrier" even for the poor; and (3) the law exempts poor people from the court fees based on the doctrine of Esar.

Time Spent

The long delays associated with dispute resolution within the Iranian justice system are considered a barrier to justice (CCA, 2003). Long delays present an obstacle in resolving injustices and deprive people of their rights by not taking legal action to counter legal problems. Although there is no research to provide consistent data on the actual time a user of justice may spend on resolving a case in Iran, the time spent and long delays seem to have a significant effect on an individual's decision about whether or not to take legal action.

Moreover, the inevitable delay is a fundamental issue regarding the expenses that seeking justice may incur as it includes the time that an individual spent, the money spent during this long period of time, and the cultural and emotional costs. While the assessment of time spent as a value is context-dependent, it

[25] This entry shows GDP on a purchasing power parity basis divided by population.

might be summarised that the amount of time (days, months, or years) that a user of justice has to spend is actually the cost of access to justice.

However, I disagree with the general theory that people with higher incomes will put a higher value on time compared to those whose time is less valuable in a country like Iran.[26] I think people with higher incomes are more likely to benefit from access to legal assistance, which is not as costly as it is for users of justice in Western societies.[27] Therefore, they are able to save more time (and spend less) in dealing with other barriers such as the ineffectiveness of the delivery of justice, corruption, or lack of information.[28] It seems that the poor or those with lesser earnings need to spend more time (and more money) on the different levels of the path to justice starting with data collection. In short, those seeking justice spend time on different priorities, beginning with the collection of legal information, seeking help from professionals, filing the case, awaiting hearings, and travelling, in addition to many other actions.

Research showed that delays are an inherent part of any judicial process (Lind and Tyler, 1988). In fact, Iranian legal culture has accepted lengthy delays as an inherent element of access

26 "In general, it could be hypothesised that people with higher earnings will place a higher value on time compared to those users whose time is less valuable" (Gramatikov, 2008: 16).

27 The bylaw "compensation for legal services performed by lawyers" that went into effect on 18 July 2006 limits lawyers' fees. The law (which was suggested by the Bar Association and confirmed by the head of the Judiciary) governs the terms under which lawyers can accept fees. According to this bylaw, a fee charged for a lawyer's services is calculated as a percentage of the client's case. Therefore, a lawyer's fee shall not exceed more than 7 percent in the monetary cases and 5 percent in the nonmonetary cases (not more than 4 percent in the family-related cases and maximum 5 percent in the criminal cases).

28 The findings of the survey study presented in Chapter 6 supports this line of argument.

to justice.[29] However, as a Persian proverb illustrates: "justice delays but never denies"; there is a strong cultural perception that even though the demand for justice is delayed, justice will never be denied. This is because public legal culture perceives justice as an equivalent concept with a right (haqq), which is inherent and inviolable. It is interesting to note in this connection that I ran a simple Google search and came up with almost 102,000 results. Almost all of these Internet pages quoted the Persian proverb to reflect a clear message: "No matter how long it takes, justice will be done." Also the analysis of a survey in Chapter 6 shows that most of the respondents innately perceive accessing justice (haqq) to take a long time but nevertheless, justice (haqq) will always be realised. The belief is that individuals have certain inherent and inviolable rights and justice is one of them. It therefore seems that the phrase "justice delayed is justice denied" might not be true in all sociolegal contexts, at least not in Iran.

It is important to acknowledge that such lengthy delays (*etaleh dadresi*) have been extensively studied by the Ministry of Justice and in academia. Notably, these studies (which are described in the following paragraphs) have examined some of the key dimensions considered as a barrier to access to justice. The purpose of this section is to provide a quantitative and demographic portrait of some of the main issues in relation to time spent between 1996 and 2008. Most of the data analysed are from the 2006 Census of Population and some complementary information from other sources (for the most part data published by the Ministry of Justice) is also used. Results presented in this section summarise the trends observed across Iran and may not reflect provincial trends.

[29] Supporting views are reported in the local press that delays are inherent in the judicial process. For a ready reference, see Fardanews, "Long Delay," accessed 10 June 2010, available online at http://www.fardanews.com/fa/news/126097.

The most recent quantitative research that can provide a general idea of average time spent on legal concerns is a sample study by the Ministry of Justice in 2007.[30] This study sampled almost 10,000 civil and criminal cases for a study to assess total time spent. Of these 4,375 civil cases, 4,375 criminal cases and 797 were appeal cases. The average minimum amount of time taken, from cases being brought to court and passing through all the levels of the appellate system for litigants in civil cases, was 463 days (1–2 years) and for criminal cases, 274 days (1 year). The average maximum time was reported to be 4,367 days (12 years) in civil cases and 3,313 days (9 years) in criminal cases. As claimed by the Minister of Justice,[31] the minimum average time was reduced by the necessary measures to fifty-seven days in the court of the first instance and thirty-one days in the appeal court. Yet the average maximum amount of time for a litigant who goes through all levels of proceedings is two to five years and could be as many as ten years.[32] In my personal experience, a land dispute took five years to resolve after passing through all first instance and appellate processes.

The most serious concern involves inefficiency in dealing with the large number of litigations. Most local research studies on the lengthy delays have emphasised the large numbers of cases and inefficiency in handling the case load. The huge numbers of unheard cases are claimed to be the main reason for such long delays.[33] It was revealed that 8–9 million cases were brought

[30] Islamic Republic of Iran Department of Justice (2007), *The Impact of Directives on Long Delay*. Tehran: Judiciary Printing Office.

[31] The Report of 10 Years Judicial Reform presented by the Minister of Justice, accessed 10 July 2010, available online at http://www.dolat.ir/NSite/FullStory/?id=178514.

[32] The comment was made by the head of the judiciary, Ayatollah Larijani, in an interview with the national TV (channel 1), accessed 22 June 2010, available online at http://www.bornanews.com/vdcgnw9w.ak9774prra.html.

[33] Although there is no official data of out-of-court settlement, it seems that the rate of out-of-court settlement is very low.

Table 2. Cases of Public Courts and Courts of Appeal

Year	Public Courts	Courts of Appeal
1996	3,120,589	178,219
2002–2003	5,041,712	421,898
2004	4,236,636	450,575
2005	3,249,853	476,056
2006	3,217,670	506,086

to the courts in 2008.[34] The shocking data that was proclaimed through the national media publicised that, each year, 20 million Iranians are in court.[35] Table 2 indicates the number of cases before the public courts and the courts of appeal (excluding the special courts) between 1996 and 2006 (1375–85).[36]

More telling, during the period 1996 to 2006, the total number of cases filed before the courts of appeal increased by almost 30 percent. The total number of cases before the public courts has increased by almost 50 percent over the period 1996 to 2003 but decreased between 2007 and 2008. There are a number of factors involved with the falling number of cases. The computerisation of the case filing system has had a great impact on avoiding filing cases that have been previously processed. Electronic case filing has automated the index book system in the civil and criminal registry of the Public Court. This system makes a note of new cases entering the registry, the parties involved, the date and time the document is filed and by whom, as well as the type of document. In addition, the Ministry of Justice, during the period 1996–2008, issued more than 385 directives to provide better access to justice.

Most of these directives have a direct link with the decrease in the delay. The most prominent regulation that had a great

34 The data given by the Justice Minster Deputy on 8 November 2008, accessed 12 February 2010, available online at http://www.fararu.com/vdcjihev.uqemhzsffu.html.

35 Ibid.

36 2006 Census of Islamic Republic of Iran.

deal of influence on decreasing the time spent was passed on 25 April 2005. This bylaw required the parties to have an attorney in civil proceedings; thus, the litigants of a new case entering the civil registry must introduce their lawyers. Moreover, the document must be filed by an attorney to be registered as a civil case. Obviously, the users of justice with better legal information are more likely to spend less time compared to those with less information. Therefore, compulsory legal assistance in civil proceedings reduced the chances of filing completed legal documents incorrectly and as a result, litigation derived from an inaccurate claim. To enable the poor and other vulnerable groups to have free legal assistance, the Ministry of Justice has provided legal aid clinics in all of the public courts. The Bar Association also had to introduce free legal assistance to those who were referred by the court as Mosar or an applicant for exemption based on Esar, as explained earlier.

Inadequate Human Resources

Another important barrier to access to justice with particular reference to delays arises from an insufficient number of skilled staff and competent judges. This section presents a demographic portrait of justice personnel and their evolution between 2000 and 2008 in order to examine some related issues of inadequate human resources. The main group described here is that of the court personnel. Table 3 shows the number of judges in Iran.

As Table 3 indicates, the number of judges has increased from 4,322 in 2000 to 7,939 in 2008. As a result, the number of judges per 100,000 habitants has increased from 6.8 to 10.9 in 2008.[37] Nevertheless, there is an unequal gap in the distribution of judges across the country. In small cities, per 100,000 habitants

[37] Islamic Republic of Iran's Planning Deputy of the Presidential Office (2009), *Development Report of the Judiciary*, accessed 15 July 2010, available online at http://www.spac.ir/barnameh/317/p-1.htm.

Table 3. Number of Judges in Iran

Year	Judges	Judges per 100,000 Capita
2000	4,322	6.8
2001	5,801	8.9
2002	6,300	9.5
2003	7,231	10.8
2004	7,330	10.7
2005	7,429	10.7
2006	7,528	10.7
2007	7,947	11.1
2008	7,939	10.9

there is only one judge dealing with varying categories of cases, including criminal and civil procedures.[38] Moreover, the judiciary faces a serious shortage of personnel, which has been addressed as one explanation for the lengthy delays. The latest published data state that the number of staff in the judiciary, excluding the judges, increased by almost 13,000 between 1998 and 2008, or close to 2.01 percent.[39] In 2008, the number of nonjudicial personnel and judges was reported to be around 34,185,[40] representing less than 0.13 percent of a labour force of 25.2 million Iranians (2009 estimate).

Although most justice-related occupations require specific qualifications and educational requirements, only a small proportion of the staff are reported to have any postgraduate education. The only available data reveal that about 69 percent of nonjudicial personnel have either a high school diploma or just a middle school certificate; 30 percent, an associate or graduate degree; and only 1 percent have successfully undertaken postgraduate study.[41] The reality

[38] The figure given by the journal of the Ministry of Justice which is called Mavi, accessed 20 July 2010, available online at http://www.maavanews.ir/tabid/38/ctl/Edit/mid/384/Code/6456/Default.aspx.

[39] Ibid., n. 38.

[40] Ibid.

[41] Ibid.

is even more discouraging in terms of judges. The Constitution reveals that: "the conditions and qualifications to be fulfilled by a judge will be determined by law, in accordance with religious criteria."[42] The law on the selection of judges, adopted in 1983, stipulates that judges must be Muslim men, of legitimate birth, Iranian citizens, loyal to the Islamic Republic of Iran, *Mujtahid* (an Islamic legal scholar) or holding a law degree or Islamic law degree; they also must have a certificate confirming they have no criminal convictions, a good reputation of being fair and noble, and be between twenty-three and thirty-nine years old. The prospective candidates are expected to pass an entry exam that is held annually by the judiciary. The successful candidates are required to complete their basic judge's training, which takes 15, 18, or 24 months depending on the post they are applying for. In 2009, for instance, 358 candidates – among them seventy-three women – took part in the judge training courses, but only 117 candidates could complete the training phase successfully and join the justice system.[43] In practice, the judges are often thought to be incompetent and inexperienced, especially in the courts of the first instance.[44]

The judicial reform programs in Iran, as elsewhere, have traditionally focused on training personnel to improve the performance of justice institutions, particularly with regard to dealing with case management and delay. These personnel training programs, in spite of having been extended during the last few years, are still, inadequate. In 2008, 29,000 personnel have participated in at least one of the training programs provided by the judiciary. This figure represents almost a 53.8 percent increase in the number of personnel compared to 1999, when only 3,351 justice-related personnel were reported to have taken part in any related training programs.[45]

[42] Article 163 of the Constitution.

[43] Ibid., n. 38.

[44] Interviews in the field research support this line of the argument.

[45] Ibid., n. 38.

Also judicial personnel are required to participate in a related skill development program. Although some major advances have been made, the actual capacity of the trend toward skill development seems to be inadequate. In a very optimistic report by the Minister of Justice, nearly 6,000 judicial and 20,000 nonjudicial personnel have had the benefit of a maximum of 53.8 hours training per year. Yet, according to a group of young judges of the court of the first instance, the figure sounds rather rhetorical. In an interview, they confirmed the figure given above would only be somewhat true if the total included hours during which personnel take part in group prayers, religious ceremonies, and political speeches, along with actual hours spent at training workshops. From the critics' perspective, one major gap is the lack of credible data regarding the efficiency of these programs in any specific data relating to the impact of personnel training on court performance. Although the benefits of personnel training in providing greater access to justice are comprehensible, the outcomes of these programs in practice are unclear and unpromising.

Corruption

Access to justice seems to be a costly process for people in Iran, taking into account not only the legal fees they need to pay but also the unofficial payments. The obvious paradigm is that a corrupt judiciary can increase the cost of justice in many ways (Transparency International, 2007). In particular, vulnerable groups such as the poor, minorities, people with a poor educational background or less well connected are more likely to be encouraged to pay unofficial payments.

Although corruption within the Iranian judiciary has been subject to the strongest disapproval from the authorities of the Supreme Leader,[46] it still remains one of the main challenges

[46] On 22 December 2001, Ali Khamenei, the Supreme Leader of Iran, issued an order to fight against corruption.

for the justice system. It appears that the government's anti-corruption efforts have not been enough to tackle widespread corruption, and many consider the situation to be getting worse by the day. In fact, consistent with Transparency International, which publishes the annual Corruption Perception Index, Iran fell from 78th in 2003 to 146th in 2010.[47]

Similar to many other legal concepts, prohibition of the notion of bribery has its roots in Islamic law. The Farsi word for bribe is *rashwah*, which also has an Arabic root. This term refers to an unofficial payment to an administrator in order to influence the conduct of the recipient (Jafari-Langroudi, 1997: 335). It also means an act implying money or gift giving that achieves a goal through conspiracy.[48] The prohibition of bribery in Islam is based on the primary and secondary resources. The Quran says: "And do not swallow up your property among yourselves by wrongful means; neither seek to gain access thereby to the authorities, so that you may swallow up a portion of the property of men wrongfully while you know."[49] Allamah Tabatabei has cited a Hadith in Tafisr Al-Mizan confirming that the verse prohibits bribing the judicial authorities.[50] The Quranic hostility to bribery was

[47] The Corruption Perceptions Index (2009), accessed 20 June 2011, available at http://www.transparency.org/policy_research/surveys_indices/cpi/2010/results.

[48] Turayhi, Fakhr ud-Din, Majma' ul-Bahrain, 1416 AH, Tehran, published by Ketabfurushy Murtazawy, 1416. vol. 1, p. 184.

[49] Quran, 2:188.

[50] "The Imam said: "The Imam said: Allah knew that there would be in this ummah judges who would do injustice. He did not mean (here) judges of a just authority, but He meant those of an unjust authority. If you had a right against someone and you summoned him to the judges of a just authority, but he did not agree to it and compelled you to put your case before the judges of an unjust authority, so that they might decide in his favour, then that man would be among those who had resorted to the Judgment of the Satan. And it is the word of Allah: Have you not observed those who think that they believe in what has

reinforced by the Islamic tradition. In the Shia school of thought, corruption has also received strong condemnation through narratives originating from the words and deeds of the Prophet and Imams.

The primary point about all related narratives is that there is no distinction between who pays and who receives; indeed, all types of bribery are forbidden by the explicit texts. "Beware of bribe! It is nothing but disbelief. The one who is involved in bribe will not even smell the fragrance of Paradise" (Safinat'ul-Bihār). Elsewhere, the Prophet (S) says, "Allah cursed the briber, the bribe-taker and the mediator (meaning the one who walks between the two) in judgment. Avoid bribery as it is disbelief (*kufr*) and the bribe-taker is far from the mercy of God."[51] The same position, in confirming that bribery is negation of faith, has been taken by Imams. This position attempts to emphasise that there is no distinction between bribery to seek a right or to establish something void, impose injustice, or achieve a benefit: all of these are forbidden. Imam Ali, the first Shia Imam, states that "taking bribes (money or gift) by official authorities is forbidden (*haram*) and bribing the judges is disbelief (*Kufr*) in God."[52] The corruption in judicial proceeding amounts to disbelief in Allah.[53] Also based on fatwa, non-official payment to public servants is forbidden (*haram*).[54]

Despite the prohibition of corruption under Sharia and national law, justice systems are often warped by corruption. "We

been sent down unto you and what was sent down before you? They intend to resort to the Judgment of Satan, though they were commanded to deny (reject) him (4:60)." Tabatabaei, Muhammad Husayn. Al-Mizan, vol. 2, p. 52, under verse 188 of surah Baqarah.

51 Al-Majlisi (2000), vol. 24, p. 24.

52 Ibn 'Abd al-Malik Muttaqi, Kenz Al-Amal, vol. 6, p. 112.

53 Hadith from Imam Sadiq at al-Hurr al-Aamili (1998), vol. 18, p. 162.

54 See Ayatullah Ruhollah Musavi Khomeini (2001), vol. 2, chapter of judgment, issue 6; Ayatullah Fazel Lankarani (2006), vol. 1, question 972; Ayatullah Safi Golpaygani (1997), vol. 2, question 1540.

do not deny the existence of corruption": Judiciary Chief Ayatollah Sadeq Amoli Larijani made this remark in response to an MP, who said that all judges receive bribes.[55] He also added, "but it is not fair to say all judges are corrupt."[56] Although there are examples of initiatives that were designed to tackle corruption, these legislations and governmental policies did not appear to have any major impact to prevent and contain judicial corruption. Note, for example, the law for Severe Punishment for Perpetrators of Embezzlement, Corruption and Fraud adopted in 1988 by the Expediency Discernment Council.[57] This bill includes a definition of administrative corruption and its punishment. However, the judiciary does not even reveal how many anticorruption cases have been ground-breaking with successful results. Another example is the United Nations Convention against Corruption (UNCAC)[58] that was been ratified by the Islamic Republic of Iran in April 2009, but there has been no published data regarding the impact of this international legal instrument on combating corruption.[59]

In addition, the Supreme Court for Disciplinary Control of Judges is used primarily for any complaint charging a judge with: (1) violation of the rules of professional conduct such as judges' duties to each other; (2) violation of the Code of Judicial Conduct such as disposing all judicial matters promptly, efficiently and

55 "Not all judges are corrupt: Judiciary Chief" (Mehr News Agency, December 2010), accessed 10 June 2011, available online at http://www.mehrnews.com/en/newsdetail.aspx?NewsID=1207107.

56 Ibid.

57 The Expediency Discernment Council of the System is an administrative assembly that was created upon the revision to the Constitution in 1988 and appointed by the Supreme Leader to resolve the conflicts between the parliament and the Council of Guardians.

58 The Convention was adopted by the General Assembly by resolution 58/4 of 31 October 2003 and entered into force on 14 December 2005.

59 The implementation of the UNCAC in Iran will be reviewed by two state members appointed to the task in 2011.

fairly; (3) conviction of a felony such as corruption, which is a criminal act; (4) misfeasance or malfeasance in office; and (5) persistent failure to perform judicial duties. Nevertheless, the court has been criticised for the lack of efficiency and transparency of its procedures concerning the discipline or removal of corrupt judges.[60] It appears that the lack of accountability within the Iranian justice system exists not only because there is no legal framework or the political will to combat corruption, but mainly because there is no appropriate case-tracking or monitoring within the court system (CCA, 2003).The main concern relating to corruption is the lack of public trust and confidence in the justice system, which, in turn, creates hesitation in people with regard to the legal process.

Before concluding this section, it is important to note that corruption in the judiciary is a complex issue and needs to be addressed by a variety of policies. Long delays, for example, cause corrupt practices and influence the public perception of corruption. In Iran, users of justice more often pay bribes to speed up the litigation process.[61] The huge backlog of cases results in delayed justice; it is quite common for a case to be delayed for years. As a result, most users of justice have to pay unofficial payments, and when abuse occurs, corruption further twists the justice system. Another reason for bribing the judiciary is in order to secure a favourable result in a lower court despite the fact that the rate of corruption falls dramatically when it comes to the higher courts. It is clear that a dysfunctional justice system leads to corruption.

[60] The parliamentary research centre's decision that the Supreme Court for Disciplinary Control of Judges has been inefficient in investigating and prosecuting cases of judicial misconduct (ISNA, March 2011). Accessed 23 May 2011, available online at http://shayegh.ir/1389/12/08/لايحه-››تشكيلات-دادسرا-و-نظارت-انتظامي/.

[61] Instances are reported in the local media regarding corruption and long delay. For a ready reference, see EfaNews, "Long Delay Causes Corruption," accessed 9 July 2010, available online at http://efanews.com/?id=27153.

Inadequate Legal Assistance

The need for legal assistance, although not completely missing in Iranian legal provision, seems inadequately implemented to be assured in practice. The Constitution of 1979 Islamic Revolution guarantees that in all of the courts, both parties have the right to have a lawyer and anyone who cannot afford a lawyer will be provided with one.[62] This constitutional provision is akin to many developed countries that declare the right to free legal representation not only for indigent criminal defendants but also for indigent civil litigants (see for instance Article 29 of the Constitution of Switzerland,[63] Article 18 of the Constitution of the Netherlands,[64] Article 24(3) of the Italian Constitution).[65]

In this context, legal assistance is a positive obligation of the Islamic state to ensure access to justice for those without adequate means. This positive approach symbolises a parallel between the Iranian Islamic state and other welfare states such as the United States in the area of access to justice.[66] In Iran,

[62] Article 35 of the Constitution.

[63] "Every person lacking the necessary means has the right to free legal assistance, provided the case does not seem to lack any merit. To the extent necessary for the protection of one's rights, the person also has the right to free legal counsel."

[64] "Everyone may be legally represented in legal and administrative proceedings."

[65] "The poor are entitled by law to proper means for action or defense in all courts."

[66] The constitutional law "that the United States has most fully moved from a negative to a positive – or welfare-state in the realm of access to justice. We have seen that the right to counsel, like the rest of the Bill of Rights, was at first seen as essentially negative. And it is still seen that way in the sense that it is still viewed as a barrier against government oppression. Yet, by a curious dialectic, the right to counsel has served as the vehicle for converting American consciousness from a negative to a more positive approach to access to justice for those without the means to buy their way into our ever-expanding court system"(Cappelletti and Garth, 1978: 285).

legal assistance for criminal cases has been subjected to more detailed legislative protection. The Code of Criminal Procedure mandates that in all criminal cases, each party has the right to a lawyer,[67] that anyone accused of a crime can request a lawyer from the court, and that the government must provide the lawyer's fees.[68] Despite these protective constitutional and legal obligations, many defendants' right to counsel has been denied in practice in Iran. Many defendants are excluded from access to a legal counsel during the investigation procedure while in detention. This is mainly because, under a note to Article 128 of the Code of Criminal Procedures, defendants' access to lawyers in sensitive cases can be barred by the judges. Restrictions to the right to counsel provided under the note to Article 128 of the Code of Criminal Procedures seems to contradict Article 3 of the Law on Respect for Legitimate Freedoms and Safeguarding Citizens' rights, enacted in 2004. This law obliges the court and the prosecutor to fulfil the right to legal representation of the defendants by providing the opportunity to be represented by a lawyer during all stages of the trial. However, it has been claimed that prosecutors and courts have closed their eyes to this new legislation in order to deny the defendant's right to counsel under Article 128.[69] Thus, many lawyers have access to their clients' files just a few days before a trial hearing once the investigation process has been completed (see Amnesty International, 2010; Human Rights Watch, 2010).

[67] Article 185 of Criminal Procedure Code.

[68] Article 186 of Criminal Procedure Code.

[69] For example, the lawyer of Arash Rahmanipour, who was one of the two executed on 28 January for alleged involvement in the post-election unrest, has said that she was barred from attending all sessions of his trial and was threatened with arrest when she tried to enter the court room. In another case, Zeynab Jalalian, a member of Iran's Kurdish minority, who was sentenced to death on or around January 2009, has said that her trial lasted only a few minutes and that she was not allowed a lawyer in court (Amnesty International, 2010).

It is also important to note that the right to counsel is more restricted in the practice of so-called special courts (e.g., the revolutionary court). The UN Working Group on Arbitrary Detention report of 2003 concluded that

> through an extremely restrictive interpretation of article 128 of the Code of Criminal Procedure and of note No. 3 to the law on the selection of counsel, the revolutionary tribunals – in addition to the fact that they have no constitutional legitimacy – abuse the already questionable authority given them under these instruments to exclude counsel at their discretion from hearings in cases covered by this article, that is, those involving the internal and external security of the State, cases in which their presence is all the more necessary. This derogation is so serious that it makes these tribunals special courts.[70]

The problem is compounded by the lack of an adequate system. Free legal assistance in criminal cases takes two major forms under the Iranian legal system: mandatory defence and assigned counsel. It is noteworthy that there is no public defence service that is funded by the government of the Islamic Republic of Iran. Under this scheme, which has been widely adopted around the world, legal representation for those who are in need is provided by a governmental organisation staffed by full-time lawyers. The main benefit of the public defence schemes is that they "will not distribute resources on the basis of private economic criteria (the need for profit) and, as a result, they may be more responsive to other goals. Nevertheless, public models of provision are also prone to subjective and implicit resource allocation and may be more susceptible to budgetary restraint and political control" (Moorhead, 1998: 380). There is also the question of cost effectiveness of a public defender service as an alternative to other legal

[70] Conclusions and recommendations of the Working Group on Arbitrary Detention, mission to the Islamic Republic of Iran; E/CN.4/2004/3/Add.2, para 51.

assistance schemes. An evaluation of the public defender's pilot in England and Wales (Bridges and Paterson, 2007) revealed that cases handled by public defenders usually demonstrate higher costs than comparable cases handled via private practitioners.

The main structure of legal assistance in criminal cases under Iranian jurisdiction is based on an ex officio or assigned counsel system. The ex officio system is perhaps the oldest system to be used at some level to build up the legal aid system in quite a considerable number of countries, including, for example, the United States, Australia, South Africa, and Poland. In Iran, the traditional ex officio system is applied when the court assigns a counsel who needs to be a member of the Bar. Article 1 of the 1976 Law of the Establishment of the Financial Security of Attorneys states that ex officio appointed lawyers are assigned in criminal cases by the court. The Bar Association or the Centre for Legal Advisors, Lawyers and Legal Specialists of the Judiciary must introduce a qualified lawyer to the court. The term used to describe ex officio is *vekalat taskhiri*, an Arabic term meaning an assigned free counsel. The court, the Bar, and the Centre for Legal Advisors, Lawyers and Legal Specialists of the Judiciary are the main legal bodies to appoint ex officio counsel for defendants who cannot afford a legal representative. Attorney's fees in cases of mandatory defence in which ex officio counsel is appointed are paid by a special judiciary budget.

The mandatory defence is an obligatory order for the validity of the criminal proceedings in specific cases. Criminal trials cannot proceed in the absence of a defence counsel when the accused is charged with an offence punishable by the death penalty, retribution, life imprisonment, or stoning to death. Article 168(1) of the Code of Criminal Procedure provides that in such cases, if no defence counsel has been appointed by the accused, the court should assign a defence counsel ex officio.[71] In most cases, judges determine ex officio fees in line with the Iranian Bar Association

[71] Article 186 (1) of the Code of Criminal Proceeding.

criteria, to be paid in favour of the state's finance at the end of the trial.

The mandatory defence provision, however, does not take into account the financial status of the defendant as an indicator; in practice, those who can afford a private practitioner are more likely to have their own counsels and only indigent defendants have the benefit of the ex officio provision. This is perhaps because of the impact of popular legal culture on the public's perceptions of assigned counsel. No studies have been carried out on either a small or large scale to examine public perception of assigned counsel.

However, national media reports show that popular legal culture perceives that the assigned counsels' performance is not as good as it should be when compared with private counsels. "People think assigned counsels would not be concerned as much as necessary for their clients because they haven't been paid an adequate amount of money for the service." These are the words of the judiciary's chief legal advisor in an interview with a national daily newspaper.[72] Another commentator confirms that lack of public trust in assigned counsel performance might be the result of actual cases. This criminal practitioner claims that popular legal culture considers mandatory defence more as "a legal decor" than adequate criminal legal assistance for the defendant. This perception results largely from the performance of courts and lawyers: when a court-appointed lawyer was employed, an adequately prepared defence was not presented.[73] Based on the qualitative interviews, I also believe Iranian popular cultural representations of assigned counsels have played an important part in explaining why defendants prefer to hire their own legal

[72] Nasiri Savad Kohi, "What We Need to Know about Assigned Counsel," (Jam e Jam: April 2008), accessed 15 February 2010, available online at http://www.jamejamonline.ir/newstext.aspx?newsnum=100936530065.

[73] Ibid.

representatives even in mandatory defence, although the actual scope is subject to further scrutiny.

The main criticism here is the lack of control with regard to the qualifications of the assigned counsel and the quality of service. The traditional version of the ex officio system seems to have been refined in many countries whereby attorneys meet certain minimum qualification criteria, such as having related experience. Although one of the principles for the provision of legal aid under the Law on the Establishment of the Financial Security of Lawyers is that "there should be no difference between the quality of service provided as legal aid and the quality of service provided as legal assistance to a paying client," it appears that this principle is not put into practice.

The defendant has a right to reject legal representation only in cases involving sexual offences or cases against approved ethics.[74] In most cases, if the defendant has been granted an ex officio legal representative in the court of the first instance, the same counsel represents the defendant until the final judgement is delivered. Iranian criminal jurisdiction does not recognise any other criteria for determining whether legal representation is mandatory other than the scope of the possible punishment. The defendant's mental condition, for example, does not establish the right to mandatory defence. The Office of Legal Council and Legislative Affairs of the Judiciary provides that where a murder defendant absconds during the trial process but an ex officio counsel is present to answer the charges, the trial is not in absentia.[75]

Nevertheless, mandatory defence under Iranian criminal jurisdiction is problematic on several counts. This system is restricted to a few categories of cases; those that are left out are often those where the defendants are at risk of long years of deprivation of liberty. Moreover, mandatory defence is permitted only when the investigation has been completed and so, during the pretrial

[74] Ibid.

[75] Opinion number 7/4853 issued 7 August 2001.

phase, any investigative procedures take place in the absence of a defence counsel. Last but not least is the lack of a clear system of regulations regarding those who can be appointed as assigned counsel. Almost any lawyer can be appointed regardless of their field of practice and specialisation.

Under the assigned counsel system or what is referred to as assistance counsel (Persian: *Vakil Mozedati*) in Iranian legal terminology, indigent criminal defendants whose offences do not fall within the remit of mandatory defence can apply for free legal assistance. The adoption of a "means" test is based on the Quranic doctrine of Esar, as noted earlier in the explanation of cost barriers. Therefore, under the Iranian Code of Criminal Procedure, the defendant must provide evidence of the lack of sufficient means on the basis of income or not having access to financial resources during the trial. Once the defendant has proved Esar, the court must appoint an ex officio counsel. The main evidence that should be submitted involves providing at least four witnesses who can testify to the lack of financial means of the defendant.[76]

However, the provision remains inadequate since the law provides no further explanation as to the minimum or maximum level of income that should be established and proved. The lack of consistent standards of the "means test" can cause conflicting decisions by courts in similar situations. In most cases, judges may pass judgements based on their knowledge of one of the veritable means of proof that the law requires in the Shia school of thought. In some cases, judges also require further local investigation from within their neighbourhood to prove financial difficulty of the defendant. Under Iranian jurisdiction, it is not the eligibility tests that result in the instances of potential free legal assistance being low but the punishment for false claims. Under Article 30 of the law of Esar, in filing a false claim, applicants may

[76] Article 23 of the Law of Esar. However, Article 506 of the Code of Civil Procedure provides that the testimony of two witnesses would be enough to prove the mean test.

face one to six months' imprisonment. The main problem with the assigned counsel scheme is that there are no clear systems obliging the authorities to inform the defendant of the right to free legal counsel. It seems that the majority of criminal defendants fall into the self-representation category. The private criminal law practitioners appear expensive and unaffordable for many defendants who are mainly from the poorer sections of the population.

One of the related concerns here surrounds the lack of a culture of counsel; most criminal defendants do not request legal assistance. The UN Working Group on Arbitrary Detention, reporting on its visit to Iran in February 2003, noted: "the absence of a culture of counsel, which seriously undermines due process. The Group notes that many ordinary law prisoners have no understanding of the role of counsel and do not request the assistance of State appointed counsel. The latter are in any event few in numbers and largely unmotivated owing to the low pay."[77]

Legal assistance in civil litigation fares no better. As previously mentioned, even though the Iranian Constitution provides for a right to legal assistance in both criminal and civil cases,[78] there being clear legislative protection to guarantee obligatory legal representation in civil litigation, the legal aid system, in civil cases, seems to be inadequate and insufficient in providing free legal services for indigent civil litigation. The main legislative protection for legal assistance in civil litigation has placed the emphasis on the legal profession. Article 23 of the 1954 law on the Bar provides that lawyers must represent at least three civil cases per year on a pro bono basis. The law, however, does not provide a clear and sufficient procedure regarding the right to

[77] Amnesty International report (June 2007), p. 11.

[78] Article 35 of the Constitution declares that "both parties to a lawsuit have the right in all courts of law to select an attorney, and if they are unable to do so, arrangements must be made to provide them with legal counsel."

free legal assistance. Also Article 21(2) of the implementing bylaw to Article 187 of the Law of Third Economic, Social and Cultural Development Plan (adopted in May 2000), guarantees that judicial legal advisors must provide free legal representation for three civil cases per year.

Critics raise more pragmatic objections to Article 187's legal advisors, mainly regarding the independence of the legal profession in Iran. Under Article 187, the judiciary "shall be authorised to confirm the competence of the law's graduates who shall be granted licences for the establishment of legal advisory institutes." Therefore, Article 187 authorises the judiciary to introduce a new generation of lawyers beyond the Bar's power to provide free legal assistance in civil litigation. The legal advisors' institute operates under the supervision of the judiciary, having a totally different examination and traineeship process from the Bar. So Bar Association lawyers and the judiciary's legal advisors are permitted to present all types of cases in court under the Iranian legal system. Estimates by the Minster of Justice show that, from 2001 to 2009, approximately 32,000 legal advisors under Article 187 have been admitted to practice.[79]

Legal profession institutions such as the Iranian Bar Association remain "extremely concerned about Article 187 legal advisors and believe they constitute a serious threat to their own independence" (International Bar Association, 2007: 10) and the International Bar Association observes that "the power of the judiciary to grant and repeal licences is likely to result in Article 187 legal advisors being strongly influenced by the judiciary. The relationship may also affect judicial independence and impartiality" (ibid.).

[79] Gholam Hossein Elham, "Achievements of Judicial Development in Ten Years" (speech presented by the Minister of Justice at the national conference for the judiciary, June 27, 2009), accessed 10 March 2010, available online at http://www.dolat.ir/NSite/FullStory/?id=178514.

Therefore, low-income civil litigants who are unable to secure legal representation on their own may fall under the scheme of Esar and request an assigned counsel (Persian: *Vakil Mozedati*). In theory, civil indigent litigants are required to file an Esar case before the court, requesting free legal assistance that is subject to "means" tests. Successful litigants may refer to the Bar or to the Centre for Legal Advisors, Lawyers and Legal Specialists of the Judiciary to appoint a lawyer who will represent them on a pro bono basis. In practice, indigent litigants who, in most cases, are not familiar with the law and the judicial process must file the Esar request with the assistance of a legal advisor. Moreover, the provision of legal assistance for civil indigent litigants is widely underused, as there are no adequate specified procedures for appointing a lawyer. The right to be granted free legal representation applies only after litigation has commenced, and it is only at this point that a litigant or respondent may file a legal aid application with the court.

A major improvement facilitating free legal assistance in civil litigation was a bylaw, passed on 25 April 2005, requiring the parties to have an attorney in civil proceedings. As mentioned previously, the litigants of the new case entering the civil registry must introduce their lawyers. Moreover, the document must be filed by an attorney to be registered as a civil case. To enable the poor and other vulnerable groups to have free legal assistance, the Ministry of Justice provided legal aid clinics in all of the public courts, while the Bar Association also had to introduce free legal assistance to those who were referred to by the court as Mosar or an applicant for exemption based on Isar, as explained earlier.

Compulsory legal representation in civil litigation came to an end through the Supreme Court in its judgement No. 714, dated 2 March 2009. In order to arrive at this conclusion, the Court conducted a review of the constitutional provisions. The judgement in particular refers to Article 34 of the constitution, which states that "it is the indisputable right of every citizen to seek justice by recourse to competent courts. All citizens have right of access to such courts, and no one can be barred from courts to which he has a legal right of recourse." The judgement provides that "the mandatory legal representation in civil litigation functioned as barrier to justice for Iranians."

Conclusion

This chapter began by classifying the various categories of barriers to access to justice in Iran. It explored some of the common issues in order to give breadth and depth to the study of the different dimensions that incorporate the criteria, which create circumstances in which barriers to access to justice might be experienced. The analysis in this chapter shows that many of the barriers are applicable to all disadvantaged groups in different communities; however, some of the barriers from the Iranian user perspective include the cost of justice, lengthy delays, the insufficient numbers of judges and skilled staff, corruption, restrictive legal aid eligibility guidelines, and also limitations in terms of pro bono legal service provision.

The chapter also exposes the limits of legal assistance as an effective mechanism for providing wider access to justice. It highlights the fact that despite the existence of constitutional and legislative provisions, the reality on the ground appears to reflect that many Iranians who are facing significant legal problems do not have access to affordable legal assistance. Many individuals of limited means, who are unable to afford legal advice, are forced to confront their legal problems without legal assistance. This analysis has helped enrich our understanding of access to justice in Iran, with particular reference to the barriers to access to justice and also to see if any law and policy have been adopted to facilitate overcoming these barriers. Even though there are examples of legislation or policies that were designed to tackle barriers, these initiatives did not appear to have any significant impact in overcoming any obstacles. The lack of research exploring the nature and incidence of such barriers and also the lack of understanding, between related law and policy bodies such as the Ministry of Justice, of ways and mechanisms to provide better access to justice, seemed to reflect a lack of law and policy focus.

4 Access of Women to Justice and Legal Empowerment

The analysis of women's access to justice, with particular reference to their legal empowerment in the setting of an Islamic state such as Iran, is not an easy task. However, I want to suggest that it is equally important to distinguish and highlight the impact of sociocultural dimensions of inaccessibility that women face on their path to justice. In light of the discussion in the previous chapter, which reviewed barriers to access to justice without any particular reference to women, the present chapter examines gender-specific barriers to access to justice. The chapter also provides a conceptual analysis of empowerment and specifically attempts to conceptualise the legal empowerment of women. The chapter first presents a detailed analysis of the key components that constitute Iranian women's access to justice. Second, it analyses some of the key gender-specific barriers women might face in the quest to solve their problems and then explains how the concept can be reduced to measurable elements to maximise the access of Iranian women to justice.

Women, Justice, and Access

The discussion about access to justice becomes extremely complicated when it focuses on women in Iran. The analysis of "women's access to justice" is most often merged with "women's unequal status" in Iran as a Muslim country located in the Middle East. Controversial key words such as women, justice, Iran, Islam, and the Middle East can lead any potential discussion to a biased conclusion that there is no substantive justice under Islamic law for women. This impression, however, might appear unfair and incorrect to those academics who are familiar with the notion of access to justice, and yet it appears to be the fundamental understanding of many. Note, for example, a number of Iranian women activists (especially those in exile) believe that the lack of substantive justice is a result of legal and political Islam.[1] Inside Iran also "secular women, who wielded no influence with the Islamic regime, launched their dialogues publicly through print publications (weeklies, monthlies), often arguing that Islam is unable to deliver justice to women" (Hoodfar and Sadr, 2009: 892).

To understand how true these impressions and statements are, we need to examine what elements constitute the degree and quality of Iranian women's access to justice. There are four main components to which I want to draw attention. The first part deals with the notion of justice and equality embodied in the law. It questions substantive justice and the existence of equal remedy for women in the law and other regulatory frameworks. The second component deals with institutions of justice, looking

[1] For example, Mehrangiz Kar, a well-known Iranian feminist now living in the United States, believes that the Iranian legal system is inherently incompatible with the Convention on the Elimination of All Forms of Discrimination Against Women (CEDAW). She says, "the Iranian government is based upon Islam, and its constitution states that laws cannot contradict the Sharia. Given that the Sharia does not consider men and women's rights as equal, its joining the Convention would be problematic" (Fathi, 2007, BBC World Service).

at procedural justice to examine whether or not the legal system is able to provide access to equal and effective remedies for women. The third element is about cultural norms and social context, which affect and determine the extent to which legal rights may be realised. Finally, the fourth component pertains to the human agency of access to justice, dealing with the issue of legal empowerment.

This book, however, does not claim to provide a complete analysis. The main objective here is to provide a contextualised understanding of the key elements associated with women's access to justice in Iran. My second qualifying remark concerns information provided regarding discriminatory laws, which is reflected within the framework of substantive justice without attempting to develop a conceptual framework for women's human rights in Islam, since most of the laws presented next are based on Islamic law. The reason for not including an analysis of women's rights under Islamic law is because of the various interpretations of the Islamic sources and also the multifaceted sociolegal structures of Muslim societies. The complex nature of women's rights in Islam thus requires a comprehensive study that is beyond the scope and rationale of this book.[2] It is important also to note that the focus of this study is on the formal legal system, which is referred to as the "justice system."

Women and Legal Justice

The discussion regarding Iranian women's access to justice is most often faced with a substantive question: to what extent have the equal rights of women been protected by constitutional provision and domestic legislation? This section therefore looks

[2] An extensive academic and legal scholarship has been produced about the nature of Islamic law and whether it limits women's rights. For example see Ali (2000); Ahmed (1992); Kandiyoti (1991); and An-Na'im (1990).

at a list of discriminatory laws affecting equal access of women to justice. As noted elsewhere, a journey to justice for women is built upon the existence of equal remedy by international, constitutional law and by a legal and regulatory framework.[3] With regard to international instruments, Iran has not ratified the Convention on the Elimination of All Forms of Discrimination Against Women (CEDAW).[4] Under the previous president, Mohammad Khatami, the parliament passed a bill in favour of joining the convention, but the Guardian Council vetoed it on the grounds that the bill contradicted Islamic principles. This claim was made even though some Muslim-dominated countries such as Afghanistan, Azerbaijan, and Tajikistan have ratified CEDAW without any reservation. Also most of the Muslim states have joined the Convention, such as Bangladesh, Egypt, Algeria, Saudi Arabia, Malaysia, the Maldives, Morocco, Iraq, Jordan, Kuwait, Libya, Pakistan, Tunisia, Turkey, and Indonesia, albeit some with substantial reservations. States that have used adherence to Islam as justification for including reservations in the Women's Convention include Bangladesh, Egypt, Iraq, Kuwait, Libya, Malaysia, the Maldives, and Morocco. Tunisia and Pakistan have not expressly cited Islam as a reason for reserving their position, but the religious argument may well be inferred from the text of what appears to be a general reservation (Ali, 2006: 86).

Countries that have ratified CEDAW are obliged to provide equal remedy for women in the case of discrimination. They also agree to eliminate discriminatory laws, in keeping with the principle of justice and equality within their legal systems. It seems that the Constitution of Iran has replicated the key provisions of CEDAW such as "equality before the law" even though it is not a

[3] For a detailed analysis of legal protection of access to justice, see Chapter 3.

[4] Adopted at New York on 18 December 1979; Entered into force on 3 September 1981. UN GA Res. 34/180, 34 GAOR, Supp. (No. 46) 194, UN Doc. A/34/46, at 193 (1979), 2 U.K.T.S. (1989); 19 I.L.M. (1980) 33.

state party to the convention. However, there are still several discriminatory laws against women that hinder their equal access to justice, as we shall discuss later.

The first promise of substantive justice is based on constitutional provisions. The constitution of Iran recognises equality among citizens in conformity with Islamic law. Article 20 of the constitution states: "All citizens of the country, both men and women, equally enjoy the protection of the law and enjoy all human, political, economic, social, and cultural rights, in conformity with Islamic criteria." This general protection is narrowed down in Article 21, which places obligations on the state to ensure women's equality. The state "must accomplish a prescribed list of social goals related to women's role in society including, inter alia, the growth of women's personality, the protection of mothers, and special insurance for women without support."[5] As stated earlier, the Iranian Constitution guarantees access to justice within fair trial provisions without any discrimination between women and men.[6] Beyond the constitution, Iranian women's legal status in the Penal Code and the Civil Code[7] clearly appears unequal to that of men, as shown in the key examples of discriminatory laws listed below.

The Penal Code is marked with unequal treatment of the two genders based on the following key issues. First, criminal liability for girls commences six years prior to that of boys. Under the Penal Code, juveniles are immune from prosecution for committing a crime.[8] The law does not determine the age for criminal responsibility; however, it defines a child as a person who has not yet reached the age of puberty. The age of puberty (known as *boloogh*) is set at age fifteen for boys and nine for girls in the Civil Code.[9]

[5] Article 21 of the Constitution of the Islamic Republic of Iran.

[6] For a detailed discussion, see Chapter 3.

[7] References about discriminatory articles in the Penal Code and the Civil Code are provided in the following discussion.

[8] Penal Code, Article 49.

[9] Civil Code, Article 1210.

A second issue relates to the unequal rights of women regarding testimony in criminal matters. The Penal Code has a long list of crimes in which women cannot testify, including drinking alcohol,[10] sodomy, homosexuality,[11] and organised prostitution.[12] In other cases, the testimony of two women usually equals that of one man. For example, to prove adultery[13] or unintentional murder,[14] a man's testimony is worth the testimony of two women. A third issue relates to unequal punishment. According to Article 209 of the Penal Code, "if Muslim man commits first-degree murder against a Muslim woman, the penalty of retribution shall apply. The victim's next of kin, however, shall pay to the culprit half of his blood money before the act of retribution is carried out." Therefore, the punishment (*Qisas*)[15] is based on sex of the offender of the crime, which violates Article 14 of the Islamic Penal Code that reads: "a punishment that should be equal to the crime." Another issue pertains to *Diyat* (blood money), which is a financial punishment pronounced by a judge.[16] The law, however, considers a woman's life to be worth half that of a man. "The blood money for the first- or second-degree murder of a Muslim woman is half of that of a murdered Muslim man."[17]

In relation to family law, the Iranian Civil Code includes a discriminatory category of regulations where women and men appear unequal. Regarding marriage, for example, the law says that the marriage of a virgin girl [even after puberty] requires the permission of the father or paternal grandfather. If the guardian

[10] Penal Code, Article 170.

[11] Penal Code, Articles 117, 119, and 128.

[12] Penal Code, Article 137.

[13] Article 76.

[14] Article 237.

[15] Under Islamic criminal law, *Qisas* crimes (murder, intentional and unintentional physical injury, and voluntary and involuntary killing) involve the sanctions of retaliation or compensation.

[16] Islamic Penal Code, Article 15.

[17] Islamic Penal Code, Article 300.

refuses to give permission without a valid reason, the court can grant permission.[18] On the subject of divorce, "A man can divorce his wife whenever he wishes to do so" (Article 1133, Civil Code). Yet the wife is able to initiate a judicial divorce (referring to the court) in only a few cases. When it is proved to the Court that the continuation of the marriage is likely to cause difficulties, the judge can compel the husband to divorce his wife to avoid more harm and difficulty. If this cannot be done, then the divorce will be granted with the permission of the Islamic judge.[19] Also, if the husband refuses to pay the cost of maintaining his wife, and if it is impossible to force him to make payments through the court, the wife can initiate divorce. The same stipulation exists in the case where a husband is unable to provide for the maintenance of his wife.[20] The law also recognises *khula* and *Mubarat*.[21] Another issue relates to the equal rights of women concerning inheritance. According to the law, women inherit half of what men would usually inherit in comparable situations.[22]

This list of laws, which are unequal in terms of their treatment of women is not exhaustive; nevertheless, the above-mentioned laws appear to be the most significant with reference to access to justice. These statutes clearly have an adverse impact on women's equality and deny their equal access to justice. For example, imagine a path to justice for two women who are victims of

18 Article 1042, Civil Code.

19 Article 1130, Civil Code.

20 Article 1129, Civil Code.

21 According to Article 1146 of the Civil Code: "A *Khula* divorce occurs when the wife obtains a divorce owing to dislike of her husband, against property which she cedes to the husband. The property in question may consist of the original marriage portion, or the monetary equivalent thereof, whether more or less than the marriage portion." Article 1147: "A *Mubarat* divorce occurs when the dislike is mutual in which case the compensation must not be more than the marriage portion."

22 Civil Code, Article 907.

organised prostitution. If they want to report the crime, their testimony will not be heard by the court. They also might be charged with adultery if they cannot prove that they have been forced into prostitution. Now imagine what would happen if the victims were men. Under the law, with the testimony of two men, the crime of pimping and organised prostitution can be proved.[23]

The discriminatory laws on divorce and custody of children cause a vast range of physical and emotional barriers for women in accessing justice. It is relatively clear that women find it difficult to deal with the fear of losing custody of their children if they initiate divorce. According to the law, "A mother has preference over others for two years from the birth of her child for the custody of the child and after the lapse of this period custody will devolve on the father except in the case of a daughter who will remain under the custody of the mother till 7 years."[24] And "If the mother marries another man during her period of custody, the custody will devolve on the father."[25] The unequal custody rights upon dissolution of the marriage are terrifying enough to discourage women from seeking justice for their family-related problems.

Discriminatory laws create a sense of powerlessness among women because "every person should receive a just and fair treatment within the legal system" (Muralidhar, 2004a: 1). The discrimination that women often face with regard to family law, property, inheritance rights, employment, and so on limits their legal entitlements and so acts as a barrier to justice. This "unjust" and "unfair" access to laws and regulations reflects the necessity of making rights equal so as to ensure legitimacy and credibility of a justice system. Especially for women, a lack of access to equal rights results in a lack of courage and self-confidence, which seem often the greatest obstacles to challenging the injustice.

[23] Penal Code, Article 137.
[24] Civil Code, Article 1169.
[25] Civil Code, Article 1170.

A "fair treatment" by the legal system is based on substantive justice that aims at eliminating legal discrimination. However, substantive justice needs to extend its scope from a narrow concept of formal equality to initiate laws and policies for gender equality and justice. The realisation of substantive justice requires the positive obligation of the state to ensure equality without distinction on the basis of gender. Therefore, whereas equal treatment by law is essential, the State needs also to address causes, impacts, and outcomes that can marginalise and disadvantage women's rights and interests. Providing nondiscriminatory legal remedies and effective protection of women's rights by law thus is a substantive element of access to justice that also promotes gender equality.

Women and Administration of Justice

A black letter law, even where it protects a substantive right, is not enough to provide women with access to fair and effective justice. The law clearly can set a legislative norm to protect women's interests and rights. However, the access of women to justice also requires access to an effective and fair administration of justice that is able to provide easy access to equal remedies. In Iran, as elsewhere, the quality of justice women receive is equally pertinent in providing fair access to justice. The laws in Iran, while rather diverse and nonbiased, still may fail to protect women's rights because of the failure of the justice system to provide effective and fair enforcement.

The gender-related barriers to accessing justice are closely associated with the capacity of law enforcement agencies to provide effective legal remedies for women. The barriers, as we discussed in the previous chapter, affect the access of both men and women to justice. It seems, however, that men have easier access to justice than women.[26] The institutionalised gender biases and

[26] Most of the respondents of the survey study presented in Chapter 6 thought that men have easier access to justice.

discriminatory norms appear to permeate the administration of justice in particular and therefore create more multilayered barriers that women must overcome in order to access justice. Table 4 illustrates the key barriers and their implications for Iranian men and women in accessing justice.

One important barrier that must be briefly discussed here is the lack of gender sensitivity. In the context of access to justice, gender sensitivity within the justice system is of special significance in a sociolegal setting in which women may have nowhere else to seek protection of their rights. Gender sensitivity generally refers to the ability to recognise women's equal rights and also to understand the diverse perceptions of gender roles. Most policies concerned with gender sensitivity and access to justice are related to improving women's capacity to access resources and opportunities in order to overcome barriers to accessing justice. Some policies are also linked to the proportion of female staff within the justice system.[27]

Gender sensitivity within Iranian justice delivery agencies seems to be minimal. The number of female personnel working within the justice institutions, such as judicial officers, judges, and police and prison officers, although increasing, is still much lower than the number of male personnel (CCA, 2003). This low representation is especially problematic because women are officially barred from being judges. Prohibition started immediately after the 1979 Islamic revolution; this was when women judges were barred from practice. This practice was legalised later on by adding a clause to the constitution, which indicated that only men may become judges. The same clause was approved by the provisional government in 1979 and was added to the

[27] For a detailed discussion, see UNDP (2007), "Gender Equality and Justice Programming: Equitable Access to Justice for Women," accessed 25 March 2010, available online at http://www.undp.org.ir/gender/Equitable%20Access%20to%20Justice_EN-EBOOK.pdf.

Table 4. Barriers to Access to Justice for Women and Men

Barriers	Women	Men
Lack of legal protection	Lack of legal protection obstructs access to justice for both women and men. However, unequal status of Iranian women reflected in some gender-biased laws increases the hurdles that women must overcome in accessing justice.	Lack of legal protection bars access to justice for both women and men. However, the male-dominated law protects men's rights and interests.
Lack of de facto protection	There is a considerable lack of de facto implementation and enforcement of women's rights.	De facto implementation and enforcement is considerably greater for men.
Cost of justice	Cost of justice obstructs access to justice for both women and men. However, women have less access to financial resources to pay the costs of justice.	Cost of justice obstructs access to justice for both women and men. However, men have more access to financial resources to pay the costs of justice.
Lack of physical access	Most women cannot afford transport to the agencies or even the time to travel to the justice system to take legal action.	Men mostly can afford the transport or time to travel to justice institutions.
Long delays	Long delays obstruct access to justice for both women and men.	Long delays obstruct access to justice for both women and men. However, men feel more confident to negotiate the timing of their case with the staff of the court.[a]
Lack of legal assistance	Lack of legal assistance obstructs access to justice for both women and men. However, poverty and cultural gender biases constrain women's economical capacity to afford legal assistance.	Lack of legal assistance obstructs access to justice for both women and men. However, it seems men as heads of household have greater access to financial resources to afford legal assistance.

(*continued*)

Table 4. (*continued*)

Barriers	Women	Men
Lack of confidence	Gender discrimination, poverty, and lack of contacts in the public sphere decrease women's trust in the justice system.	Corruption and poverty reduce men's confidence in the justice system.
Lack of legal knowledge	Despite more Iranian women enrolling in higher education than men, having fewer contacts in the public sphere seems to negatively influence their level of legal knowledge.	Men are in greater contact with the public sphere, where they have more chances to learn about the law and the legal system.
Lack of gender sensitivity	Low representation of women in justice institutions has contributed to a lack of gender sensitivity.	The traditional assumptions regarding the roles of men sometimes have a negative effect on men.
Lack of balanced gender representation	The justice system is male-dominated and culturally less accessible for women.	The male-dominated justice system is more welcoming and accessible for men.
Social and cultural constructions	Discriminatory cultural norms provide obstacles to the ability of women to take legal action. Also the legal system under the control of gender biases fails to provide equal remedies for women.	Cultural values privilege men on the path to justice.

[a] This negotiation is an informal part of Iranian court procedure. Women are usually powerless and less confident to negotiate, and any attempt made is based on building sympathy.

constitution[28] and, as a result, judgeship became an exclusionary position for men. The ratification was also included in the

[28] Article 163 of the constitution lists the characteristics of judges without specifying a man or a woman.

1982 judges' employment law, which stated: "judges are only appointed among qualified men" (Article 2).

The law reform in 1992 facilitated a means for women to sit as assistant judges in some civil courts, but still women were prevented from becoming judges. The judiciary, however, uses "female judges" as an accepted term for those women who sit as assistant judges, judicial advisors, and deputy to the prosecutor. The number of female judges has been reported to be 528 in Iran, out of which 7 are the deputy to the prosecutor, 13 are the judicial deputy, 442 are assistant judges, and 86 serve as judicial advisors.[29] Therefore, the number of female judges comprised less than 5 percent of the 7,939 judges that were reported to be service in 2008.[30]

A related issue needs to be addressed here with regard to the unequal power relationships between men and women judges, which also have an adverse impact on women's access to justice. In a survey study of how female judges experienced working within a male-dominated system, forty-five respondents were asked to reflect upon their experiences in Tehran, of which thirty maintained that they had to overcome considerable difficulties to become a judge and felt that they were marginalised in the decision-making process (Moazami, 2007). Almost all participants mentioned the unequal power relationships that exist between male and female judges, illustrating examples such as male judges having forced female judges to make official decisions against their own judgement (ibid.).

In addition to the small number of female personnel within the justice delivery organisations, a limited appreciation of women's rights and an inadequate understanding of gender roles by the male staff of the justice system also negatively affect equal access

[29] Statistic provided by the Ministry of Justice in year 2008, accessed 23 April 2011, available online at http://isna.ir/isna/NewsView.aspx?ID=News-1677323.

[30] Ibid.

of women to justice. The crucial role of judges, prosecutors, and police is particularly important in view of gender-based discrimination and violence against women. In the case of domestic violence in particular, family court judges in general are indifferent to women threatened by violence (Nadjafi, 2007); thus the reluctance of justice officials to pursue investigations leaves women without any protection from the law. Voiced and unvoiced discrimination by judges or discriminatory practices in law enforcement and by justice officials explain how assumptions regarding gender roles can affect the law and its practice.[31]

Unfair treatment as a key constituent of procedural justice is more evident concerning accused women and female offenders.[32] Discrimination in the treatment of female offenders by the justice system "not only resulted in decreasing the age of those imprisoned, but has also contributed to an increase in the number of women convicted for petty crimes" (ibid., 13). Also, many female offenders believed that "double standards do exist and women are charged with greater severity than their male counterparts" (ibid.). A similar result has been shown by the survey study of women's access to justice in Afghanistan (Women and Children Legal Research Foundation, 2008), where 75.7 percent of the respondents reported facing some kind of problem with the

[31] As stated by former Chief Justice of India, "In recent years, the role of judiciary has extended beyond issuing directions on social issue concerns to ensuring effective and fair implementation of the same. As a judge this requires elimination of subtle ways in which the courtroom perpetuates discrimination and violation of women's right.... As judges we need to be proactive and take charge of our courtroom to ensure that the subtle ways of discrimination through spoken and unspoken words are eliminated" (Anand, 2004: 12).

[32] Procedural justice examines both formal procedures (e.g., laws and legal proceedings) and informal procedures (e.g., being given permission to be heard) to measure whether the fairness of procedures has lead up to the distribution of certain outcomes (Van den Bos, 2005: 273–300).

police or the wider judicial system. The most frequently reported problems – 21.6 percent – have been an absence of hearing or "believing" women's stories (ibid., 36).

This effect is called the "voice effect," which is one of the most robust effects in justice literature (e.g., Folger, 1977). Most of the women that I interviewed during my survey study placed an emphasis on the fairness of the process. Other correlated studies have also shown that people attach a perceived fairness to procedures that lead to certain decisions (Van den Bos, and Miedema, 2000). Research studies regarding gender and procedural justice explain that women place more value on procedural justice than men in different contexts (e.g., Sweeney and McFarlin, 1997; Tata and Bowes-Sperry, 1996). In my fieldwork, examples given by the respondents more often reflected the issues that relate to whether a woman has been given the opportunity to voice her claim. Court procedures, especially the way cases proceed to a hearing and the way women are treated, have an effect on how the female user of justice has experienced fair as opposed to unfair procedures.

Women and Cultural Barriers

This section identifies the debate with regard to social and cultural settings and its significance for the access of women to justice. It discusses how culture imposes on women's equality beyond substantive and institutional justice. Even when the laws are just and inclusive and operate adequately, women may face enormous difficulties in accessing justice because of discriminatory cultural norms. Any related analysis thus should be able to address cultural paradigms to understand how justice and access have been defined beyond law and order in the social context.

The influence of cultural considerations on women's access to justice can be determined from the fact that making a legal claim is still not an easy decision to make for many women in

Iran. Those women who take legal action are often stigmatised by the community, particularly if they claim against their spouses. Statistics suggest that the divorce rate has gone up steadily, rising by 15.7 percent in 2009 compared with the previous year, against a 2.1 percent increase in marriages, yet divorce is considered socially taboo. Women are more stigmatised by divorce, as illustrated in a Persian proverb: "a woman enters her husband's house with a white wedding dress and leaves it in a white burial shroud." In criminal or civil cases initiated by women against male members of their family, there is always a fear of losing face in society and also losing support from the family upon whom women may be economically dependent. As the following case studies illustrate, social stigmatisation creates a sense of powerlessness and emotionally deters women from seeking justice. These are stories of women for whom access to justice was denied by what I would like to call the "culture of injustice."

The first case involves a young girl who was the victim of gang rape as a form of honour revenge in South East Iran (Sistan and Baluchistan Province). The girl (said to be twelve or thirteen years old) was kidnapped from her school; her teacher and classmates were witnesses to this. The victim was released in her neighbourhood a few hours after the kidnapping. The day after, the police, having been informed by the school, approached the victim's family but the family denied that any crime had taken place. The police believed that the victim's family and the gang of rapists were both involved with drug trafficking, which had caused long-held hostility between the two families. The school headmaster later reported the case to the advisor of the province's governor of women's affairs. She (the advisor) had several meetings with the victim's family, begging them to report the crime and in particular to allow the authorities to conduct a medico-legal examination of the crime. The family rejected the request, quoting tradition and cultural norms. To them, seeking legal justice could be used as confirmation for their community that their daughter had been a victim of rape, and her lost virginity could greatly damage the reputation of the family. The case was brought by the advisor of the province's governor to the National Legal Committee for Women's Rights in 2004. At that time, I was a member of the committee, which was instigated by the Ministry of Interior to examine the issues regarding the legal protection of women in the different provinces of Iran. In the above-mentioned case, the main question was how to overcome the cultural obstacles in providing access to justice for women where legal protection and administration of justice has the ability to provide a just remedy.[33]

A more recent case involves Mina, whom I met in 2008.[34] Mina was the mother of a four-year-old son, Kamyar, from her marriage to Amir. A few months after their wedding, Amir started to sexually abuse Mina in their home in Karaj (located 20 km to the west of Tehran). "He forced me to do things that I didn't want to." And when I asked her what sort of things, she replied: "things that prostitutes do in some brutal videos." She reported that even during her pregnancy, she was subjected to serious sexual abuse by her husband. "I couldn't tell anyone. It was a great dishonour for me and my family." She could bear the violence until she realised her husband was sexually assaulting their four-year-old son. "I saw my poor baby with no clothing on, sitting on the devil's lap ... I suddenly realised why my Kamyar was terrified to be alone with his dad whenever I had to leave the house." A few days later, Mina left the house with Kamyar and went to her father's house. "I couldn't tell them what he had done to us. What would my father or brothers think of me? It disgusted me to see myself through their eyes ... I just told them I wanted a divorce. I told

[33] All case documents are archived by the National Legal Committee for Women's Rights, the Ministry of Interior in 2004. Despite several attempts to gain access to the case documentation, official reports were not available to the researcher.

[34] The names have been changed to protect the parties' confidentiality and privacy.

them Amir had beaten me ... they said that, even so, it could not be serious since I had no bruises on my face." She desperately wanted a divorce and custody of her son, but her family insisted that she had to return to her husband's house before "people start to say things that would ruin her reputation."

Mina came to me for help. She did not want to take legal action against Amir based on sexual violence and abusing their child. "People will stigmatise my poor son and that may remain with him for years. I don't want to damage his reputation in future ... he needs to be a man of honour." We had several meetings. I persuaded her that even if she obtained a divorce, the court could award custody to her husband unless he was proven to have been sexually abusive toward the child. Mina's fear for her son's safety helped her overcome her fear of social stigmatisation. I arranged an informal meeting with the head of the related family court that had jurisdiction over Mina's case. Fortunately, the head and his deputy showed support and sympathy. Since marital sexual assault cases are very often extremely difficult to prove in court, they organised a medico-legal examination to provide enough evidence before it was too late (the examination usually needs to be carried out within 72 hours of a sexual assault). A physical examination documented both extra-genital and genital injuries and marks.

I asked Mina to arrange a meeting with her family where we could raise the issue regarding their understanding and support. A day later, her mother called to warn me about "disturbing Mina's life and dishonouring her family." She said "the law and the court can't bring justice to Mina when she has to face blame from society and feel guilty for the rest of her life." I was not able to contact Mina anymore. I was told that Mina and her son were living in her paternal home. Her extended family was told that Mina and her husband had issues over incompatibility but no legal action was made for divorce and obviously no crime of sexual assault toward Mina and her son was reported. In 2010, I was informed that Mina and her son were still living with her parents, with no sign of redressing violence and injustice.[35]

These case studies might sound extreme, as they illustrate women in critical situations, but they reflect the fact that many Iranian women often have to overcome cultural obstacles because of traditional gender bias and social stigmatisation in accessing justice. Further empirical evidence concerning gender bias and cultural values and whether or not women perceive cultural norms as a barrier to access to justice are also examined in Chapter 6, which presents the results of the survey study undertaken for this study.

Human Agency in Access to Justice

I begin this section by looking at definitions of empowerment and women's empowerment. I then move on to the literature that covers legal empowerment to examine how legal empowerment is related to women's access to justice. I would like to suggest that formal law cannot be an adequate path for women to access justice in the presence of customary practices and sociocultural norms.

Women and Empowerment

The term "empowerment" has been used in various fields, such as education (Freire, 2000), women's studies (Morgen and Bookman, 1988), and development (Friedmann, 1992; Narayan, 2002), among other subjects. Empowerment has also become popular in the development field since the mid-1980s. This was a "new buzzword" in international development language but is often poorly understood (Oxaal and Baden, 1997). Numerous academic studies

[35] To maintain ethical principles, in particular confidentiality and privacy of the victims, the researcher is not able to provide complete reference.

have been conducted to define empowerment but so far little agreement has been reached (e.g., Friedmann, 1992). Most of the related international documentation often uses empowerment to promote various social inclusion policies rather than providing a comprehensive conceptual analysis.[36] There have also been a large number of research studies regarding the possible measurement of empowerment (Alsop et al., 2006; Narayan, 2002). These studies have attempted to examine how empowerment can be reduced to measurable components.

From a measurement perspective, empowerment is mainly about opportunities that people can use to make effective choices and take action. For example, research involving five countries[37] and conducted by the World Bank measures degrees of empowerment by examining the capacity to make an effective choice. This capacity "is primarily influenced by two sets of factors: agency and opportunity structure. Agency is defined as an actor's ability to make meaningful choices; that is, the actor is able to envisage options and make a choice. Opportunity structure is defined as the formal and informal contexts within which actors operate" (Alsop et al., 2006: 6).

Literature regarding empowerment most often uses common concepts such as power, control, participation, and making choices to define empowerment. The notion of empowerment in particular has been emphasised through people's ability to make choices (Kabeer, 1999). In this context, empowerment is a process of change in the power relationships whereby marginalised and disadvantaged populations make their own life decisions. In other words, "the term empowerment refers to a range of activities from individual self assertion to collective resistance, protest and

[36] See some of the United Nations documents, particularly about women's empowerment such as the Association for Women in Development (Everett, 1991), the Declaration made at the Micro-credit Summit (RESULTS 1997), (UNICEF 1999), and DFID (2000).

[37] Brazil, Ethiopia, Honduras, Indonesia, and Nepal.

mobilisation that challenge basic power relations. For individuals and groups where class, caste, ethnicity and gender determine their access to resources and power, their empowerment begins when they not only recognise the systemic forces that oppress them, but act to change existing power relationships."[38] The notion of control also has been emphasised in social work studies originally used by Barbara Solomon (1976). Solomon defines empowerment as the process by which disadvantaged groups increase power by accessing psychological and material resources, and begin to take control over their lives.

Another line of thought takes into account the different approaches to the process of empowerment. The top-down and instructive approach has been emphasised in the field of welfare reform in the late 1970s. In this perspective, existing social structures, such as neighbourhood, family, church, or voluntary associations, give instructions with regard to what poor people should do for their empowerment because they assume that poor people are powerless and need to be given power (Berger and Neuhaus, 1996: 158). The "bottom-up" approach, on the other hand, operates from below and involves a participatory process toward development (Oxaal and Baden, 1997; Narayan et al., 2000). Therefore, empowerment is a bottom-up process and cannot be operated from the top down.

On the subject of women's empowerment in particular, a study by the World Bank reviews some of the related literature and underlines some similarities between the definitions of women's empowerment such as "women's agency" and "process" (Malhotra et al., 2002). This study distinguishes empowerment from power to highlight that women themselves must make choices and exercise control over their lives to be considered empowered. Women's agency has most often been described by the related literature as an ability to make decisions and exercise control over resources and their lives. Woman's agency thus is "a capacity or ability to

[38] Batliwala (1994).

make meaning within a given set of cultural practices which fail to offer a clear and consistent formula for life, but are marked by contradictions" (Naffine, 2002: 86). Process, as another vital element of empowerment, has been emphasised by many writers on the subject (Kabeer, 1999; Rowlands, 1995). Process is the progression from gender inequality to gender equality.

Several different efforts have been made in recent years to develop comprehensive frameworks outlining the various dimensions within which women can be empowered (Malhotra et al., 2002). One commonly used index is the Gender Empowerment Measure (GEM), which measures gender inequality in the areas of political participation and decision making, economic participation and decision making, and power over economic resources. The index refers to women's empowerment as a similar concept to gender equality by measuring women's participation at a national level and thus does not include an individual basis. The GEM ranking for Iran is 87 and the value is 0.347; this includes the share of seats in parliament held by women (4.1); female legislators, senior officials, and managers (16); female professional and technical workers (34); and the female economic activity rate (0.39).[39]

It appears that the GEM provides a very limited reflection of women's empowerment. An increased percentage of female administrators and managers, for instance, does not represent whether or not Iranian women are empowered in their personal, familial, economic, and political lives. Empowerment of women in Iran includes numerous factors contributing to women's lives at both national and individual levels.

Legal Empowerment

In recent years, international organisations and development agencies have developed strategies for using the law to help

[39] UNDP (2006), *Human Development Report 2006*. New York: Oxford University Press.

disadvantaged populations have more control over their lives. Although these approaches vary in structure from legal literacy to public interest litigation, they are similar in embracing empowerment as processes.

The concept of legal empowerment emphasises the process and strategies that use "legal services and related development activities to increase disadvantaged populations' control over their lives." The phrase "legal empowerment" was suggested by Stephen Golub as a response to the failure of the "rule of law orthodoxy." Golub argued that Western advocacy for the rule of law has several problems; first, it employs a top-down approach by concentrating on building state-dependent legal institutions. Second, it assumes legal reforms should aim at smoothing the function of the market to eradicate poverty. Third, developing countries are employing international approaches without contextualising those strategies. Fourth, it fails to guarantee access to justice for all by bringing the judiciary to meet people's needs (ibid., 7–21).

Building on Golub and McQuay (2000) and Golub (2003), legal empowerment has been defined as a "process" that increases disadvantaged groups' control over their lives through use of the law, legal information, and action. Legal empowerment also has been seen as a "goal," referring to the actual achievements of the disadvantaged groups through the use of law. "The distinction is important, because the process of legal empowerment can proceed even if the goal has yet to be achieved" (Golub and McQuay, 2000: 26).

In a similar vein, the Commission on Legal Empowerment of the Poor[40] in its final 2008 report, Making the Law Work for Everyone, defined legal empowerment as "the process through which the poor become protected and are enabled to use the law to advance their rights and their interests, vis-à-vis the state

[40] The Commission on Legal Empowerment of the Poor was established in 2005 by UNDP, and after three years of research, the commission suggested strategies for empowering those living in poverty through providing voice, identity, access, and protections of rights.

and in the market" (2008). The commission recognised two key conditions for legal empowerment; identity and voice. "The poor need (proof of) a recognised identity that corresponds to their civic and economic agency as citizens, asset holders, workers, and businessmen/women. Without a voice for poor people, a legal empowerment process cannot exist" (ibid., 26).

In this context, legal empowerment can be defined as a subjective as well as an objective phenomenon. Most of the related research studies seem to emphasise creation of empowering opportunities such as providing legal aid, legal information, and legal institutions reform (see Narayan, 2002; Golub and McQuay, 2000). Thus, the objectives of these result-based projects have been categorised as "empowerment." However, "opportunities are external to the impoverished person, and although providing these opportunities may alter the person's potential reality, they are not empowering in and of themselves unless they enter into that person's actual reality" (Brown, 2003: 1). Subjective legal empowerment refers to processes that empower individuals to use the law. "In order to be legally empowered a person has to see herself as capable of using legal means for solving the problem" (Gramatikov and Porter, 2010: 6).

Beyond objective or subjective approaches, legal empowerment fundamentally is about power. However, most definitions of legal empowerment avoid "power" and use the term "control" instead. In this perspective, "control may relate to priorities such as basic security, livelihood, access to essential resources, and participation in public decision-making processes" (Golub and McQuay, 2000: 26). The question here is whether legal empowerment is only about taking legal action and participating in public decision-making processes. This question seems crucial when examining the access of women to justice in Iran. Women should be able to recognise themselves as entitled to make choices and take action. Legal empowerment consequently must include the processes and mechanisms that enable women to perceive themselves as entitled to make choices.

This book defines legal empowerment as a subjective phenomenon that must result in functional objectives. Thus, legal empowerment refers to processes that result in enhancing the self-belief of individuals and, in particular, disadvantaged groups to perceive themselves as citizens entitled to make choices and take action on their own behalf and change the power relationship to have better control over their lives. Law and legal institutions may not always be able to provide access to justice for women, as we discussed earlier in this chapter. Legal empowerment thus seems a promising paradigm for women to have a better understanding of the use of the law in their surroundings and of the sociolegal factors that may make them powerless and marginalised: "when they recognize systemic forces and oppressive surrounding conditions, they step in the process of their empowerment and commit to activities" (Morgen and Bookman, 1988: 4). This notion of women's agency is also relevant from the point of view of women's access to justice in Iran, for women who have to face not only substantive and institutional inequality but also cultural gender biases that hinder their access to justice.

The present study uses "woman's agency" in relation to the ability and strength that Iranian women have demonstrated on their path to justice. However, I do not suggest that Iranian women are responsible for their own actions and have personal duty to be empowered. Certainly there is an urgent need to promote gender equality through law reform, institutional improvement, political recognition of women's rights, and also to enhance women's access to resources. These positive changes, while vital in enhancing the access of Iranian women to justice, are not adequate enough to provide equal access to justice, as discussed earlier. Therefore, my emphasis on human agency in access to justice, as the defining criterion of legal empowerment, is mainly related to Iranian women's individual or collective ability to identify their rights and interests and make strategic choices on their path to justice. From this perspective, the choices that Iranian women make can be highlighted as women's agency. The "strategic life choices"[41] women make on their path to justice, as we see in the survey chapter, show that Iranian women are not powerless and weak in negotiating for justice and standing up for their own individual lives and for the sake of their families. Women's perceptions of access to justice, also presented in the survey chapter, can lead us to identify their abilities as an agency struggling against gender inequality.

The survey study, however, does not deny the difficulties that women may face in seeking justice. Discriminatory laws, failure of the justice system to provide effective and fair enforcement of rights, biased cultural values, and other barriers as mentioned in this research hinder women's ability to take legal action. Yet, it is important to appreciate the strengths of women in Iran who struggle to have access to a justice they perceive is more strategic for their families and children. Going to court, for example, may not be considered as a strategic choice for women when dealing with a family-related problem, but talking to a family advisor might be regarded as a strategic action. Most women interviewed in the current study reflected on their role as active agents in negotiating their rights and making strategic choices. The evidence of the current study thus strongly challenges the stereotype image of Muslim women portrayed in Iran as victims of their religion.[42]

Women's agency is also a fundamental element of legal empowerment by emphasising women's strengths, resistance, and strategies to deal with their legal problems. A brief word may be added here regarding some potential aspects of a legal empowerment model in Iran, even though providing a detailed discussion about programming legal empowerment, tools, and

[41] "Strategic life choices" refers to decisions that affect women's lives such as decisions related to marriage, divorce, childbearing, education, and employment. Empirical studies often suppose that the ability to make strategic choices will be demonstrated in an ability to make day-to-day decisions (Malhotra et al., 2002).

[42] To read more about Muslim women as active agents see Starr (1992).

mechanisms is beyond the boundaries of this research. Promoting legal empowerment of women may involve a range of different approaches and methods. In this section, however, we shall focus on those approaches and tools that aim at strengthening capacity of women to use the law in their path to justice.

It is important to note that there is no single model for legal empowerment. Legal empowerment programs are likely to vary in different contexts, cultures, and communities of Iranian society. A legal empowerment model for women in Tehran must be different from women legal empowerment in Baluchistan, for instance, where development indicators are much lower than the capital. A road map to women's legal empowerment in Iran includes three main dimensions:[43] (1) the importance of law reform to promote gender equality should be acknowledged; however, focusing on law reform should not reject opportunities to empower women to use the "existing law"; (2) legal services provided by the justice system should be based on the rights and needs of women; (3) the capacity of women as "users of justice" should be strengthened.

Building on the work of Anderson (2003), I have used the phrase "capacity of women as users of justice" to include the following categories of capacities: capacity to identify legal rights, capacity to identify legal problems, capacity to identify how to claim legal rights, and capacity to identify how to enforce legal rights. Anderson (2003) suggests different stages of access to justice, as Table 5 demonstrates.

One potential approach to strengthen the capacity of women as "users of justice" to use the law and legal system is to educate them to deal with legal matters. Most of the respondents in the current study, although, could identify the right they were entitled to but they did not know how to enforce their rights.

Another promising mechanism is developing efficient legal aid systems, which need to emphasise legal assistance provided

[43] The suggested "model" is based on the findings of the survey study presented in next chapter.

Table 5. Stages of Access to Justice

Naming	Identifying a grievance as a legal problem
Blaming	Identifying a culprit
Claiming	Staking a formal legal claim
Winning	Getting rights and legitimate interests recognised
Enforcing	Translating rights into reality

From Anderson, 2003: 2.

by paralegals and legal aid clinics. As the study presented in Chapter 6 shows, almost all of the respondents had no experience using legal aids and also did not know that some courts and the Bar Association actually provide free legal aids for the poor. Expanding legal aid systems facilitate accessibility of the judicial procedures for women, who have no legal representation. One possible mechanism is establishing paralegal programs at the community level that are missing from Iranian law society. In many countries such as the United States[44] or United Kingdom,[45] paralegals are not qualified as solicitor or barrister but receive specialised legal training to provide legal advice and assistance. They can supply basic information and legal advice and also assist with representation in administrative processes and litigation.

[44] "A legal assistant or paralegal is a person qualified by education, training or work experience who is employed or retained by a lawyer, law office, corporation, governmental agency or other entity who performs specifically delegated substantive legal work for which a lawyer is responsible." Under this definition, the legal responsibility for a paralegal's work rests directly and solely upon the lawyer"(definition by American Bar Association, accessed 27 February 2011, available online at http://apps.americanbar.org/legalservices/paralegals/def98.html).

[45] "A person who is educated and trained to perform legal tasks but who is not a qualified solicitor or barrister" (United Kingdom's National Association of Licensed Paralegals, accessed 27 February 2011, available online at http://www.nationalparalegals.com/nalp.htm).

Beyond expanding legal services to the poor by paralegals, legal aid clinics and clinical legal education can involve law students who provide free legal advice for disadvantaged groups. Clinical Legal Education (CLE) has emerged as a reaction to the failures of the traditional legal education during the last thirty years. This term can be defined as an interactive teaching methodology that aims at learning by practicing and also creating justice values.

In Iran, law school study consists of four years of academic work. There are around 2,390 higher education institutions in Iran, and most of them teach law as a graduate major. Most law schools also adopt an analytical approach to the law as logical doctrine taught principally through lectures. The teaching methodology thus includes lecturing while students read the law from textbooks. Some law schools also use the Casebook Method with focus on judicial decisions and the Socratic Method, which teaches the skill of legal analysis, both derived from American legal education in the nineteenth century.[46] From a personal perspective, I also have been trained by a traditional approach to legal education during my graduate study in Iran. I learned about clinical legal education while completing a master's degree at the Central European University. Upon my return to Iran, I initiated several national projects on the law school's capacity, building on clinical legal education,[47] and also started the first Iranian CLE course in Mofid University, Qom. The course adopted an active learning

[46] See McManis (1981).

[47] In January 2007, I did coordinate a visit of Iranian law schools and Bar Association of the Campus Law Clinic and Street Law program at the University of KwaZulu-Natal in Durban, South Africa. The South African experience provided the Iranian delegation with a pragmatic overview and general idea about clinical legal education. On 19 June 2007, the First International Conference on Clinical Legal Education was held in Shahid Beheshti University, Tehran. A brief summary of the conference is available online at http://www.sbu.ac.ir/Default.aspx?tabid=552&ctl=Detail&mid=1612&Id=730, accessed 25 May 2011.

methodology to teach practical legal skills to the students. The students could apply to work with the Mofid University Legal Clinic where they assist lawyers with family law cases.[48] Apart from Mofid University, none of the other Iranian law schools offer "clinical legal education" courses where students act as lawyers under the direction of a faculty member. Therefore, most students have to take a bar examination in one of the provinces upon graduation from law school to be able to practice law. These restrictions on who may provide legal services present an obstacle to more accessible forms of legal services such as paralegals and legal clinics.

There are some problems, however, with developing clinical legal education in Iran. These challenges include: (1) there is a fear that a legal clinic may upset the law school's relation with the local legal community; (2) there are limited resources regarding qualified clinical teachers, textbooks, financial support, and infrastructural facilities; (3) there is a limited capacity to accommodate interested students within the clinical education program; (4) no credit is given to students who take part in the community work; (5) the local community and especially women are not aware that the law schools provide free legal services; (6) there is a legal restriction on faculty to practice in a court of law and also on students to represent clients in the court; (7) there is a problem with supervising students to provide legal aid; and (8) there exists a lack of involvement of the Bar and the Judiciary. Beyond these problems, there is a great danger that the legal aid services provided to the vulnerable women by the law school may not be adequately gender-sensitive.

[48] The legal aid clinic of Mofid University has since been developed to teach students effective legal skills. The Mofid clinic also renders assistance to indigent clients on family law, labour law, and criminal law. See legal aid clinic of Mofid University, accessed 10 February 2011, available online at http://lcmu.ir/.

However, it may thus be concluded that clinical legal education remains as one of the key themes for enhancing women's access to justice in Iran. This is mainly because legal aid clinics may provide legal services to women at no cost, especially when Iranian lawyers are not required by law to fulfil any commitment to public service by mandatory pro bono. Clinical legal education may also inspire a commitment to social justice and public interest among the students. Many of my former students from Mofid University continued to contribute to access-to-justice by educating women about their rights and performing pro bono work. Besides, clinical programs may contribute into strategies such as public interest litigation that reflect change in the law itself. As a final point, legal clinics may help explore methods for more effective representation of clients' interests.[49]

Conclusion

This chapter has attempted to contextualise the access of Iranian women to justice by examining substantive and procedural justice, sociocultural barriers, and legal empowerment. It reviews gender-specific barriers to access to justice and also illustrates the limits of formal law as a mechanism for providing equal access for women to justice in the presence of discriminatory institutional practices and social norms. The chapter presents similar interrelated components of empowerment, women's empowerment, and legal empowerment, and suggests that legal empowerment can provide better access to justice for women in Iran. One important conclusion drawn is that women's empowerment and, in particular, women's legal empowerment is a multidimensional process and is difficult to measure. Legal empowerment also has different meanings in different contexts; a variable that indicates empowerment in one sociolegal setting is likely to be different in another

[49] For a detailed discussion see Charn (2003).

setting. This chapter concludes the first part of the book regarding the conceptual framework and also a contextualised analysis. Part II of the research study includes two chapters that discuss the methodology, access to justice measurement models, and the findings from the survey study with reference to women's perceptions of access to justice in Iran.

PART II

One of the main points of emphasis in this book is that any possible discussion of access to justice should be able to include the wide range of social and cultural contexts, since the meaning of what is defined as justice often varies in different contexts. Therefore, in order to appreciate the contextualised analysis of access to justice in Iran, it is important to study how people at the community level perceive access to justice. With this background in mind, Part II sets the stage for the case study on the perceptions of women regarding access to justice in Iran. To this end, empirical data were collected to support the main research question, that is, whether legal empowerment alternatives can provide wider access to justice for women in Iran. Part II includes two chapters to discuss first how to measure perceptions of access to justice, and then present the results of a survey study on women's perceptions of access to justice in Iran. Chapter 5 initiates the discussion by linking the methodology with the theoretical and contextual framework developed in the previous chapters and presents the basis for conducting the survey study. The chapter reviews some of the most applicable research findings to identify which methodological framework should be incorporated into a measurement model for the purpose of this study. It further argues that legal empowerment is the most practical model for measuring women's perceptions of access to justice in Iran. To assess the issue of women's perceptions of access to justice in Iran, Chapter 6 explains the research strategy and presents results of the survey study.

5 Methodology

How to Measure Access to Justice

Now that we've discussed the various conceptual and contextual dimensions of access to justice, the focus of the discussion can shift to one of the main topics of the book; that is, how to measure women's access to justice in Iran. Which method of measurement is more appropriate for the purpose of this research? How can women's access to justice be evaluated in order to test the study's hypothesis regarding whether legal empowerment can provide broader access to justice?

This chapter attempts to develop a measurement model for women's access to justice in Iran, which was used to develop the survey presented in the next chapter. Legal empowerment is the most practical model for measuring women's access to justice in Iran. The rationale of the "legal empowerment" model used to develop a survey study is to test the research assumption with regard to whether legal empowerment can provide broader access to justice for women in Iran.

Measurement Models

Earlier we reviewed the various sociolegal barriers such as lengthy delays, bureaucratic and costly procedures, lack of legal knowledge, and insufficient legal representation, that hinder people in Iran who are seeking justice. However, little is known about the main barriers to access to justice from the Iranian women's perspective. This chapter attempts to explore whether Iranian women have a greater tendency to experience discrimination or dissatisfaction with the justice system, even where the law provides equal protection. How do they perceive their legal rights? How do they perceive justice? How do they perceive legal problems? Do women have sufficient confidence in the justice system to pursue their legal rights? How do they perceive the quality of the procedure and outcome of access to justice? What are the cultural or emotional costs that women have to bear when they are seeking justice? How do they perceive the gender sensitisation of the administration of the justice system? Do they have a basic legal knowledge of legal institutions or legal actions? What amount of time do they spend taking legal action?

A lot of similar questions can be posed; however, since each of these questions covers a different aspect, measuring women's access to justice remains a very complicated area of study. This is not only because indicators may methodically fail to generate data about the experiences of population subsets and neglect women's perceptions as a vulnerable group, but also because of Iranian sociolegal and political settings.

The difficulty in measuring women's access to justice is not limited to the Iranian context; measuring the performance of justice is often perceived as a difficult undertaking (Sudarshan, 2003). It is also almost infeasible to measure people's experience when they seek access to justice (Carfield, 2005). Amidst the paradoxical nature of measuring access to justice, the measurement of access to justice in Iran specifically appears to be a multifaceted study since it is concerned with multiple factors. These factors include substantive justice (e.g., equal legal protection, discriminatory laws); institutional indicators (e.g., the effective administration of justice, gender sensitisation); user-based indicators (e.g., legal awareness, perceptions); needs-based indicators (e.g., types of legal action, legal service); development-based indicators (e.g., poverty, security); and culture-based indicators (e.g., gender bias, discriminatory traditions).

In the last half decade, several empirical research projects have been carried out to examine whether justice is accessible when people seek remedies to their legal problems. Most of the earlier studies employed a qualitative approach, examining access to justice as access to court or access to legal aid (Cappeletti and Garth, 1979). One of the primary large-scale empirical research studies is the "Comprehensive Legal Needs Study" conducted by the American Bar Association in the 1970s. Thereafter, access to justice was more often measured by surveying "paths to justice" to examine what types of actions people usually take to deal with their legal problems (American Bar Association, 1994; Coumarelos, 2006; Currie, 2007; Genn and Beinart, 1999; Genn and Paterson, 2001; Pleasence, Balmer, and Buck, 2004). These studies also examined the costs and outcomes of the different mechanisms from the user's perspective (American Bar Association, 1994; Genn and Beinart, 1999).

Different methodological models, such as measurement of the efficiency of the justice system, have been used to evaluate access to justice (European Commission for the Efficiency of Justice, 2005). Assessment of the various legal services is one of the most appropriate methods used in evaluating access to justice. The evaluation of the "Public Defender Service in England and Wales," for example, provides a comprehensive analysis of cost effectiveness, quality, patterns of case conduct, independence of thought and behaviour, client satisfaction, efficiency, and accountability of management structures, among other points (Bridges and Paterson, 2007). In short, most of the measurement models of access to justice consist of different categories of indicators to assess inputs (fee, time, and delay), quality of outcome, and quality of procedure.

In developing countries, most of the ongoing studies are trying to measure the connection between the rule of law and access to justice,[1] to observe "the citizen's use of institutions of law as deliberative force in which private and public dominations can be contested and debated" (Parker, 1999: 47). Specific aspects of the rule of law, including the role of the legal profession, ombudsman offices, the police, equal treatment, and accountability, are the aspects the rule of law methodology measures. In the Asia-Pacific region, where Iran is located,[2] several research studies have been conducted to measure access to justice. This research has been led mainly by the international development organisations, namely, the United Nations Development Program (UNDP), the Asian Development Bank (ADB), the World Bank (WB), and the Ford Foundation.

The UNDP Asia-Pacific Rights and Justice Initiative advocates for a rights-based approach (RBA) for greater access to justice (UNDP, 2004). A rights-based approach involves two key parties: claim-holders and duty-bearers. Therefore, most of the access to justice indicators developed by the UNDP define the lack of respect for human rights as the main obstacle in accessing justice; a "lack of normative protection guaranteeing the existence of a remedy for grievances, as well as the incapacity to seek such remedies even where they formally exist, or the incapacity to provide them when sought" (UNDP, 2003: 7). In the same way, the World Bank (WB) employs multiple indicators in relation to the institutional dimension of access to justice. These indicators include the structure of judicial institutions, jurisdiction, the legal framework, personnel, and salaries (Maru, 2009). The World Bank also provides statistics on the number of judges, lawyers, claims, and

[1] More details about the critical approach on how laws can make justice more accessible can be found in the writings of Parker (1999) and Heywood (2000).

[2] The United Nations regional category for Iran is the Asia-Pacific. Middle East as a regional category for Iran gained broader usage after the 1950s; "The term 'Middle East' gained broader usage in Europe and the United States, with the Middle East Institute founded in Washington D.C. in 1946, among other usage" (Held, 2000: 7).

legal services, and based on these statistics, related indicators have been developed to measure access to justice (Djankov et al., 2003; Ranis et al., 2005).

The Asian Development Bank (ADB) and the Ford Foundation focus more on legal education and legal empowerment. The Ford Foundation's Global Law Programs Learning Initiative (GLPLI) advocates law as a tool that not only brings "concrete benefits to marginalised groups, advancing their human rights, and promoting their development, but raises their capacities to generate, participate in, and sustain social change on their own" (McClymont and Golub, 2000: 6). The ADB uses legal empowerment as a key policy for greater access to justice. From the ADB's perspective, legal empowerment basically "involves the explicit or implicit use of the law (for example, through training, counselling, or litigation) or relates to public decision-making processes that have a specific legal dimension (for example, equipping citizens or communities with the skills and confidence to appear before an administrative tribunal or to inform local policy development). It frequently combines such activities with initiatives that are not inherently law-oriented, such as community organising or livelihood development. While they typically include education, most advanced legal empowerment initiatives aim to do more than simply teach people about law" (Asian Development Bank, 2001: 8).The legal empowerment approach is an example of how access to justice can be improved by bottom-up policies (Golub, 2003). Other examples of the bottom-up approach include paralegal programs mostly organised by the Open Society Justice Initiative (OSJI), community justice projects, and advocacy for informal justice systems (Hammergren, 2007; Meene and van Rooij, 2008; Lundy, 2008; Commission on Legal Empowerment of the Poor, 2008).

To my knowledge, no empirical research has been carried out to measure access to justice, which has been either led or conducted by international organisations in Iran. The only related project is the Human Rights for Greater Access to Justice undertaken by the UNDP-Iran.[3] The project includes several initiatives focusing mainly on human rights education. The output to access to justice that is most closely related is the establishment of ten pilot legal aid clinics within law schools and Iranian civil society organisations. It is worth noting that this project brings together, for the first time in Iran, eight key national human rights players, including the Centre for Human Rights Studies at the University of Tehran, the UNESCO Chair for Human Rights, Peace and Democracy at the Shahid Beheshti University, the Centre for Human Rights Studies at the Mofid University; the Islamic Human Rights Commission, Centre for Training and Research of the Judiciary of the I.R. of Iran; the Iranian Bar Association; the Organization for Defending Victims of Violence; and the Association of Iranian Journalists. The main criticism of the project is the lack of any empirical research regarding access to justice since the project takes more account of advocacy methods rather than functioning as a research scheme. This is unfortunate because three out of four of the leading Iranian universities are national partners of the project. Despite this, the project remains unable to produce any credible scholarly analysis of access to justice in the country.

User and Institutional Perspectives

As outlined earlier, various international organisations have utilised different indicators to measure access to justice. In the following sections, we will see that academic and scholarly research has also employed many variable indicators. Although scholarly

[3] In September 2005, the Ministry of the Foreign Affairs of the Government of the Islamic Republic sent official approval to the United Nation Development Program country office in Tehran for the signing of the UNDP–Iran supported cluster project on human rights and access to justice 2005–2009. The project document is available at http://www.undp.org.ir/index.php/component/content/article/71, accessed 8 June 2010.

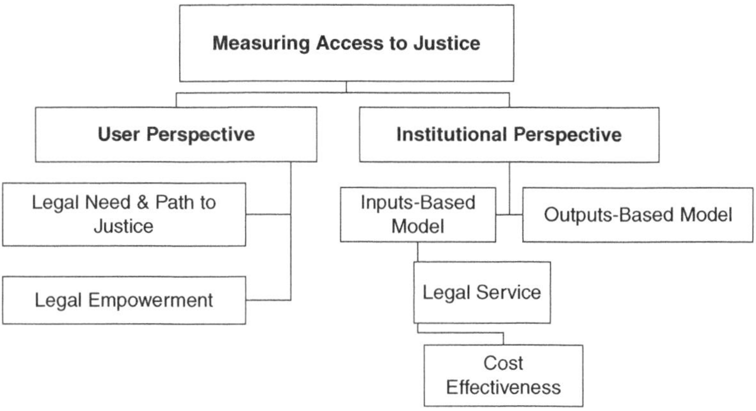

Figure 1. Methodological Framework for Measuring Access to Justice.

indicators for measuring access to justice are primarily context-dependent, they can nevertheless be identified either by measuring specific aspects of access to justice (the legal service, legal awareness) or measuring access to justice in general (path to justice, legal needs).

The indicators are also useful in understanding that any conceptual framework used to measure access to justice can be structured by two key dimensions, which take account of both the user's perspectives and institutional perspectives. The user's perspectives explore the barriers and difficulties that users of a specific justice system associate with access to justice. The measurement models based on the user's perspectives can be categorised into two general groups, including legal needs and legal empowerment. The measurement model derived from institutional perspectives can include either an input model or an output model. Based on my own observation, Figure 1 outlines the main methodological framework for measuring the accessibility of justice. The concepts indicated here will be elaborated upon in subsequent discussion.

Studying the user's perspective is essential for exploring the barriers to access to justice. The user is defined as a person who takes a legal action (formal or informal) to deal with a legal problem. The measurement models based on the user's perspective can be divided into two main methods. The first is surveying the legal needs or path to justice. This is an empirical tool that evaluates the perceptions of the people (users) who use a specific mechanism to obtain justice to resolve their disputes. The second method can be referred to as legal empowerment, which evaluates the public's perceptions of law and legal institutions to explore their legal awareness.

As previously mentioned, several large-scale studies surveyed "legal needs" as a measurement model for access to justice (e.g., American Bar Association, 1994; in the United Kingdom (e.g., Genn and Beinart, 1999; Genn and Paterson 2001; Pleasence et al., 2004); New Zealand (Maxwell et al., 1999); China (Michelson, 2007); and Australia (Coumarelos, 2006). The term legal needs is often used in the context of access to justice to refer to common problems that people face in their everyday lives (e.g., Genn and Beinart, 1999; Pleasence et al., 2004). These legal problems cover different matters such as employment, social benefits, health, and education. They are derived from the legal rights[4] of people within an existing "legal system" (Schetzer, 2003).

Related research studies before the 1990s defined legal needs as those legal issues for which people typically seek legal advice.[5] The broader interpretation of legal needs, as in the actions that people take to deal with these needs, is described as "paths to justice." A path to justice is a course of required action that users

[4] Legal rights or statutory rights are defined as rights that exist under the rules of a specific legal system.

[5] The Comprehensive Legal Needs Study by the American Bar Association used the term "legal need" in two ways: "first, people sometimes find ways of dealing with circumstances they face without turning to a lawyer, a mediator, or the courts. These circumstances are still considered 'legal needs' although there is no implication they must of necessity be brought to the justice system. Secondly, some 'legal needs' arise from changes in society and from the effects of the civil justice system itself on society" (ABA, 1994: 4).

of justice experience to facilitate dealing with their legal needs (Gramatikov and Porter, 2010: 9). This definition of path to justice extends to both formal and informal processes.

The legal needs studies differed in terms of the number and type of legal issues they surveyed[6] as well as the definitions of a legal issue they provided. However, the key concern relates to how a legal need can be identified. In fact, little is known about the related indicators used to identify legal needs, aside from seeking dispute resolution or reviewing the legal problems that are usually taken to lawyers (Griffiths, 1977). Most of the applicable indicators miss those legal problems that may be solved by non-formal mechanisms or those that remain unresolved (Genn and Beinart, 1999).

In Iran, legal problems are sometimes solved through informal mechanisms; in addition, a large proportion of legal problems remain unsolved. These non-formal solutions do not fall within the definition of formal justice system. They include informal mechanisms such as talking to the other party involved in the dispute or involving a third person from the family in deliberations.[7] The identification of legal needs in Iran therefore seems to be an infeasible undertaking if it relies on those indicators in relation to seeking legal advice. In many cases, people do not seek advice for their legal problems. It is not clear, though, whether this is because they do not trust the judicial system or because they are not aware of the law and the legal process.

With regard to legal needs, it must also be noted that the term "justiciable events" used by Genn and Beinart (1999) includes those legal issues that often are not identified as legal problems

[6] For instance, some legal needs studies focus on civil legal issues and exclude criminal and family problems. See Rush Social Research Agency (1999).

[7] The Asia Foundation survey has included nonformal solutions in the assessment of the citizen's perceptions of the Indonesian justice sector (AC Nielsen and Asia Foundation, 2001: 141).

as a result of lack of legal awareness, and also those legal problems that remain unresolved or are resolved by nonlegal mechanisms. Justiciable events are circumstances that "raise [civil] legal issues, whether or not people recognize them as being legal and whether or not they respond to the event by using some part of the civil justice system" (Genn and Beinart, 1999: 12). Research has shown that only a small number of problems are resolved via the formal justice sector (Genn and Beinart, 1999; Moorhead and Pleasence, 2003; Genn et al., 2003; Pleasence et al., 2004; Currie, 2007).[8] These studies have shown that the decision people make to solve a problem is a complex process that relies on different factors, such as the nature of the problem as well as the type of person making the decision.

Although evaluating how people deal with justiciable problems has not been the subject of any large- or medium-scale research studies in Iran, some of the findings of the paths to justice studies seem to be relevant to the Iranian context. For instance, these studies demonstrated that people feel negatively about the justice system and so are unwilling to become involved with the courts, or the people's opinion of the courts is formed by media stories. The survey that I conducted in Tehran presents the same results.[9] I looked at how women deal with a legal problem in the Iranian context. Relationships between gender and the rate of

[8] The Paths to Justice study in England and Wales (Genn and Beinart, 1999), for instance, considered "access to justice" beyond the use of legal services to realise court-based resolutions. This study was replicated in Scotland (Genn and Paterson, 2001). Both studies used quantitative and qualitative research methods to explore what people do and think when faced with "justiciable events." These surveys also analysed whether respondents took any action, what motivation they had for not taking action, what kind of action they took, whom they consulted, what their perceptions were in terms of barriers to access to justice, and what their experience was of the legal proceedings.

[9] Please see Chapter 6 for the survey study on women's perceptions of access to justice.

legal problems have been reported by several studies (e.g., Genn and Beinart, 1999; Genn and Paterson, 2001; Maxwell et al., 1999; Pleasence et al., 2004). For instance, the Task Force on Civil Equal Just Funding in Washington, DC (2003) stated that women from low- and moderate-income households experience an unequal percentage of legal problems, mainly related to family law and domestic violence. Gender also has been found to be a factor in the incidence of specific categories of legal problems. Pleasence et al. (2004), for example, reported higher rates of family and clinical negligence problems for women.

The above-mentioned studies have been conducted in Western societies; therefore, there might be many marked differences between the Iranian (as a Muslim society) and the Western context, most importantly about the legal and social status of people (user of justice), nature of the dispute (legal problem), how to deal with a problem (legal action), and mechanisms for dispute resolutions. However, there are clear similarities between any paths to justice studies analysis in these two different contexts, principally about how people think about the legal system and also the notion of barriers they might experience in their path to justice. For example, analysis of empirical evidence of people and their justiciable problems in England and Wales showed that ignorance about legal rights and lack of familiarity with the court process exist across most social groups, and people generally are not educated about their legal rights (Genn and Beinart, 1999: 102). The survey study of women's perceptions of access to justice in Iran also confirms that most women were ignorant about the legal and administrative systems and thought the law and legal system were too complex to be understood. Another example of a similarity between the two cultures is exemplified in an interesting study conducted in Australia. The study found that women were more likely to experience family-related problems and disputes concerning housing, loans, and government departments (Fishwick, 1992). Iranian women also seem more likely to experience those legal problems in relation to their families.

These research studies underscore the importance of public perceptions in developing effective legal policies for the community to maximise access to justice. In Iran, the main problem is most likely the lack of quantitative information needed to examine people's legal needs and perceptions. It should be mentioned nevertheless that the judiciary has conducted several national research projects regarding the delay in court proceedings (*etaleh dadresi*). These studies, based on qualitative methodologies, provide data related to the numbers of court cases, types (civil, criminal, or nonlitigious affairs), and also the subjects of the cases. I should add that I also searched the databases of Iranian universities to examine whether any academic research or book had been undertaken regarding legal needs and found that no specific research had been conducted. The fact that the Iranian legal community, including the academic institutions, has not yet shown any strong interest in exploring the actions that people take to address their legal needs is attributable to several factors, among which that they are unfamiliar with the related research methodologies and because access to justice is a recent subject for them.

However, the measurement model derived from an institutional perspective measures the quantity and quality of resources invested for access to justice (inputs) and also the quantity and quality of the results (outputs) realised from the inputs. The measurement model that examines the quantity and quality of resources derives from the notion of procedural justice and focuses on the institutional dimension of access to justice.

In the Western context, most of the recent studies have elaborated upon procedural justice within an organisational context and found that the very same indicators of procedural justice used in the legal context are applicable in the institutional context (Lind, 1990; Colquitt et al., 2001. These studies have often shown that people are concerned with the quality of the procedure (Lind and Tyler, 1988; Tyler, 2006a) even more than the quality of the outcome (Lind and Tyler, 1988). People were found to consider it a fair outcome if the procedure was fair, and they were also more satisfied with a negative outcome if the procedure was viewed as fair (Tyler, 1996). Extensive research shows that procedural justice plays a greater role than distributive justice in structuring people's perceptions of justice (Lind and Tyler, 1988; van den Bos et al., 1998). The same findings have been confirmed by Iranian women. As we discuss later, most of the survey's respondents also understood better justice to be fairness of process.

The first dimension of an input-based measurement model for access to justice is that of cost-effectiveness. The previous chapter regarding barriers to access to justice details the costs of taking legal action (fees, expenses, long distances and lengthy delays, the actual costs of engaging a lawyer, social, cultural, and emotional costs) all of which exclude the poor and other marginalised groups from justice. The different categories for litigation costs, including transaction costs, transfers costs, total amount of money expended, total defence expenses, and total litigation costs, were also discussed (Cohen, 2000; Miller, 2002). Repeated studies show that the most important factors in determining whether people are able to use the available legal remedies are the costly litigation process and access to financial resources (Galanter, 1974; Cappelletti and Garth, 1979; Woolf, 1996). Chapter 3 regarding barriers to access to justice explains that the cost of litigation is said to be a barrier in Iran, as in many other developing countries (Commission on Legal Empowerment of the Poor, 2008).

Access to justice seems to be more expensive for women because the cost of taking legal action also includes social and cultural costs such as the potential loss of social status, income, or family protection. Perhaps one of the most important issues in connection with measuring Iranian women's access to justice lies in exploring what category of costs is more effective for women in taking legal action. Are they monetary costs and the lack of access to financial resources? Is it the social and cultural costs that make women unable to use the available legal remedies? Or the emotional costs? These questions have also been incorporated into the survey study in order to understand the impact of cost barriers on women's access to justice in Iran.

Another important aspect pertaining to the institutional perspective is evaluating the quality of legal services including legal aid plans. The conventional definition of legal services is limited to the legal representation, legal advice, legal assistance, and legal information provided by a lawyer. However, recent research studies have shown that people use all sorts of legal and non-legal advisors and do not limit themselves to conventional legal advisors (Genn and Beinart, 1999; Maxwell et al., 1999; Pleasence et al., 2004). It has been emphasised that the definition of legal services must include all individuals and organisations that people usually refer to for advice in dealing with their legal problems (Pleasence et al., 2004). I also support the proposal that the definition of legal services must include all individuals, groups, and organisations that people refer to for legal advice. In Iran, people seem to use a very wide variety of sources and do not limit themselves to lawyers. Although there are numerous types of advice providers such as community groups, local Imams, religious authorities, charities, NGOs, the Judiciary Legal Assistance Bureau located in public courts, and the Bar Association Legal Assistance Bureau, it appears that the first point of contact is most commonly family and friends. An important question that should be asked here is regarding the methodology of measuring the quality of legal services. In fact, different frameworks have been applied to define and assess the quality of legal services. The evaluation of "the Public Defender Service" in England and Wales, for instance, adopts the peer review methodology to measure the quality of criminal defence work. The peer review framework involves "the assessment of files using a standard criteria and ratings system to determine the quality of advice and legal work provided to clients in a particular category of work. Following consideration of the files using the criteria, an overall judgment on the quality of advice and legal work is made" (Legal Services Commission, 2005: 7). The peer review was first attempted in

"Quality – The Legal Agenda" (Sherr et al., 1994) at the beginning of Legal Aid Franchising. It was adopted later in the research "Improving Police Station Legal Advice" (Bridges, 1998).

Assessment of the quantity/quality of output is another aspect of the measurement model based on an institutional perspective. Research into organisational justice links several dimensions of justice to the quality of outcomes (Colquitt et al., 2001). These include procedural justice or fairness of decision-making processes (Leventhal and Kenneth, 1980), distributive justice, or fairness of outcomes and international justice (Greenberg, 1993) that cover interpersonal justice (respect) and informational justice (adequate explanation). More recent work has focused on developing a methodology for measuring four dimensions of organisational justice, namely distributive justice, procedural justice, interpersonal justice, and informational justice (Colquitt et al., 2001). Some scholars have also developed the criteria for the measurement of outcomes from different justice theories (Konow, 2003; Törnblom and Vermunt, 2007). However, there is not yet a comprehensive measurement methodology for the quality of outcomes of paths to justice.

Indicators

One of the main methodological challenges is that of developing appropriate indicators that can be incorporated into a practical measurement framework. The indicators, from a social science perspective, are significant tools in measuring the performance of a duty holder (input indicators), the process of a program (process indicators), and the level of success or failure of a particular program (outcome indicators).

The development of indicators for measuring access to justice and for other sociolegal concepts requires a "sociological imagination" (Bulmer, 1984). In particular, if the measurement framework requires conducting a survey, "we must translate any concepts into a form in which they are measurable" (DeVaus,

2002: 43). Therefore, constructing an indicator is "the process of converting concepts into their empirical measurements or of quantifying variables for the purpose of measuring their occurrence, strength and frequency" (Sarantakos, 1993: 46). Indicators aim to examine the adjustment of an ongoing program. They can also be used to determine the status of an ongoing program (Sudarshan, 2003).

An interesting paper about access to justice indicators in the Asia Pacific region (Teehankee, 2003) adopts a rights-based approach as the dimensions for the classification of the indicators, including (1) existence of remedy; (2) capacity to seek remedy; and (3) capacity to seek effective remedy. The paper distinguishes the qualitative or quantitative nature of the indicators based on their types; the indicators that measure the quantity/quality of resources provided for access to justice (input scheme), the indicators that measure the quantity/quality of outputs, the indicators that measure the quantity/quality of results created through outputs (outcome scheme), and finally, the indicators that measure the extent to which broader goals are achieved through program outcomes (impact scheme). These indicators are collated from a range of sources that include governmental, civil society, and international development organisations. International development agencies are increasingly developing indicators of access to justice mostly to establish the link between justice and development. The World Bank, for instance, has developed a wide range of indictors, including the structure and function of judicial institutions, the selection mechanism for the head of the judicial institution, jurisdiction, legal framework, personnel and salaries, alternative dispute resolution mechanisms, and public legal education (World Bank, 2003). The United Nations Development Program, with a rights-based approach, focuses on legal empowerment, legal awareness, legal aid, and provision of effective remedies (La Salle Institute of Governance, 2003).

These indicators often have focused on a well-functioning legal and judicial system based on the rule of law assumptions, such as boosting independence and accountability rather than considering the specific justice needs of people at the local level. Another clear failure involves the lack of impact evaluations of access to justice interventions by the international development organisations such as the United Nations Development Program and the World Bank. Most of the available evaluations of access to justice interventions often are limited to numerical significance, such as number of judges, skilled staff, or users.

Yet the evaluation of effective access to justice policies and mechanisms has been encouraged by academic institutions. One study of interest is a research project entitled "Measuring Access to Justice in a Globalising World, the Hague Model of Access to Justice." The main objective of this research project is to develop a framework for measuring access to justice in international and in national settings. The project has produced a number of interesting papers about different aspects that are involved with measuring access to justice, such as cost (Gramatikov et al., 2008), quality of outcome (Verdonschot et al., 2008), and priorities for the justice system (Barendrecht et al., 2008).

Upon closer examination, however, it is important to question whether "Measuring Access to Justice in a Globalising World" can provide a model that is globally applicable. In fact, almost all of these studies are more concerned with the Western contextual framework, mainly North Europe and the United States. The literature also is dominated by more of a regional model of access to justice rather than a global applicable model. Use of the term "developing countries" has been limited to a few instances to allow for inclusion of the rest of the social and legal contexts that are not "developed." The project nevertheless has discussed a number of concepts that can be used in different contexts. For instance, in one of their working paper series, a thought-provoking shortlist has been suggested. This shortlist, presented in Table 6, provides the indicators and criteria required for a measurement tool to evaluate the quality of outcomes "across various settings, such as a negotiated agreement about compensation of damages between

Table 6. Indicators, Criteria, and Items of Quality of Outcomes

Justice Type	Indicator	Criterion	Item
Distributive justice	Equity	The outcome is proportionate to the contribution of the parties.	To what extent was the other party's contribution to the problem taken into account in the outcome? To what extent was your contribution to the problem taken into account in the outcome? To what extent did the outcome consider the efforts the other party made to resolve the problem? To what extent did the outcome consider your efforts to resolve the outcome?
Distributive justice	Equality	The outcome gives both parties an equal share.	To what extent did you and the other party pay or receive an equal share in the outcome?
Distributive justice	Need	The outcome considers the needs of the parties.	To what extent were the other party's needs considered in the outcome? To what extent were your needs considered in the outcome?
Restorative justice	Restoration	Emotional and material harms have been repaired.	To what extent were your monetary harms repaired as a result of the outcome? To what extent were your emotional harms repaired as a result of the outcome?
Restorative justice	Reintegration	The future compliance with the law of the other party is increased.	To what extent was the outcome effective in ensuring that the other party will avoid similar behaviour in the future?
Transformative justice	Transformation	The conflict was reframed in terms of relationships. The outcome reflects the interests of the parties.	To what extent did the outcome improve the damaged relationship with the other party that resulted from the problem? To what extent was the outcome favourable for you?

Informational justice	Justification	The parties received a thorough explanation of their outcome.	To what extent did you receive an explanation of the outcome from the neutral person? To what extent were you satisfied with the explanation you received?
Legal pragmatism	Anti-foundationalism	The outcome was pragmatic.	To what extent did the outcome solve your problem?
Legal pragmatism	Instrumentalism	The consequences of the outcome were taken into account.	To what extent were the chances that the outcome would be enforced taken into account? To what extent were you satisfied with the outcome? To what extent did you find the outcome fair?
Formal justice	Formal equality	The outcome and the outcome of others are transparent in such a way that they can be compared in terms of equal treatment.	To what extent was it possible for you to compare your outcome with the outcome in similar cases? To what extent was your outcome similar to the outcome of people in similar cases?

Source: Verdonschot et al., 2008: 15–16.

a seller and a buyer of a car, the result of a process to obtain identity documents, or the outcome of a process part of a crime victim reparations program" (Verdonschot et al., 2008: 15).

An important conclusion to draw from Table 6 is that measuring access to justice is a complex subject matter comprised of variable scopes, meanings, and aspects across context and sociolegal forces. The indicators can also be very different and multifaceted. Therefore, any attempt to develop indicators for measuring access to justice in Iran should take into account the sociolegal context, while acknowledging the fact that "there is no holistic objective theory or model for assessing access to justice" (La Salle Institute of Governance, 2003: 41).

Measuring Iranian Women's Access to Justice: A Legal Empowerment Model

As noted previously, legal empowerment can be seen as one of the subcategories of the user-based model for measuring access to justice. In my view, a measurement model based on legal empowerment theory consists of three key dimensions: first is public perception, second is legal awareness, and third is the capacity to take legal action. Although the notion of "empowerment" seems to be qualitative, a variety of qualitative and quantitative indicators can be incorporated into a legal empowerment measurement model. These indicators are comprised of, for example, public knowledge of rights, legal institutions, or legal procedure, legal literacy, literal language of the law, availability of a community legal awareness program, legal aid, and public interest litigation. The public's perceptions are defined from the point of view of prospective beneficiaries or actual users of the justice sector.

A good example is the survey study on citizens' perceptions of the Indonesian justice sector (AC Nielsen and Asia Foundation, 2001). This study specifically has provided an important background to my survey study. For obvious reasons, I've used their model in developing the methodological framework of the survey study. The similarities between Indonesian and Iranian contexts include common factors such as level of development, impact of religion, and culture. As discussed earlier, Iran is among the high human development category as quantified by the human development index (HDI, 2010).

Although Indonesia is less developed and is categorised among the medium human development countries (rank 108th out of 169 countries), both countries face social and economic inequality among the population (CCA Iran, 2003; CCA UNDP Indonesia, 2007). Another significant equivalent characteristic is that Iran and Indonesia are predominantly Muslim. With wide cultural and ethnic diversity across Indonesia, the majority of Indonesians are Muslims, although it is not an Islamic state. The study on citizens' perceptions of the Indonesian justice sector (ibid.) relies on qualitative and quantitative data collection methods and explores citizens' understanding of law and legal institutions, their basic legal knowledge, the key factors that influence people's preferences in choosing between formal and informal resolutions mechanisms, and their level of satisfaction with their chosen course of action. The study gives a broad definition of the justice sector, including the judiciary, law enforcement agencies, administrative tribunals, legal education institutions, the legal profession, and civil society organisations working on legal issues.[10]

[10] The survey findings indicate that Indonesian perceptions of the legal system at a community level involve a combination of positive impressions and unfulfilled expectations. "The positive impressions include the belief that the legal system can be improved, that the government cares about the views of ordinary citizens, and that citizens can in turn help the government to make the legal system fairer. While many of the beliefs expressed by respondents are in no way supported by actual experience, they reflect important perspectives on the need for legal reform strategies to take citizens' views and expectations into account and to secure increased space for citizens to inform the national legal reform agenda" (AC Nielsen and Asia Foundation, 2001: 113).

The assessment of a citizen's capacity to seek a legal remedy can be incorporated into a legal empowerment model. The capacity to seek legal remedies is also related to the institutional perspective of measuring access to justice, in particular legal services methodology. Poor and disadvantaged groups are often prevented from seeking formal justice mainly because their capacity to do so is influenced by their legal awareness and also the lack of access to legal services.

These examples explain why legal empowerment has been used as the measurement model. In this research, legal empowerment is defined as "the use of legal services and related development activities to increase disadvantaged populations' control over their lives" (Golub, 2003: 25). The main dimension of the above-mentioned definition is the "capacity to seek remedy," which is influenced by three main dynamics: legal knowledge of the justice system, legal advice (including legal aid), and the existence of alternative dispute resolution mechanisms. All of these refer to the resources provided for access to justice, an input notion. The legal empowerment indicators include mainly the citizen's knowledge of fundamental rights, familiarity with legal institutions, legal literacy, and literal language of the law, paralegal, public interest litigation, and legal aid.

Building on the study of citizens' perceptions of the Indonesian justice sector (Golub, 2003), a list of indicators has been produced. These indicators seek to evaluate whether Iranian women are legally empowered with particular reference to access to justice. Table 7, based on my own observation, illustrates some of the key indicators with particular reference to Iranian women from the perspective of legal empowerment.

These indicators provide a basis for the questionnaire used in the survey study that is presented in next chapter. The main objective of the questionnaire is to enhance the possibilities for gathering a broader range of data for overall analysis of the research questions, particularly regarding legal empowerment. It is a closed questionnaire with clear and brief questions representing

Table 7. Legal Empowerment Indicators (With Focus on Iranian Women)

Item	Hypothesis	Explanation	Indicators
Do women know their political, social and civil rights?[a]	Women are usually found to have little understanding of their rights that restricts or impairs their ability to seek justice.	This is a qualitative indicator which measures women's knowledge of basic rights.	Women's knowledge of fundamental rights, women's knowledge of fundamental rights inherited in Islamic law
Do women know the legal system?	The majority of Iranian women have a basic understanding of the obligations of legal institutions (the police, courts) and the procedures for claiming these obligations.	This is a qualitative indicator which measures women's knowledge of the legal system.	Women's knowledge of legal institutions; women's knowledge of legal procedure; women's knowledge of justiciable disputes
What are the sources for women's information about law and the legal system?	The sources of information about law and the legal system are not diverse and responsive to the population of women.	This indicator can be a qualitative and quantitative indicator, which measures the quantity/quality of resources provided for raising women's legal awareness of law, rights, and the legal system.	Television and radio, print media, websites and weblogs, cultural centres, legal aid clinics, hotlines, women NGOs, mosques, religious ceremonies
Is there any legal aid provided for women?	The absence of an efficient legal aid system does not only impair women's access to legal representation but also fails to respond to their need to seek free legal advice.	This is a quantitative indicator, which measures the existence of legal aid programs provided for women.	Existence of legal aid organisations and existence of legal aid clinic within the law schools

(continued)

Table 7. *(continued)*

Item	Hypothesis	Explanation	Indicators
Is there any public legal education program?	Raising public legal awareness contributes in two dimensions for building women's capacity to seek legal remedy: (1) women's legal knowledge and (2) the community's knowledge about women's rights.	This indicator can be qualitative or quantitative, which measures the resources provided for raising public legal knowledge.	Television and radio programs, family education programs, community-based training, legal aid, public interest litigation, training of government officials
Do women trust the justice system?	Lack of confidence in the justice system hinders women's ability to claim their legal rights.	This can be a qualitative or quantitative indicator, which measures if women trust the justice system.	The numbers of women-initiated legal cases and women's confidence in the justice system
What is the impact of culture on women's access to justice?	Traditional gender biases hinder the ability of women to take legal actions. The justice system, also under control of gender bias, fails to support women's rights.	This is a qualitative indicator, which measures the impact of culture on women's access to justice.	Impact of culture on women's self-confidence to seek justice, impact of culture on the justice system, impact of culture on the community
What is the role of family in relation to women's access to justice?	Lack of family support decreases women's confidence in seeking justice.	This is a qualitative indicator which measures the role of family in relation to women's access to justice.	Role of family in women's self-confidence building.

[a] See Chapter 6.

the major dimensions of access to justice. The questionnaire also includes two open-ended questions: What are their experiences of the litigation process? (How user-friendly is it?) And is there any way in which the service can be improved?

The questionnaire targeted one hundred respondents, including women, at the community level. As discussed earlier, one of the sources for the questionnaire is the survey study on citizens' perceptions of the Indonesian justice sector (AC Nielsen and Asia Foundation, 2001). Also the survey study of women's access to justice in Afghanistan contributed to drafting the questionnaire.[11] The Women and Children Legal Research Foundation survey team distributed the questionnaire among 450 male and 900 female respondents in five provinces of Afghanistan. Also, numerous focus group discussions were conducted to provide a more detailed analysis of women's access to justice in Afghanistan. This study confirmed that Afghan women's perceptions of the justice system were mainly negative. These were based on the actual experience of women who either had been accused of committing crimes or who had sought help from the justice system at large (WCLRF, 2008: 39). The study also revealed that the formal barriers for most of the respondents included lack of affordable legal representation, abuse by authorities, delays in the justice system, weak law enforcement, lack of remedies provided by law – particularly in cases of violence against women, lack of de jure protection, and lack of legal aid. In addition, the traditional gender biases, and cultural values were confirmed by a majority of Afghan respondents to obstruct the ability of women to file legal claims (ibid.). The fact is that Iran and Afghanistan both share common language, religion, history, geographical location, and also culture. Iranian and Afghan women may face common concerns about the discrimination to some extent, although Iranian women are much more educated and liberated. As shown in Table 8, these indicators closely reflect the questions of the survey study.

[11] I was involved with this study as a consultant.

Table 8. Indicators and Questions

Indicator	Question
Women's knowledge of rights	Q1.Which of the following do you consider a right of women by the law? Becoming a minister Establishing a trade union Requesting the right to divorce at the time of marriage
Women's knowledge of Islamic rights	Q2. Which of the following do you consider a right of women in Islam? The right to negotiate marriage terms of her choice The right to have her own property The right to ask for divorce
Women's knowledge of legal action	Q3. What action do you take when confronting a family dispute such as inheritance, cost of maintenance, or marriage portion? Refer to the family Refer to the Family Advisor Service Refer to the court Not take any legal action I will be patient because the problem can be resolved if given time
Women's knowledge of legal procedure	Q4. Which of the following issues can be filed as a criminal case before the court? Verbal abuse Beating Sexual abuse
Women's knowledge of legal procedure	Q5. Which of the following issues can be filed as a civil case before the court? Family dispute over choosing a place to live Husband refuses to pay the marriage portion (dowry) Husband is unable to perform his marital duty
Women's knowledge of legal institution	Q6. Which of the following institutions are you aware of? Police General Court Legal aid agency The Forensic and Legal Medicine Agency
Cultural obstacles	Q7. What do you think about women who claim their rights by taking legal action? I think women who take legal action are at the end of their tether and have no other choice I think women who take legal action are brave and empowered

Indicator	Question
	I would avoid going to court; it's not a right place for women to go
	I think women and men have the same difficulties in litigation
Cultural obstacles	Q8. How do you consider the social attitudes toward a woman who takes legal action against her husband?
	A bad-mannered wife
	A brave woman
	I think the social attitude toward those men and women who take legal action against their spouses is the same
	Most women prefer to not take any legal action because of cultural considerations and fear of losing face
	Most women are patient and long-suffering with their husbands
Women's perceptions of seeking justice	Q9. Why aren't there as many women litigants as men?
	Lack of social acceptance
	Lack of financial resources
	Lack of general information about the law
	Lack of family support
	Lack of legal protection
Women's perceptions of the justice system	Q10. What do you think about the justice sector?
	The justice sector is corrupt
	The justice sector fails to protect women
	The justice sector should protect women equally
	The justice sector can be improved
	I don't trust the justice sector
Women's perceptions of seeking justice	Q11. What do you think about litigation?
	Bringing legal problems to the court is likely to make them worse
	Women will not have equal access to justice
	The legal system can protect my equal rights if I go to court
	Only people with wealth, power, and the right connections have access to justice
	Litigation should be the last course of action for dispute resolution
Sources for women's knowledge of law	Q12. Which of the following sources do you use to learn about law and the legal system?
	Television and radio
	Print media
	Websites and weblogs
	Cultural organisations

(continued)

Table 8. *(continued)*

Indicator	Question
Legal aid	Q13. Have you ever sought legal advice from any legal aid organisations?
	Yes, I have sought legal advice from a legal aid office in the public court
	Yes, I have sought legal advice from the legal aid office in the Bar Association
	Yes, I have sought legal advice from a legal aid NGO
	No, I have not experienced legal aid
	I was not aware of the existence of legal aid agencies
General perception	Q14. What do you think about women's access to justice?
	There are no equal legal protections for women
	Women can have access to justice if they want
	The main barrier for women's access to justice is that they don't know their legal rights
	The justice system does not apply equal protection of women's access to justice
	Women face more barriers than men in accessing justice
Path to justice	Q15. What is your experience of the litigation process?

Conclusion

The literature review shows that measurement models adopted by various studies capture different dimensions of access to justice. Each model of measurement reflects a particular perspective, such as the user perspective or institutional perspective. I also review the measurement models adopted by international agencies in developing countries and in particular the Asia Pacific region to argue that their models have primarily linked access to justice to strengthening the capacities of legal and judicial institutions. Thus, the measurement models based on the rule of law hypothesis have a major focus on institutions and the use of the institutions by the people, rather than an emphasis on the individuals.

Most of the measurement models are founded on the institutional perspective, measuring the quality and quantity of the resources invested in access to justice such as legal service, litigation cost, and long delays (input scheme). But the measurement models based on the user's perspective primarily survey legal needs and assess the user's perception in selecting a specific mechanism or institution when seeking justice. The main focus, therefore, is on the procedure that a user experiences in seeking justice, called a path to justice. It is uncertain, however, whether the institutional approach pursued by most international organisations can share real benefits with women in a Muslim country like Iran. This is because most of the barriers to access to justice that Iranian women might experience seem to originate from limited legal knowledge and also cultural obstacles.[12] The present study therefore suggests that the legal empowerment model used to measure women's access to justice in Iran should differ from similar models at an international level. It should emphasise equal normative protection and the existence of equal remedies through constitutional laws, legal regulatory frameworks, and customary norms.

[12] During the in-depth interviews, almost all respondents expressed their approval of limited legal knowledge and cultural norms as "key barriers" to Iranian women's access to justice. Note, for examples, Ahmad Salari, a Program Analyst and Head of Democratic Governance and Trade Program Cluster (Access to Justice National Project) in UNDP Iran, interviewed on 15 April 2010; a criminology professor of Tehran University, Shahla Moazami, interviewed on 12 April 2010; and a semi-structured group interview with three NGO activists on 22 April 2010.

6 Women's Perceptions of Access to Justice

We examined the theory underpinning this book in the literature review (Chapter 2), the research context (Chapters 3 and 4), and the methodological approach in Chapter 5. In this chapter, we review the setting for this study from a methodological point of view and present the findings of a survey study with regard to women's perceptions of access to justice in Iran (Tehran), conducted as an important component of this book. The chapter presents the results of the quantitative phase of the research, for which the survey described in the Appendix is the main method for data collection.

This study is designed to focus on Iranian women's basic legal knowledge – their knowledge of Islamic rights and of legal action; familiarity with the role of the courts, police, and other formal institutions; familiarity with the legal procedure, perceptions of cultural barriers, issues that influence their preference for mechanisms of formal or alternative forms of dispute resolution, and their level of satisfaction with the chosen course of action. It is important to note that this is the first study of its kind to assess women's perceptions of access to justice, and its findings are by no means exhaustive. Although the study highlights several major aspects of women's access to justice in Iran, there is a considerable range of insight and in-depth analysis yet to be examined from the quantitative and qualitative data by further research on the subject.

This chapter is structured in four sections. The first section provides the rationale for the research strategy, which was implemented through the use of a questionnaire-based survey. The second section describes the procedures used to define the population for this study and presents descriptive data of the survey respondents using frequencies, percentages, and means. Third, variables are analysed using percentages and statistical significance testing. Where appropriate, the results are illustrated diagrammatically. Finally, conclusions drawn from this analysis are linked to the theoretical framework of the book.

Designing Sampling Strategies

A questionnaire-based survey was chosen as the main data collection method for this study. Although surveys and questionnaires are said to be different, the terms are often used interchangeably. Surveys tend to focus on broad issues that aim to answer research questions, while questionnaires tend to focus on a central theme or notion that aims to test specific hypotheses (Wiggins and Stevens, 1999). Most of the listed studies regarding access to justice used questionnaire-based surveys to collect hypotheses-related information.[1] Most of these studies have used the survey (in preference to the questionnaire); therefore, for the purposes of this study, the term "survey" is used.

Also, a survey study is self-administering and minimises the distance between respondents and the researcher. Surveys have been the most common methodology by which researchers in different subject areas collect data (Tull and Hawkins, 1987). In addition, the survey method allows the investigation of intangible phenomena that cannot be observed directly by the researcher (Bagozzi, 1996).

1 As indicated in the previous chapter, surveys are by far the most widely used method of research for studies into perceptions of access to justice (AC Nielsen and Asia Foundation, 2001).

This survey study, as with any other form of qualitative survey, encountered a number of difficulties. Challenges were linked primarily to defining questions that would adequately measure the women's perceptions with reference to access to justice. Another difficulty was related to the issue of the representativeness of Iranian women. The political sensitivity surrounding women's access to justice was another concern. Therefore, it was important to design a sampling strategy to overcome these challenges and also provide impartial and unbiased results.

One of the most common sampling strategies in qualitative investigations is purposive sampling or a nonrandom sample where the criteria employed to select respondents is more important than the sample size, depending on resources and research objectives (Wilmot, 2005). Purposive sampling is more successful when analysis is completed along with data collection. Although there are different methods of purposive sampling, this research employs "theoretical sampling." Theoretical sampling provides an opportunity for the researcher to change the sample design and also to examine the data as the sampling progresses to ensure that a robust theoretical framework is generated (ibid.).

The decision to use theoretical sampling was made after realising that there was no empirical data measuring Iranian women's perceptions of access to justice. It was an inevitable process since "unlike the sampling in quantitative research, theoretical sampling cannot be planned before embarking on a grounded theory study. The specific sampling decisions evolve during the research process itself" (Corbin and Strauss, 1990: 192). In the sampling process also, theoretical sampling provides more space for a multifaceted study, in which there are no restrictions to the types of data obtained, data collection technique employed, or the method by which the data are analysed. "In theoretical sampling, different kinds of data give the analyst different views to understand a category and to develop its properties; these different views we have called slices of data" (Glaser and Strauss, 1967: 65).

At this point, it is important to understand why theoretical sampling is an appropriate technique for the present research. The study of women's access to justice as qualitative research employs nonprobability sampling that does not intend to generate a statistically representative sample.[2] Here, my research objective was not to generalise the findings statistically but rather to generalise the findings theoretically. However, no attempt was made to construct a representative sample across Iranian women because the information required to weight the sample in proportion to the female population was unavailable.

Regarding the sample size, several factors were involved including research hypothesis, data collection methods, financial resources, time, political constraints, the number of variables examined, and the degree of accuracy needed. Theoretically speaking, the researcher cannot predict how many people will need to be sampled; rather, the purposive sample sizes are often determined on the basis of theoretical saturation in grounded theory.[3] In addition, qualitative research such as this endeavours to simultaneously achieve depth and breadth which, in this research, meant conducting several in-depth interviews alongside a survey. According to Glaser and Strauss, this method allows "data collection for generating theory whereby the analyst jointly collects, codes, and analyses his data and decides what data to collect next and where to find them, in order to develop his theory as it emerges" (Glaser and Strauss, 1967: 45).

[2] Probability sampling aims at producing a statistically representative sample so members of the sample population are selected randomly and have a known probability of selection.

[3] This term refers to a situation in which "no additional data are being found whereby the (researcher) can develop properties of the category. As he sees similar instances over and over again, the researcher becomes empirically confident that a category is saturated ... when one category is saturated, nothing remains but to go on to new groups for data on other categories, and attempt to saturate these categories also" (Glaser and Strauss, 1967: 65).

The survey was conducted during April and May 2010 in Tehran. It attracted 135 women, aged eighteen to sixty-five years covering North West and South Tehran. After missing responses were eliminated, there were 120 respondents remaining and all statistics described in this section are calculated on the basis of a total sample size of 120. It is important to note that this number cannot be considered a small sample due to the socially and politically sensitive atmosphere in Tehran surrounding women's issues at the time of the research. Moreover, qualitative sampling is often small because a phenomenon needs to appear only once to be considered valuable. However, it is not possible to estimate the response rate in percentages because of the uncertainty regarding the size of the total population of women in Tehran and also to whom the survey was advertised.

Regarding the areas that the survey randomly covered, North West Tehran was selected not only because there was more accessibility for the researcher but also because of the high level of education in the neighbourhood. Conversely, there is a lower level of education and considerably higher levels of poverty in South Tehran. An effort was therefore made to try to represent as far as possible the varied socioeconomic status of the women respondents. A more detailed description of the survey respondents is provided later in this chapter.

On the subject of the issues regarding sampling, one concern was that a nonresponse bias may occur when nonresponse is correlated to the research topic. The nonresponse bias occurs when a large number of people in the survey sample fail to respond and have relevant characteristics that differ from those who do respond (Dillman, 2000). Despite this issue, there seems to be no agreement on the maximum acceptable proportion for missing cases and nonresponse. For this study, no testing was done on missing information and nonresponse. Overall, none of the questionnaires were missing more than 5 percent of information. Therefore, it is possible to claim that the nonresponse rate would not have biased the study findings. In addition, it is also possible that errors in the survey may occur during an interview or may be a result of the manner in which the questions were worded.

The survey data collected were incorporated into computerised databases using SPSS for Windows version 18.00.[4]

Descriptive methods of analysis are employed to present qualitative data and describe perceptions of the surveyed respondents using frequencies and percentages. The distribution of responses for each independent variable is summarised using a bar chart and a frequency table. Numerical data from the questionnaire are also coded into SPSS to expose whether statistically significant differences of perceptions occur between respondents according to their backgrounds. The technique of data analysis applied in each section is different. The data are then analysed in different stages: sample characteristics; descriptive statistics; reliability; and validity testing. Descriptive statistics are used to review the data regarding the distribution of responses for each variable and the relationships between them.

Regarding survey design and construction of the variables, almost all of the variables used in this study are based on the perceptions of the respondents and are created from responses to the survey. Therefore, the following variables needed to be constructed in order to conduct this study: knowledge of rights and the legal system; sources of information regarding the law; preferred approaches to resolving justiciable problems; perceptions of gender bias and cultural values; access to legal aid; perceptions of the barriers to access to justice; perceptions and actual experience of the legal system.

[4] The Statistical Package for Social Science (SPSS) is a software package that was developed in the 1960s and has been widely used by social scientists to conduct a series of statistical analyses. In this study, SPSS was used to analyse the correlation between dependent and independent variables. Responses to the survey's questions for each respondent are carefully input into SPSS. Once all the data have been entered into SPSS, tabulation is concluded and the raw data summarised for future analysis.

Description of the Survey Respondents

The sample included 135 women from Tehran. Those who had missing socio-demographic variables were excluded, resulting in a final sample size of 120. The respondents were chosen mostly from among women who participated in community religious ceremonies and morning group exercises in public parks and universities.

Religious gatherings traditionally take place separately for men and women in different places such as mosques, private homes, or religious buildings. Women's religious rituals in Shia tradition often include Quran readings, *dua* readings (prayers of supplication), and involve celebrating the Prophet Muhammad and Imams' birth anniversaries and commemorating the martyrdoms of Imams. Women also take part in such events to enjoy social interaction, entertainment, exchange of ideas and informal chats, emotional support, charitable activity, and the joy of food. I was given a chance to briefly explain my research to women who were at the gatherings, usually during the refreshment breaks.

Respondents interviewed during morning group exercises in the public parks of North West Tehran were more diverse and from different demographic backgrounds.[5] The response rate was considerably higher among women to whom the survey had been advertised in the public park compared to the religious gatherings. This was mainly because of the degree of trust and interaction developed through some of my family members who were active members of the morning workout group.

[5] It is interesting to note that a lot of outdoor exercise equipment has been permanently installed in the parks in Tehran and most other cities. This equipment is free to use by both men and women of all ages and is accessible to everyone. Many women and men also attend the early morning workout groups in Tehran parks. I was amazed to see how many people would get up early in the morning to participate in these group exercises. The morning group exercises are also a source of social intimacy and verbal interaction for women.

Respondents who were university students were chosen in order to include the perceptions of the educated younger generation of Iranian women. In addition, approximately 20 percent of women interviewed were chosen from employees of public and private sector organisations in order to survey the views of employed women with potential access to more independent financial resources.

The survey requested some demographic information, including age, marital status, education, and employment status. Education was categorised into five groups based on the Iranian educational system: illiterate, poor literacy, secondary school diploma, graduate, and postgraduate. Employment status coding was derived from the socioeconomic surroundings of women in Iran and also the coding method of the National Statistics Center. This included employed (e.g., working for the public or private sectors), self-employed (e.g., hairdresser or running a family business), housewife (consistent with the statistics of the Iran Statistical Center in year 2006, about 16 million women were considered to be housewives, meaning occupied in household work and affairs), and student (academic entities or religious schools). In an effort to capture marital status, the variables were coded to define five different marital situations, including single, married, divorced, widow, and married but not living with husband (e.g., husband working away or husband living with second wife). The age grouping used consisted of 18–25 years, 26–35 years, 36–45 years, 46–55 years, and 56–65 years. It is possible to argue that in this study, the researcher might have had more success in attracting female respondents by not asking their exact age. However, the researcher prefers to avoid using stereotypical language as it seems totally inaccurate to perpetuate the cliché that, culturally, Iranian women are not comfortable about their age.

The following section provides the general descriptive statistics of the background variables of the survey. As Figure 2 shows, the majority of respondents are between 25 and 35 years old.

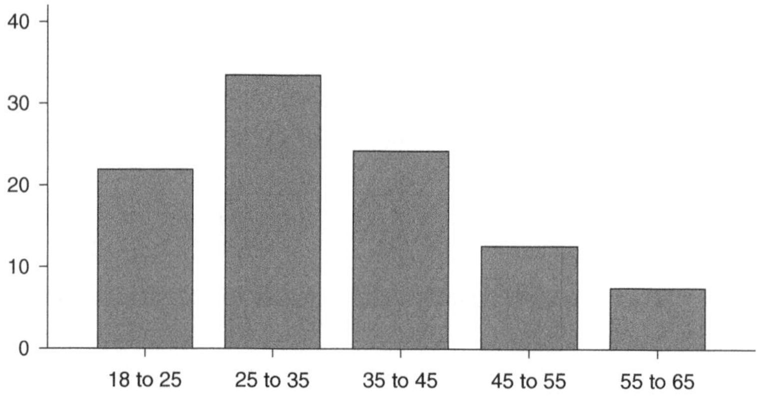

Figure 2. Age of Respondents.

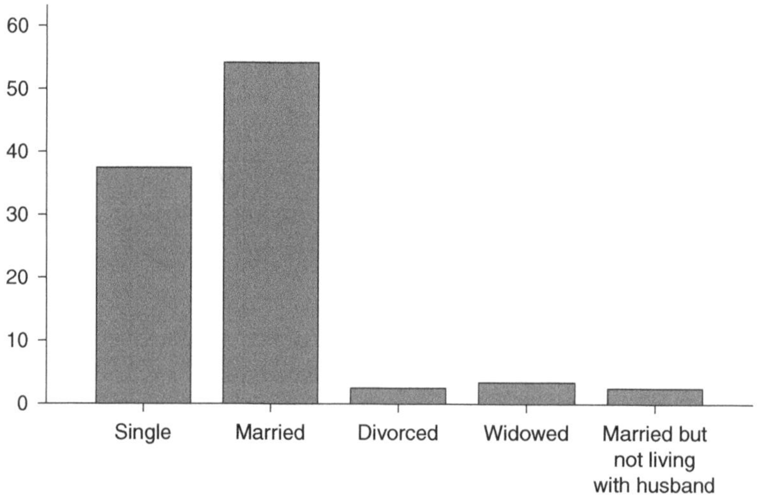

Figure 3. Marital Status of Respondents.

As noted earlier, Iran has a very young population, 70 percent of whom are between 15 and 64 years of age. The marital status of the respondents is illustrated in Figure 3; slightly more than half of the respondents (n = 65, 54.2%) were married. Only 2 percent were divorced and married but not living with their husband.

As shown in Figure 4, the sample contained a relatively high proportion of respondents with a higher education (58.3%, no for graduate = 46, no for postgraduate = 24). Of the remainder,

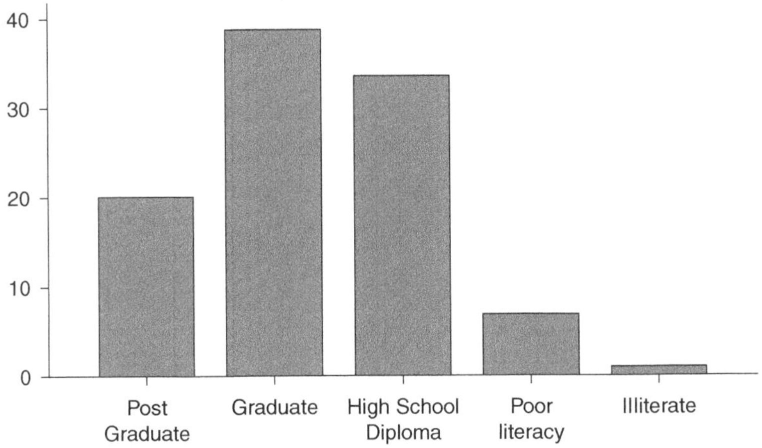

Figure 4. Educational Background of Respondents.

38.3 percent of the respondents had completed graduate studies, and an additional 20 percent had completed postgraduate studies in the form of a Masters degree or PhD. This can be explained by the fact that Iranian women account for almost 70 percent of the student population in Iran's higher education system. Also the Iranian female high school graduates' share of those participating in the nationwide universities' entrance exam increased from 42 percent in 1983 to 65 percent according to a report by Iran's Parliament (*Majlis*) Research Center.[6]

The employment breakdown of respondents is illustrated in Figure 5: most respondents were housewives, 34 percent were employed by private or public institutions, and less than 4 percent were self-employed. It is important to note that, as defined by the Iran Statistical Center, a housewife is a person who is not employed. However, 2.5 percent of the respondents identified themselves as "unemployed," that is, as a person who is not a housewife but is looking for a job.

[6] The 2008 report by the Research Center of the *Majlis* (parliament) to the administration of President Mahmud Ahmadinejad confirmed that women outnumber men in Iran's higher education. Available at http://rc.majlis.ir/fa/news/show/765155, accessed 20 June 2011.

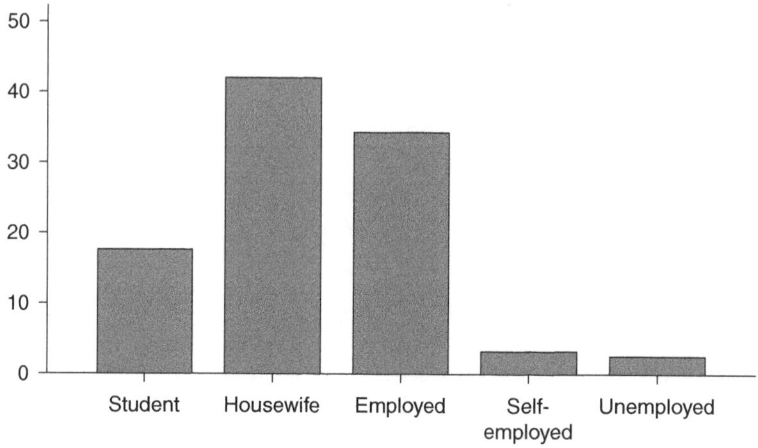

Figure 5. Employment of Respondents.

Having discussed the background variables, the following section presents the findings regarding the respondents' knowledge of their rights and the legal system. The central focus was to examine women's basic legal knowledge, their understanding of Islamic rights, familiarity with legal action and the role of the courts, police, and other formal institutions.

Knowledge of Rights and the Legal System

The survey consisted of several questions to measure women's knowledge of rights, Islamic law, and the Iranian legal system. An equally important question pertained to women's knowledge of their personal rights. Respondents were given three examples: an example of political rights (being a minister), an example of socioeconomic rights (the right to establish a trade union), and an example of family rights (the right to ask for a divorce).

Interestingly, most respondents were knowledgeable about their rights (75%); however, they demonstrated a better knowledge of the right to ask for divorce at the time of marriage (family rights) and also of political rights in comparison with their socioeconomical rights. One possible explanation for their greater awareness of political rights could be because of the appointment of the first female minister in the history of the Islamic Republic on September 2009, just a few months before the survey was conducted. In fact, it was the public debate on Mahmoud Ahmadinejad's nomination of three women to join his cabinet that led to the appointment of Marzieh Vahid Dastjerdi, the female health minister.

It might be interesting here to briefly present a portrait of Iranian women in power. Since 1963, when Iranian women obtained the right to vote and to participate in parliamentary elections, female members of Parliament have played an active role in questioning and debating various legal, economic, and political issues relating to the family, such as the Family Protection Law. Female participation in recent national and local elections has also been very high. In 2006, during the City and Village Councils elections, 7,106 women participated as candidates, which resulted in 1,491 of them being elected as council members. In the 2009 presidential election, of the 475 proposed presidential candidates, forty-two were women. Nevertheless, despite the gradual increase in female empowerment, women are still largely underrepresented at most levels of the governance structure, especially at ministerial and other senior executive levels. There are only eight female members of Parliament out of a total of 290 members. Amidst the paradoxical nature of women's role in social and political power sharing and decision making, Ahmadinejad's nomination of three women to join his cabinet was the topic of public debate.

Another important aspect of legal awareness for women living under any codified interpretation of Islamic law is the knowledge of women's rights in Islam. The survey, therefore, included a question to evaluate women's knowledge of their rights in Islam. Respondents were given specific examples of the rights of Muslim women. The list consisted of the right to negotiate marriage terms, the right to own property, and the right to ask for a divorce. The study findings show that most of the respondents were aware of their rights in Islam (n = 75, 62%). Interestingly enough, more respondents (12 out of the 75 who were aware of the fundamental rights) specified the right to own property as a woman's right in Islam, but few mentioned the right to negotiate marriage terms (4 respondents).

The question is, then, why did respondents show a better understanding of property rights than the right to negotiate marriage? The answer lies in the relationship between women and property, which requires examination from a sociolegal perspective. To contextualise the issue, two different dimensions need to be addressed. First is an increase in the rate of employment for women from lower-income groups. Iran's empirical evidence indicates a rise in the employment rate among women following the Islamic revolution. The censuses of both 1986 and 1996 show that the ratio of employed women had increased from 5.1 percent to 7 percent and also that urban female employment had increased from 8.8 percent to 11.3 percent. This is in spite of the state policies that defined women's major role as homemakers and mothers, where, under the constitution, women came to be viewed primarily as "mothers." Wider access to economic resources, therefore, requires practising those socially recognised economic rights that are defined by the right to property ownership. Nevertheless, women still make up a significant proportion of the unemployed in spite of a higher educational rate, so there are many inequalities between men and women in terms of access to economic resources, employment opportunities, and income.

A different dimension suggests the existence of an internalised fear of insecurity among Iranian women that leads them to want to protect and maintain their right to property. Most of the examples provided by the women interviewed in relation to their access to justice having been denied were about being denied the opportunity to inherit housing, land, and property, or their lack of economic resources. In most interviews and focus group discussions I conducted, not only women but also men indicated that women need to secure access to economic resources by having ownership of a house or land. Although, culturally speaking, the husband is responsible for his wife's living costs, in reality, the woman has control over family spending and savings.

An interesting observation from this survey was that respondents showed a better knowledge of their rights in law (Civil Code in particular) than the rights of women in Islam. This finding, however, requires considerable interpretation. A possible rationalisation is that, because most respondents had a high level of education, their general familiarity with their rights by state law was better than their familiarity with women's rights in Islam.

It is also useful to note here that the formal Iranian educational system is based on a curriculum in which religious education – the Quran courses (*Motale'ate Ghorani*) and purification within the framework of the Shia school of thought – is given priority. However, I conducted a brief review of textbooks relating to various subjects within primary, secondary, and higher education but found very little if any teaching regarding women's rights in Islam. On the contrary, textbooks and teaching methods reinforce stereotypes that confine women to the home as mothers and homemakers.

Another key paradigm of legal awareness is familiarity with the legal system and legal procedure. The questionnaire included categories that alluded to different family-related problems to measure respondents' knowledge of the legal system. These questions were aimed at assessing women's knowledge of legal problems that respondents identified as being subject to legal action. I use the term "justiciable events" to include those legal issues for which the Iranian legal system provides a remedy or those legal issues that are not often identified as legal problems because of a lack of legal awareness.[7] The list of criminal matters included verbal abuse, beating, and sexual harassment. These were followed

[7] According to Moorhead and Pleasence (2003), people may have different perspectives at various stages about a justiciable problem such as whether they perceived an issue to be a problem; whether they sought a solution; whether they had knowledge of what might be done to resolve it; the type of response sought; and above all whether a legal remedy was sought.

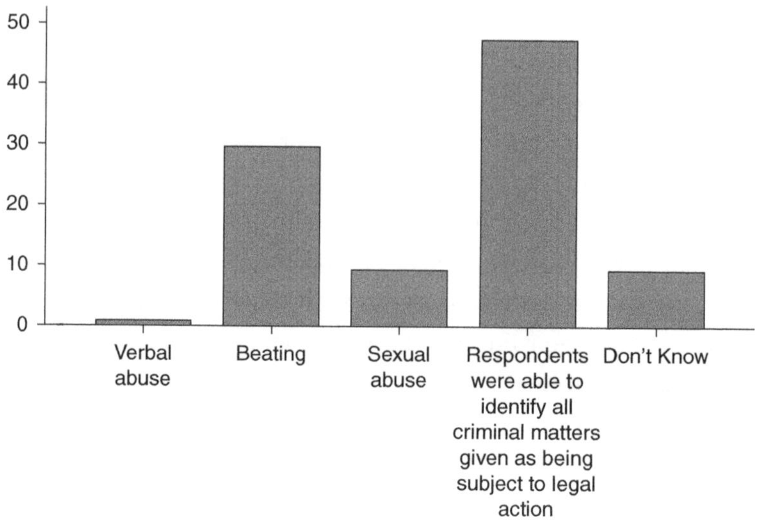

Figure 6. Understanding of Criminal Matters.

by a number of civil disputes: family disputes over choosing a place to live; cases in which the husband refuses to pay the marriage portion (dower); and instances in which the husband is unable to perform his marital duty.

Figure 6 shows that respondents (46%) have a slightly better understanding of criminal matters as being subject to legal action as opposed to civil legal problems (45%). In criminal matters, the number of respondents who agreed that beating (n = 35) was subject to legal action was much higher than those who indicated that sexual (n = 11) or verbal abuse (just one respondent) was a criminal matter.

In civil disputes as shown in Figure 7, the majority of respondents highlighted the husband's refusal to pay the marriage portion as being subject to civil dispute (28.3%). Less than 2 percent of the respondents indicated that a dispute over choosing a place to live was a justiciable issue. The number of respondents who said that they did not know about either criminal or civil legal problems (n = 29) was slightly more than the respondents who were not aware of fundamental rights (n = 24). However, an

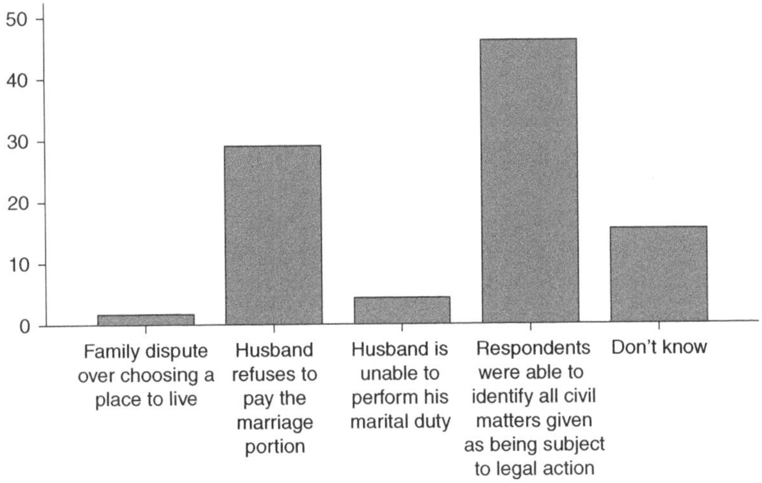

Figure 7. Understanding of Civil Matters.

awareness of justiciable problems increased consistently in line with a higher educational background. Last but not least, most respondents were not able to distinguish between criminal and civil matters or civil and criminal courts.

Knowledge of rights and legal procedures is of no use if a user of justice does not have sufficient knowledge of the legal institutions that regulate public life. The assessment of the general awareness of legal institutions suggests that respondents were, for the most part, unfamiliar with the legal institutions. The list given to respondents included the police, general courts, legal aid agencies, and the Forensic and Legal Medicine Agency because these are main legal institutions that a justice user would be most likely to face if they were to take any action in Iran. The findings of the present study confirm a common lack of awareness of the legal institutions. Of all the respondents to the main questionnaire, almost half stated that they did not know anything about the legal institutions indicated in the list.

As indicated in Figure 8, respondents who stated that they knew about the judicial system were primarily those most familiar with the police (two respondents). A small group of respondents

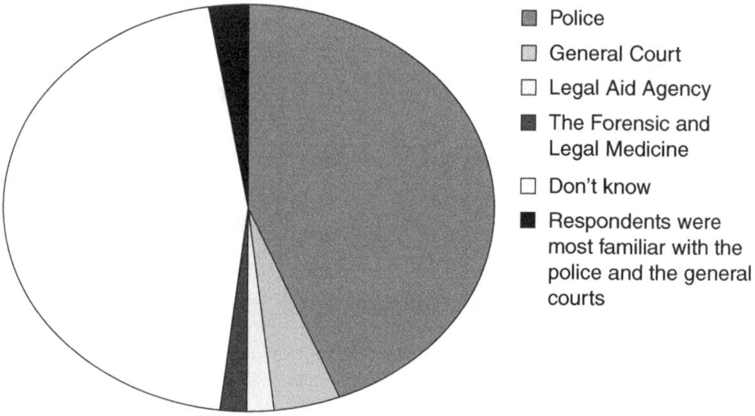

Figure 8. Awareness of the Legal Institutions.

were familiar with the general courts (less than 5%). In fact, very few respondents had ever been in a court or appeared before a judge. Their general knowledge of what a court looks like or how it works is commonly shaped by the televised representation of criminal tribunals. Their perceptions of judges therefore were "old-fashioned" and "contradictory." For instance, in some of the qualitative interviews, respondents thought the judges' need to wear wigs and gowns was simply not part of the real picture of Iranian courts. Some others felt that judges were, for the most part, *Mullas'* trained by religious schools.

This common lack of awareness of the legal institutions is an important matter, since public knowledge of the judicial system is a crucial requirement of their journey to justice. It is a simple fact that the police or courts have a major responsibility to protect the rights of people and sustain social order. Widespread ignorance of the legal system influences women's perceptions of justice. Several studies show that people's knowledge of judicial procedures, legal institutions, rules, and their rights all have a positive effect on their perception of justice (Van den Bos et al., 1998). This concept is similar to that of informational justice, which refers to the information about and explanation of legal procedures and their outcomes. Research findings show that informational justice

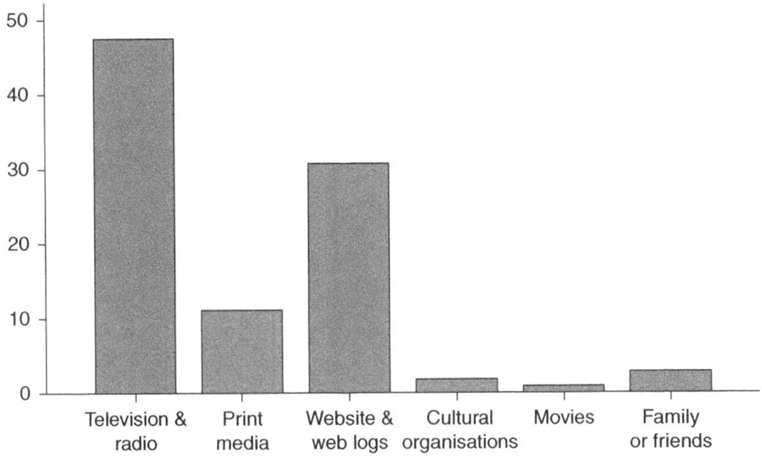

Figure 9. Source of Information.

is an important issue in the psychological process of shaping justice perceptions (Klaming and Giesen, 2008; Wenzel, 2006; Bies and Shapiro, 1987).

Sources of Information on the Law

Referring to earlier remarks regarding women's knowledge of rights and the legal system, this section focuses on the respondents' reported sources of information about the law. As Figure 9 shows, nearly half of the respondents stated that TV and radio are their main source of information about the law, rights, and the legal system. The question here is: how are women and their rights portrayed on Iranian state television and radio?[8] National

[8] According to Article 175 of the constitution, the appointment and dismissal of the head of the Radio and Television of the Islamic Republic of Iran rests with the leader, the highest ranking political and religious authority in the country. A council consisting of two representatives each of the President, the head of the judiciary and the Islamic Consultative Assembly shall supervise the functioning of Islamic Republic of Iran Broadcasting (IRIB) to guarantee it is in keeping with the Islamic criteria and the best interests of the country.

television is widely known to represent and reinforce the Islamic revolutionary values and conservative Shia ideology. While televised representations of women have changed to a great extent during the last ten years compared to the years following the 1979 Islamic Revolution and also during the Iran-Iraq war (1980–1988), women's rights activists have constantly criticised national TV and radio programs for portraying women as passive mothers or wives busy doing housework with no interest in either their rights or the law.

Most activists that I spoke with denounce women's roles on TV series. A female law lecturer I interviewed gave an example of a typical TV image of a decent woman as being one who forgives her husband as he marries a second wife, even though she has endured long-term suffering and emotional pain because of her marriage to him. The dilemma is not only in reinforcing traditional gender roles but also in the portrayal of the law and legal system on television. Family disputes and, in particular, those staged in a police station (*kalantary*) are commonplace on TV. The representation of the police, although it differs from reality, provides some level of familiarity with the atmosphere and procedures of a police station. This perhaps offers an explanation for the findings in the present study, which show that respondents were more familiar with police than with any other legal institution. Court proceedings are not typically shown on TV. The number of crime series or law and order TV dramas produced is low in comparison with the huge number of TV crime shows in some Western countries, such as the United Kingdom or the United States. Television programs seem to mislead and cause confusion about court proceedings, and thereby provide a false impression. What a trial might look like in a television drama is far from the reality of a court. Images of a trial lawyer marching around the courtroom, provoking everyone, or a female defendant who gives a poetic speech and shares her extensive story of suffering with a patient judge with a high level of listening skills – and apparently a great deal of free time – is just not part of the paradigm that most people experience in court. However, some TV series were successful in raising public awareness of the law and the judicial system.

A recent popular crime drama, *Zire Tigh* (Under the Blade), widely watched by Iranian viewers, showed the lives of two extremely close families torn apart by an accidental killing. This crime drama, even though it focused more on the social and cultural consequences of the crime and did not feature the courtroom as such, resulted in generally improved public awareness, particularly with regard to mandatory defence and free legal assistance in criminal cases. Moreover, it did not present misconceptions regarding the legal process, as the staged courtroom was fairly realistic and written legal briefs were portrayed based on criminal code, as the arguments that were presented were derived from facts and evidence.

The second source of information regarding access to justice cited by more than 27 percent of respondents was the Internet, mainly websites and blogs. These were indicated more by single and employed respondents who held higher educational qualifications.

It is important to note that during the last decade, Iran has experienced one of the largest growth rates of Internet users in the world,[9] more than 23 million in 2008. Persian is one of the most common blogging languages in the world. In a country with the youngest population in the region, access to the Internet has provided a space for free expression. Various blogs are written by law professors, judges, barristers, or law students about the law and the legal system. Anonymity in cyberspace has also provided protection, digital identity, recognition, and acceptance for users. A third source of information about the law and legal

9 Tehran, September 13, 2008, IRNA; the report by the ministry's Public Relations Department stated that the number of Iranian Internet users stands at 23 million. The report also claimed that Iran ranks 17th among the top 20 countries with the highest numbers of Internet users.

system indicated by some respondents (10%) was printed media. This may reveal the lack of a newspaper-reading culture among women. Last but not least, a small number of respondents (2.5%) mentioned family or friends as their main source of information about the law.

Preferred Approaches to Resolve Justiciable Problems

In an attempt to construct a general overview about the preferred approaches to the resolution of legal problems adopted by Iranian women, this survey focused more on examples of the behaviour and perceived strategies of respondents in dealing with family disputes including inheritance, cost of maintenance, and dower. Family disputes were suggested as a specific type of legal problem in order to gain a better understanding of the barriers to taking legal action. Also, it was important to examine the reasons, processes, and situations that influenced women's decision making in adopting any kind of strategy. Respondents, therefore, were asked what actions they take if and when faced with family disputes. The following strategies were proposed to respondents as examples of possible preferred approaches: referring to family; referring to the family advisory service; referring to the court; not taking any legal action; and being patient because the problem may be resolved over time.

The information provided by respondents, although useful in providing a general perspective of the choices of action taken by women, requires consideration in analysing the survey's data. The main issue here is linked to the notion of family disputes and also to how family values influence the decisions women make when faced with legal problems. The factors involved in women's decision making before adopting any possible strategy to deal with legal problems are multifaceted and complex. However, how the different sociolegal factors can be distinguished and how their roles and impacts can be defined seems to be a serious challenge. Related studies have shown that the possibility of some action is highly dependent on the nature of the problem and, to some extent, on the person experiencing the problem (Genn and Beinart, 1999; Genn and Paterson, 2001).

In this research, the most dominant course of action that emerged for women to deal with family-related legal problems was to seek help from nonlegal professionals. Therefore, the most common point of contact was with the Family Counselling Service (n = 51, 42.5%). The family counselling services are provided by private consultants, community organisations, or low-cost publicly funded clinics. Anyone holding a PhD in clinical psychology can apply for permission from the State Welfare Organization to set up an establishment. These services include early intervention services to couples and families, counselling, family therapy, information, support, therapeutic intervention, and referral. A very interesting finding was that a smaller number of respondents reported the family as their first line of defence (n = 17, 14.2%). Many people may still assume that the first step for women when faced with a family-related dispute is to contact their family; however, it seems that women's sense of powerlessness motivates them to seek more independent sources of advice with better quality dispute-solving skills in family-related disputes.

This research confirms that most women prefer not to take legal action. The few respondents who reported being likely to approach the courts amounted to less than 5 percent. However, a significant number of respondents (36.6%) said that they take no action at all to resolve their problems; sixteen out of 120 indicated that women should not take any legal action if they face a problem (13.3%). About two-thirds of respondents indicated that the best strategy is trying to be patient because the problem can be resolved if given time. In my opinion, these women should not be considered as submissive wives who have given up their rights because they take no action to resolve their problems. Quite the opposite – their strategic behaviour is an active decision to allow an extended period of time to pass before adopting any kind of strategy to seek advice or resolve disputes.[10] These women with a strategically active approach need to be distinguished from those respondents who adopt an inactive approach and do nothing at all about their problem. Nevertheless, further examination of strategies in relation to demographic factors suggests that the preferred approach related not only to educational qualifications but also employment status. In other words, women with higher education qualifications as well as those in paid employment were more active in seeking a resolution to their legal problems.

Access to Legal Aid

This section aims to examine access to the free or low-cost legal advice available to women, including legal services provided by the judiciary, the bar ssociation, community legal centres, or pro bono legal services provided by NGOs, in order to understand whether respondents sought any legal services or could obtain legal advice to resolve problems and where they went to get that advice. I also wanted to expose the extent to which any or all of these organisations were contributing to women's access to justice. Attention was focused mainly on legal empowerment in order to obtain a better perception of the situations of those women

[10] Feminists have noted that women's silences should not be read as an indicator of passivity and powerlessness in social linguistic encounters (Gumperz, 1982; Gal, 1991). In this understanding, purposive uses of silence should be taken into account as a transformative agency. Several studies suggest that women use silence in strategic ways to challenge sociolegal inequalities. Susan Gal (1991), for instance, notes cross-cultural research to demonstrate that women's enjoyment of sociocultural practices such assong, poetry, gossip, etc., is used to question dominant male discourses. In the context of Iranian women, I think it is important to acknowledge the significance of silence as an aspect of empowerment. The strategic silence of women should not always be interpreted as the absence of protest in the face of injustice.

seeking legal aid, and also the circumstances under which free legal advice is sought.

It is also useful to note that several sociolegal empirical studies examined legal services in the late 1960s and 1970s in the United States, Canada, England and Wales, the Netherlands, and Australia (Curran and American Bar Association, 1977; Australian Legal Needs for the Poor, 1975; Abel-Smith et al., 1973). These were mainly survey studies exploring whether the public had sought legal advice to deal with their legal problems. Some critics suggested that these surveys addressed a narrower scope of problems compared to those that were generally taken to lawyers.[11] However, an American legal needs study conducted by Barbara Curran in 1977 employed a broader scheme, examining the circumstances that influence respondents' decisions to seek advice. The same approach was adopted by the American Bar Association focusing on low- and moderate-income members of the public. Specific research on women's access to justice, Equality before the Law: Justice for Women, examined bias and discrimination in the law, and gender inequality within the justice system in Australia. The report was the result of the analysis of about 600 submissions from individuals and organisations from different parts of Australia.[12]

This study, having reviewed some of the above-mentioned survey studies, adopted a different approach and instead sought to measure the levels of women's awareness of the existence of legal assistance regardless of any particular problem. It focused on examining a lack of information as being a barrier to access to justice rather than understanding the dynamic between legal needs

[11] See Johnsen (1999).

[12] Australian Law Reform Commission, *Equality before the Law: Justice for Women*, 1994, ALRC Report No 69, Part I and II, Sydney, available at www.austlii.edu.au/au/other/alrc/publications/reports/69/vol1/ALRC69.html and www.austlii.edu.au/au/other/alrc/publications/reports/69/vol2/ALRC69.html, accessed 20 May 2011.

and obtaining legal assistance. This was because the possibility of seeking legal assistance may indicate the existence of some type of legal need, but adopting a strategy not to seek legal assistance cannot be a comprehensive indicator that the need for legal assistance does not exist. As discussed earlier, the strategy of seeking legal assistance depends more on circumstances that a decision is made than the type of problem women are facing. Therefore, to avoid manipulating the response by limiting respondents to only those who may experience a problem, a statement was included in the screening survey: "I did not know that there are some organisations providing free or low-cost legal advice for the public."

More than half of the respondents (54.2%) said that they were not aware of the existence of legal aid services. This might validate the suggestion not only that legal aid schemes in Iran are inadequate but also that knowledge of the existence of these programs is extremely limited.[13] There is no need to mention that the existence of sufficient free legal aid institutions and also public awareness of these services are significant constituents in access to justice for disadvantaged groups.

The second issue that the survey sought to measure was the scope of legal aid schemes provided for women and the availability of such assistance to them when needed. The choices included in the screening survey were limited to the most active legal aid schemes within the country, including the Judiciary Legal Assistance Bureau located in the public courts and the Bar Association Legal Assistance Bureau. Respondents who said that they sought help at some level from the judiciary-established legal advice offices in the public courts amounted to about 5 percent. Just two respondents out of 120 said that they had sought advice from the legal aid office in the Bar Association. The survey also included the possibility of seeking legal assistance from NGOs, cultural organisations, or law schools. Just one respondent

[13] These data were also confirmed by Abbas Zahiri, deputy director of the Central Bar Association, in-depth interview dated 10 May 2010.

said that she had sought legal advice from cultural organisations or NGOs. No one knew about the legal aid clinic that exists in some of the law schools based in Tehran, such as Shahid Beheshti University. In total, approximately 32.5 percent of respondents mentioned that they had not taken any free legal advice or approached any legal aid agencies in the past to deal with their legal problems. These findings reveal an extremely low level of use of the free advice resources within the population of respondents. The demand for free advice among women is not comparable with the resources available.

Gender Bias and Cultural Values

This survey examines the role of cultural values in women's path to justice. A range of possible impressions was suggested to avoid manipulating responses by imposing the assumption that gender bias is an obstacle to women's access to justice. Respondents were asked about their initial perceptions: "What do you think about those women who decide to take legal action by going to court?" This was followed by additional suggestions in order to capture the respondents' gender sensitivities: "I think those women who take legal action are at the end of their tether and have no other choice"; "I think those women who take legal action are brave and empowered"; "I would avoid going to court; it is not the right place for women to go"; "I think women and men have the same difficulties in going to court."

In response to these questions, the most common feedback respondents offered respondents was that going to court is the last decision a woman might take to enforce her rights. Respondents said that although going to court is an opportunity available to women to enforce their rights, it is nevertheless the most disliked strategy of all those they could possibly adopt (n = 57, 47.5%). The next most common view highlighted a lack of confidence in the judiciary and respondents expressed the view that going to court involves the same trouble and complications for both men and women (23.3%). A number of respondents felt that women who take legal action are, in their view, empowered and brave (n = 21, 17.5%). These women thought engagement with any legal process was a sign of empowerment. Another interesting finding was that few respondents thought the court was not the right place for women to go (n = 10, 8.3%). This low percentage may be another indication of the fact that the Iranian women's sphere is no longer limited to the confines of the house (particularly in the capital and other major cities).

However, the evidence of this study noticeably demonstrates that respondents believe the cost of obtaining justice outweighs the benefits. The difficulties associated with the cost of justice, relating to both immaterial and material issues, have a great impact on women's observations about going to court. The perceptions women have of taking action, legal proceedings, or litigation are created as a result of how they see the quality and fairness of any legal procedure, such as going to court. Their observation may be the outcome of personal experience or public perception of how the Iranian judiciary, in general, treats justice users. It is also formed by the way going to court as a formal action has been symbolised for people or a specific group of the population such as women. From a cultural perspective, involvement with the justice sector has been condemned. This might reflect the continual lack of confidence in the court system that has formed people's negative attitudes regarding taking formal action. It might be interesting to note here a Persian proverb that discourages people from going to court even if they have a very pressing legal need to do so. The proverb advises that sacrificing a specific right brings more benefit for the right holder rather than engaging with the judicial process. A possible literal translation is as follows: "I wouldn't go to the court even if I left my shoes behind there" (hat in some references), suggesting that people would rather give up their personal belongings than go to court. This research did not study lack of confidence in the court system before the Islamic revolution, so the research cannot offer any indication that the

1979 revolution has impacted either positively or negatively on people's confidence in the courts. However, a general observation of Persian literature shows that people's negative attitude toward going to court has been shaped by centuries of injustice.

A further layer of complexity arises in considering how cultural values and gender biases characterise social attitudes toward female litigants. This survey suggested a critical situation where a woman has to take action against her husband, to highlight gender bias in access to justice. In fact, most women prefer not to take any legal action because of cultural considerations and the fear of losing face associated with the action of going to court (40% of respondents). A considerable group of respondents felt that most women are patient and long-suffering with their husbands (n = 33, 27%). While it would be a factual error to generalise the survey's findings to include all Iranian women, submissiveness and patience are cherished by the tradition.

Interestingly, some 15 percent (18/118) of respondents thought that social attitudes toward those men and women taking legal action against their spouses are the same. It is important to understand that, in most cases, engagement with formal legal proceedings against spouses is viewed negatively among the community, not only as a sign of respect for the institution of marriage but also to value the honour of the couple. However, the evidence of the survey findings and qualitative interviews in the present study revealed the existence of a negative perception of women who file complaints against their husbands, which may be considered a cultural obstacle to access to justice. The negative perception against male litigants expressed by a few respondents was not comparable with the negative perception of female litigants because of the difference in numbers of respondents and also the language that they used to describe these pessimistic impressions. For example, some extracts from interview transcripts have been included to show these negative impressions: "The fear of revenge by the husband may discourage women's appealing to justice, in particular with regard to family-related issues";

"Most women would not dare to lose honor by taking legal action against their spouses"; "Most of us do not have family support post-divorce, so men are in a better situation to initiate divorce"; "We have learned by our culture to be patient and have faith in the future"; "Keeping our faces red with a slap";[14] "Most women are long-suffering with their husbands no matter how good or bad they are"; "They (society) say women should not complain."

Perceptions of Access to Justice Barriers

In order to gain some understanding of the reasons for the underlying failure to take action where there is a legal problem, respondents were asked why there were fewer women litigants compared to men. This question was aimed at assessing women's perceptions of litigation as a process of engagement with the legal system to resolve their justiciable problems, and also to understand their views on the obstacles to accessing justice. Respondents were given a set of obstacles and were asked to select the relevant ones. These included cultural obstacles (lack of social acceptance), economic barriers (lack of financial resources), lack of legal information, and lack of family support. The respondents were also asked to include any other reason. The most common reason for inaction was lack of social acceptance, given by more than 30 percent of respondents. Lack of family support was another common obstacle indicated by a number of respondents (19.2%).

Some women respondents stated lack of financial support as the main obstacle to taking legal action for women (18.3%). Financial vulnerability also has implications for the type of assistance required when women seek help to deal with their problems. Another reason cited by some respondents was that taking any kind of legal action would cause problems for their family or damage their children's lives. In general, the obstacles identified

[14] This is an old Farsi proverb meaning to keep face and honour by not asking for help.

by most respondents reflected a sense of powerlessness, even though information was available about the potential possibilities for addressing legal problems. This feeling of insecurity that comprises the fear of cultural norms of exclusion and public discrimination can be an indication of a lack of legal empowerment.

What respondents thought about women's access to justice was another component of how their perceptions of barriers have been shaped. The range of problems included in the survey and the wording used to describe those problems were developed on the basis of focus group meetings followed by the piloting of the questionnaire. The question regarding respondents' perceptions of women's access to justice focused on the paths to justice, but the question about litigation, as discussed earlier, concentrated on women as users of justice. Several barriers explicitly expressed by respondents were rooted in women's sense of inequality and powerlessness. There was strong feeling about the unequal protection of law and unequal treatment by the judicial institutions.

The researcher was not aware of any studies that had been carried out on a large scale to consider women's perceptions of inequality. The research thus indicates the importance of surveying whether lay women's perceptions of unequal access to justice were conditioned via personal experiences or popular cultural references. Also, correlations between a woman's background, empowerment, and perceptions of unequal access to justice and the role of popular culture within this process need to be examined.

The perception of unequal access to justice by respondents was expressed in different ways. Some of the respondents felt that women face more barriers and difficulties in accessing justice compared with men (n = 20, 16.7%). The same impression was expressed by a similar percentage of respondents (16%) but with more specific phrasing: "The justice system does not apply equal protection of women's access to justice." A further 13 percent of respondents believed that women face inequality in accessing justice because there is no equality in terms of legal protection for the rights of women.

The second important theme, consistent with responses in the survey as expressed by several respondents, was lack of legal empowerment. Respondents believed the main barrier for women's access to justice is their lack of knowledge of their legal rights (expressed by more than 30% of respondents). There were common perceptions that lack of legal awareness among women hinders their access to justice. For example: "Women's main problem is that they don't know their rights. Women need to learn about the law. How do they fight for their rights when they don't know anything about them?"; "You've got to know the law in order to enforce rights"; "Ignorance is the main issue, there should be more training and more TV programmes to raise women's knowledge about the law and their rights." Another group of respondents thought that women "can have access to justice if they come to a decision and take action." The wording that women used was essentially based on the belief that self-determination brings positive change. Their understanding of willpower was very similar to the concept of empowerment. The perception that empowerment can provide better access to justice for women was expressed during the qualitative interviews as well.

Perceptions and Actual Experiences with the Legal System

An assessment of Iranian women's perceptions of the legal system was drawn from the research hypothesis that incorporated three different indicators: actual engagement of women with the legal system; women's perceptions of the justice sector; and women's views of taking formal legal action. Therefore, the actual experiences of respondents were analysed to examine to what extent women respond to legal problems and take their cases to court. Respondents were also asked to illustrate their attitudes by selecting a random set of comments about the legal system and legal action. The responses to questioning in this study suggest that respondents hold a varied combination of perceptions without any reference to their actual experiences.

In order to survey common perceptions of the legal system, different statements were read to all respondents, whether or not they had been involved with any litigation or taken any form of legal action to resolve their problems. Respondents were asked to select the statement that they agreed with most. The statements were based mainly on the feedback, comments, and attitudes expressed by women during focus group discussions at the piloting phase of the questionnaire.

This research shows that only a small minority of respondents had any actual experience with the legal system of any kind, such as filing a case, reporting to the police, or attending a court hearing (n = 9). Three of these respondents cited that they had taken some kind of formal action through the legal system but did not provide any further details. Six other respondents who had actual experience with the legal system said that they were not satisfied with the experience. In conclusion, the majority of respondents did not have any actual engagement with the legal system (n = 96, 80%).

Findings of the present study demonstrate that women's perceptions of the legal system reflect not only their negative impressions but also their hopes and expectations of being equally protected by the legal system; the legal system here refers to the judiciary, courts, and legal institutions. A number of respondents expressed the opinion that the legal system should protect women equally (n = 42, 35%). The expectations expressed may be considered a positive indication, since any optimistic expectation of the legal system shares, to some extent, the same impression of the hope of fairness and equality.

However, the user's expectations also seem to be formed by the unfulfilled obligation of the justice system. One of the most important obligations of any form of legal system is to protect people's rights and interests. Almost 12 percent of those interviewed agreed that the legal system fails to protect women. Even though some respondents thought that the legal system could be improved (confirmed by 5% of respondents), there was some lack of confidence and trust in the justice system. Nearly 22 percent of respondents said that they had no trust in the legal system; the same percentage of respondents believed that the legal system is corrupt. Although corruption has been subject to the very strongest disapproval from the religious perspective (as discussed in Chapter 3), it as yet remains one of the main challenges for the justice user.

The survey also asked respondents how they viewed going to court or other means of taking formal legal action. There was a strong belief that the Iranian legal system and in particular the courts, only serve the interests of the powerful and wealthy or those with the right connections (confirmed by 30%). In fact, Iranian public culture perceives wealth and the right connections as key essentials in enforcing rights. Another characteristic that public culture identifies as important is the existence of some level of self-assurance that challenges power settings. This is referred to as the three P's of success, as they all begin with the letter P in Persian. Some of these findings appear to be in agreement with some of the results of the Paths to Justice Study (Genn and Beinart, 1999) and the study of "Public Trust and Confidence in the Justice System" which was based on a survey of 1,826 Americans (Rottman and Tomkins, 1999). As a result of this lack of trust in the judicial system, a number of respondents (25.8%) assumed that even if women initiate litigation or take other forms of legal action, there will not be equal access to justice for them. That may also explain why several respondents thought going to court should be their last resort as a course of action (n = 21, 17.5%). Only a few women interviewed felt that the legal system protects their equal rights and interests if they take formal action to resolve disputes (n = 11, 9.2%).

I provide a sample of extracts from interview transcripts to illustrate women's perceptions about the judiciary: "These courts with such laws are not going to help me. The law seems to be very old"; "Not good enough for me ... the system should be based on today's world as well"; "What is my impression of the judiciary?

I think it just doesn't work for people"; "A justice system without adequate women's judges cannot help women"; "Women should know about their rights and the judiciary should respect women's rights"; "Monitoring systems should be strengthened within the judiciary"; "A just judge can bring justice for women"; "I once took a case to the court but the other part had connections, the judge was corrupt so I gave up hope in our justice system."

Conclusion

This chapter has provided a detailed analysis of the results from the survey study. The sample characteristics and descriptive statistics have been considered as the main areas of analysis. The descriptive statistics suggest that Iranian women's perception of the justice system comprises negative impressions and unfulfilled expectations. These perceptions reflect the need for legal reform strategies to secure women's rights, needs, and interests in a traditional society where cultural gender biases hinder women's access to justice.

There are four major findings of the research. The first is that women have adequate knowledge of their legal rights. Most respondents of the present study were able to identify the legal rights to which they are entitled under the codified law and also Islamic jurisprudence. However, knowledge of rights is most valuable where it is accompanied by knowledge of legal procedures and the legal system so that it can be converted into action to enforce legal rights. This research asserts that women have less familiarity with legal procedures than knowledge of legal rights. Although the majority of respondents had an acceptable level of understanding of the legal problems they face, most respondents were not able to differentiate between criminal and civil matters or civil and criminal courts. Although the majority of respondents understood that beating was subject to legal action, only a few indicated that sexual abuse was a criminal matter. The findings confirm that most respondents were not aware of the different types of domestic violence, which society and legal institutions, in general, view as a private issue for women.

The second major conclusion that can be drawn from this research is that women have inadequate knowledge of the various legal institutions, procedures, and responsibilities to which they can refer for resolving legal problems. General ignorance about legal institutions hinders access of women to justice. Another important finding is that most respondents were not aware of the existence of legal aid services. The findings suggest that legal aid schemes in Iran are indeed inadequate, hence public knowledge of the existence of legal aid is extremely low.

The third finding that arises from this research is that women lack confidence in the legal system to protect their rights and needs. The findings attest that traditional gender biases and cultural values hinder the ability of women to claim their legal rights. Perceptions stated by the respondents regarding taking action demonstrate how they pessimistically perceive the fairness of legal procedures such as going to court. Most respondents felt that going to court is a last resort for a woman to enforce her rights. The findings of this study show that most women prefer to not take any legal action because of cultural values and gender bias. The most common explanation given by respondents who took no action was lack of social acceptance. The additional factors cited included lack of family support, lack of financial support, and lack of legal knowledge.

The fourth major finding of this research is that perceptions of access of women to justice reflect a negative opinion about the unequal protection of the law and unequal treatment by the judicial institutions. Respondents believed that the Iranian justice system does not equally protect women's access to justice. The evidence of this study shows that women consider the cost of obtaining justice outweighs the benefits. Respondents also thought a lack of legal empowerment creates unequal access to justice for women. To summarise, the use of the law or legal empowerment helps women to have more control over their lives through legal knowledge and by having the courage to take legal action. Although this research demonstrates that women have basic knowledge of their rights, there is still a need to enhance women's knowledge of the legal system and legal procedures. For this to happen, women should be educated about the types of legal problems, legal procedures, and the role of different legal institutions that they can commonly expect to face. It is important that practical information is converted into the day-to-day life experience of women.

Conclusion

This book has demonstrated that any possible discussion of access to justice should be able to deal with two primary issues: how the concept of justice is defined for people on the ground, and what context has to exist in order for justice to be better realised. The research has attempted to look at these two issues from a justice user's perspective. To do so, it has surveyed women's perceptions of access to justice in Iran, as the literature reviewed explains the lack of research studies on the subject in the country.

Therefore, the original contribution of this book has been to endeavour to present a reflective insight into accessing justice in Iran. It has analysed the range of challenges that people and in particular women face when trying to take legal action to solve their problems. It has emphasised that the gradual recognition of women's rights, access to equal legal remedies, and legal empowerment are key dimensions in shaping the prospects for improved access to justice for Iranian women. It also has highlighted the efficacy of the use of the law or legal empowerment as a tool to enhance women's access to justice in Iran.

This study began with a conceptual analysis of access to justice from both Western and Islamic perspectives to claim that the

Western state-centred approach has placed a greater emphasis on strengthening the structure and function of judicial institutions to provide "access" at the national level. On the contrary, Islamic-related notions are more concerned with establishing "justice" at the individual level rather than the state maximising the "accessibility of justice" for the nation. Therefore, one of the main contributions of the current study was to provide a conceptual framework of access to justice from an Islamic perspective. My analysis highlights four constituents that might be used in structuring a possible conception of access to justice within Islamic thoughts. These include defining the following: justice by the rights-obligations theory; procedural justice or how justice as a right can be established; access or how a rights-holder can possess justice; and also alternative dispute resolutions to encourage compromise between the rights of conflicting parties though non-judicial settlement.

The contextualised study has highlighted the fact that there is a complicated interaction of different "layers" that contribute to providing access to justice in Iran. The most fundamental layer beyond law and policy involves empowerment as being disadvantaged in terms of choices, legal information, and a voice, which hinder the ability to seek justice. Another essential layer is linked to how the Iranian justice system is established (process) and how it has been developed so far (progress). A different layer, and the most publicised one, deals with legal protection and the performance of the judiciary. One possible conclusion here was that including the right to a fair trial in constitutional law alone is not enough to provide access to justice. Law can be effective only if it is effectively implemented and accessible to poor and disadvantaged groups. Last but not least is the unseen layer or social context, whereby any equal protection via laws and the legal system might fail to protect the rights and interests of a disadvantaged population because of a discriminatory culture and customary practices.

This text further explores the various categories of barriers to access to justice from the user's perspective in Iran, including the cost of justice, lengthy delays, the insufficient number of judges and skilled staff, corruption, and also the limitations of legal assistance. It highlights the fact that although some examples of legislation or policies do tackle barriers, these initiatives did not appear to be adequate mainly because there is a lack of research exploring the nature and incidence of such barriers; this is also a lack of understanding among related law and policy bodies such as parliament, the courts, and the police, in order to provide better access to justice.

The present research shows that gender-based barriers within substantive and procedural justice and sociocultural settings play a more significant role to hinder women's access to justice in Iran. This study has exposed the fact that black letter law is inadequate in providing access for women to justice in the presence of discriminatory institutional practices and social norms. It is already witnessed that, despite the protection provided by the law, women's access to justice has been violated.

The data from the fieldwork also suggest that Iranian women's perceptions of the justice system include negative impressions and unfulfilled expectations. Most of the respondents believed that the cost of obtaining justice outweighed the benefits. Respondents also reflected that the lack of legal empowerment causes unequal access to justice for women. These views speak of the need for legal reform strategies to secure women's rights and interests.

One original finding was that most of the women respondents were able to identify the legal rights to which they are entitled under the codified law and also Islamic jurisprudence. However, most women knew little about the legal institutions, procedures, and responsibilities to which they can refer to resolve their legal problems. Therefore, their knowledge of their rights could not be converted into legal action because women did not know how the legal system works. And of course the absence of sufficient legal aid makes it extremely difficult for women to enforce their rights by taking legal action.

The main recommendation of this study is that the use of the law or legal empowerment helps women to have more control over their lives through legal knowledge and the courage to take legal action. For this to happen, women should be educated about the types of legal problems, legal procedures, and the role of the different legal institutions that they commonly face. It is important that this useful information translates into their day-to-day life experience.

Legal empowerment has the potential to enhance women's access to justice in Iran. Nevertheless, strategies for legal empowerment must be able to address structural inequalities in order to improve women's access to justice. Otherwise these strategies will not significantly change existing circumstances for the majority of women. Obviously the discrimination and inequality that account for the main sources of women's lack of access to justice cannot be changed quickly, yet it is important to enforce women's equal status by law and the legal system. As a result, there is a strong need to develop sociolegal strategies to provide better access for women to justice.

The current study has produced a number of interesting insights into the perceptions of Iranian women of access to justice. However, as with any study about such a complicated subject, a number of limitations exist, and it is important to recognise these limitations and to make recommendations for future research.

This study has its limitations both in terms of methodology and application. As mentioned earlier, the survey was limited by use of a nonrandom sample. It was carried out in some areas of Tehran with a relatively small population. Future studies about women's perceptions of access to justice should cover different cities in Iran. Moreover, the questions in the questionnaires were structured based on the researcher's knowledge of the existing debates surrounding legal empowerment and access to justice literature, as cited earlier in this study. Therefore, it is fair to say that the findings presented in this study may reflect the interests of the researcher as much as the interests of the respondents.

Nevertheless, the interpretations presented in the survey findings chapter and also the various sets of questions seem to adequately indicate that the findings of this study reflect the respondents' opinions.

Last, but not least, research creates research, and this study is no exception. It is only an initial quest to explore the complex situation of access to justice from the user's perspective in Iran. For instance, this study has not covered the extent to which minorities or defendants or prisoners have access to justice. Further research would also be needed to produce more up-to-date data in relation to these issues in Iran. Considering the lack of literature regarding access to justice from the various Islamic perspectives, it would also be of great interest to explore how different schools of thought reflect on such a notion.

APPENDIX

Survey Questionnaire

All fifteen questions detailed in Table 8 (indicators and questions)[1] were included in the survey. The main questioner also included four additional questions that asked for demographic information of the respondents, including age, marital status, education, and employment status. The last question (number 20) was an open question meant to obtain respondents' feedback about how access to justice for women can be improved. The questionnaire initially was produced in English and translated into Farsi. The English version of the survey is provided here.

Questioner

Thank you for taking part in this research. Please select the responses that reflect your opinion as accurately as possible.

1. Please select your age group from the list below:
   ☐ 18 to 25 ☐ 25 to 35 ☐ 35 to 45 ☐ 45 to 55 ☐ Over 55
2. Please select your level of education from the list below:
   ☐ Post graduate ☐ Graduate ☐ High school diploma ☐ Poor literacy ☐ Illiterate
3. Please select your marital status from the list below:
   ☐ Single ☐ Married ☐ Divorced ☐ Widow ☐ Married but not living with husband

[1] See Chapter 5.

4. Please select your employment status from the list below:
   □ Student □ Housewife □ Employed □ Self-employed □ Unemployed
5. Which of the following do you consider a right of women by the law?
   □ Becoming a minister □ Establishing a trade union □ Requesting the right to divorce at the time of marriage □ All of the above □ None of the above
6. Which of the following do you consider a right of women in Islam?
   □ The right to negotiate marriage terms of her choice □ The right to have her own property □ The right to ask for divorce □ All of the above □ Don't know
7. Which of the following do you consider a right of women in Islam?
   □ The right to negotiate marriage terms of her choice □ The right to have her own property □ The right to ask for divorce □ All of the above □ Don't know
8. What action do you take when confronting a family dispute such as inheritance, cost of maintenance, or marriage portion?
   □ Refer to the family □ Refer to the Family Advisor Service □ Refer to the court □ Do not take any legal action □ I will be patient because the problem can be resolved if given time
9. Which of the following issues can be filed as a criminal case before the court?
   □ Verbal abuse □ Beating □ Sexual abuse □ All of the above □ Don't know
10. Which of the following issues can be filed as a civil case before the court?
    □ Family dispute over choosing a place to live □ Husband refuses to pay the marriage portion (dower) □ Husband is unable to perform his marital duty □ All of the above □ Don't know
11. Which of the following institutions are you aware of?
    □ Police □ General Court □ Legal aid agency □ Forensic and Legal Medicine Agency □ Don't know
12. What do you think about women who claim their rights by taking legal action?

□ I think women who take legal action are at the end of their tether and have no other choice □ I think women who take legal actions are brave and empowered □ I would avoid going to court; not a right place for women to go □ I think women and men have the same difficulties in litigation □ Don't know

13. How do you consider the social attitudes toward a woman who takes legal action against her husband?
    □ A bad-mannered wife □ A brave woman □ I think the social attitude toward those men and women who take legal action against their spouses is the same □ Most women prefer to not take any legal action because of cultural considerations and fear of losing face □ Most women are patient and long-suffering with their husbands
14. Why aren't there as many women litigants as men?
    □ Lack of social acceptance □ Lack of financial resources □ Lack of general information on the law □ Lack of family support □ Lack of legal protection □ Other
15. What do you think about the justice sector?
    □ The justice sector is corrupt □ The justice sector fails to protect women □ The justice sector should protect women equally □ The justice sector can be improved □ I don't trust the justice sector □ Don't know
16. What do you think about litigation?
    □ Bringing legal problems to the court is likely to make them worse □ Women will not have equal access to justice □ The legal system can protect my equal rights if I go to court □ Only people with wealth, power, and the right connections can have access to justice □ Litigation should be the last course of action for dispute resolution □ Don't know
17. What of the following sources do you use to learn about law and the legal system?
    □ Television and radio □ Print media □ Websites and weblogs □ Cultural organisations □ Other (please specify)
18. Have you ever sought legal advice from any legal aid organisations?
    □ Yes, I have sought legal advice from the legal aid office in the public court □ Yes, I have sought legal advice from the legal aid

office in the Bar Association □ Yes, I have sought legal advice from a legal aid NGO □ No, I have not experienced legal aid □ I was not aware of the existence of legal aid agencies

19. What do you think about women's access to justice?
    □ There are no equal legal protections for women □ Women can have access to justice if they want □ The main barrier for women's access to justice is they don't know their legal rights □ The justice system does not apply equal protection of women's access to justice □ Women face more barriers than men in accessing to justice □ Don't know
20. What is your experience of the litigation process?
21. Do you have any suggestions to enhance access of women to justice?

Bibliography

All sources are listed in chronological order, unless otherwise stated.

International Treaties and Conventions

Convention on the Prevention and Punishment of the Crime of Genocide adopted by General Assembly Resolution 260 A (III) on 9 December 1948.

Universal Declaration of Human Rights adopted by Resolution 217 A (III) on 10 December 1948.

Convention for the Protection of Human Rights and Fundamental Freedoms (commonly referred to as the European Convention on Human Rights [ECHR]) was adopted in 1950 and came into force in 1953.

Convention Relating to the Status of Refugees Adopted by the United Nations Conference of Plenipotentiaries on the Status of Refugees and Stateless Persons convened under General Assembly Resolution 429 (V) of 14 December 1950 and entered into force: 22 April 1954, in accordance with article 43.

Supplementary Convention on the Abolition of Slavery, the Slave Trade, and Institutions and Practices Similar to Slavery adopted by Economic and Social Council Resolution 608 (XXI) of 30 April 1956 and adopted at Geneva on 7 September 1956 (entered into force: 30 April 1957 in accordance with article 13).

Elimination of All Forms of Racial Discrimination adopted by General Assembly Resolution 2106 (XX) of 21 December 1965 (entered into force: 4 January 1969 in accordance with article 19).

International Covenant on Economic, Social and Cultural Rights adopted by General Assembly Resolution 2200A (XXI) of 16 December 1966 (entered into force 3 January 1976).

International Covenant on Civil and Political Rights adopted by General Assembly Resolution 2200A (XXI) of 16 December 1966 (entered into force 23 March 1976).

International Convention on the Suppression and Punishment of the Crime of Apartheid adopted by General Assembly on 30 November 1973 and entered into force: 18 July 1976, in accordance with article XV (1).

American Convention on Human Rights, O.A.S. Treaty Series No. 36, 1144 U.N.T.S. 123, entered into force 18 July 1978.

Convention for the Elimination of All Forms of Discrimination Against Women, adopted 18 December 1979, 1249 U.N.T.S. 13 (entered into force 3 September 1981).

African [Banjul] Charter on Human and Peoples' Rights, adopted 27 June 1981, OAU Doc. CAB/LEG/67/3 rev. 5, 21 I.L.M. 58 (1982), entered into force 21 October 1986.

Hague Convention on International Access to Justice, concluded on 25 October 1980 (entered into force 1 May 1988).

Convention on the Rights of the Child adopted by General Assembly on 20 November 1989 (entered into force: 2 September 1990 in accordance with article 49).

Basic Principles on the Role of Lawyers, welcomed by the UN General Assembly in 1990.

The Worst Forms of Child Labour Convention adopted by the General Conference of the International Labour Organization on 17 June 1999 (entered into force: 19 November 2000, in accordance with article 10).

United Nations Convention against Corruption (UNCAC) was adopted by the General Assembly by resolution 58/4 of 31 October 2003 and entered into force on 14 December 2005.

Statutes

Iran Civil Code, 1928 (last amended 1985)

Iran Law of *Esar*, 1934

Iran Commercial Code, 1939

Constitution of Italia, adopted in 1947 (last amended 2007)

Iran Law concerning the independence of the Bar Association, 1954

Iran Law of the Establishment of the Financial Security of Attorneys, 1976

Constitution of the Islamic Republic of Iran, 1979

Constitution of Switzerland, adopted in 1874 (last amended 1991)

Iran Law on the selection of judges, 1983

Iran Penal Code, 1991

Islamic Republic of Iran Law of Third Economic, Social and Cultural Development Plan, 2000

Iran Code of Civil Procedure, last amended 2000

Iran Code of Criminal Procedure, last amended 2000
Iran Law on Respect for Legitimate Freedoms and Safeguarding Citizens' Rights, 2004
Iran Obligatory the Lawyer Presence in Civil Cases, 2005
Constitution of the Netherlands, adopted in 1815 (last amended 2005)

Case Law

Golder v. United Kingdom, Application No. 4451/70, Judgment of 21 February 1975
Airey v. Ireland, Application No. 6289/73, Judgment of 9 October 1979
Artico v. Italy, Application No. 6694/74, Judgment of 13 May 1980
Jordan v. United Kingdom, Application No. 24746/94, Judgment of 4 May 2001
Biondo v. Italy, Application No. 8821/70, Judgment of 28 February 2002
Steel & Morris v. United Kingdom, Application no. 68416/01, Judgment of 15 February 2005
Bubbins v. United Kingdom, Application No. 50196/99, Judgment of 17 March 2005

Other Official Documents

Amnesty International (1980). "Law and Human Rights in the Islamic Republic of Iran." <http://www.iranrights.org/english/document-338.php>
United Nations Development Program (2003). *Common Country Assessment for the Islamic Republic of Iran*. Tehran: UNDP. http://www.undp.org.ir/DocCenter/reports/npd/CCA.pdf.
United Nations Development Program (2004). Lessons on Applying a Human Rights-Based Approach to Development Programming: Case Study from the UNDP Asia Pacific Rights and Justice Initiative. Bangkok: UNDP.
2006–2007 (SH 1385) National Census; Office for National Statistics.
United Nations Development Program (2006). *Human Development Report*. New York: Oxford University Press.
Amnesty International report (June 2007). "Iran: the last executioner of children." http://web.amnesty.org/library/index/engmde130592007.
International Bar Association. 2007. *Balancing Independence and Access to Justice: A Background Report on the Justice System in Iran*. Country Visit Report. London: International Bar Association, October. http://www.ibanet.org/Article/Detail.aspx?ArticleUid=8281ffa3-1ce7-4976-a93d-e488cc0fa333
Islamic Republic of Iran Department of Justice (2007). *The Impact of Directives on Long Delay*. Tehran: Judiciary Printing Office.

United Nations Development Program (2007). *Justice for All: An Assessment of Access to Justice in Five Provinces of Indonesia*. Jakarta: UNDP.

United Nations Development Program (2007). Towards Inclusive Governance: Promoting the Participation of Disadvantaged Groups in Asia-Pacific. Bangkok: United Nations Development Program Regional Centre in Bangkok.

Research Center of the Majlis (2008). http://rc.majlis.ir/fa/news/show/765155.

Islamic Republic of Iran's Planning Deputy of the Presidential Office (2009). *Development Report of the Judiciary*. http://www.spac.ir/barnameh/317/p-1.htm.

UNDP (2010). *Human Development Index*. http://hdr.undp.org/en/reports/global/hdr2010/chapters/.

UNESCO Science Report (2010). The Current Status of Science around the World.

State Prisons and Security and Corrective Measure Organization Statistical Report (2010). http://www.prisons.ir/index.php?Module=SMMPrisonStat&SMMOp=IranPrStatView&SMM_CMD=&IranPrStatYear=1388&IranPrStatFollow=All&IranPrStatMonth=12

Amnesty International joint statement (10 October 2010). "IRAN: Lawyers' defence work repaid with loss of freedom." http://www.amnesty.org/en/library/asset/MDE13/093/2010/en/d4a07c06-70a0-4409-8c57-ec7142771309/mde130932010en.html.

Human Rights Watch (2011). World Report: Iran. http://www.hrw.org/en/world-report-2011/iran

Interviews

Research interviews (open-ended discussions of relevant issues) were conducted with the individuals listed. Personal notes for recording information were taken by hand. Officials of the justice institutions such as judges agreed to be interviewed on the basis of anonymity. The other semi-structured interviews are presented in the survey chapter.

Prof. Shahla Moazami, criminology professor of Tehran University, interviewed on 12 April 2010, Tehran.

Mr. Ahmad Salari, Program Analyst and Head of Democratic Governance and Trade Program Cluster (Access to Justice National Project) in UNDP Iran, interviewed on 15 April 2010, Tehran.

Mr. Abbas Zahiri, Deputy Director of Central Bar Association, interviewed on 10 May 2010, Tehran.

Ayatollah Mohaghegh Damad, Interviewed on 12 May 2010, Tehran.

Prof. Abdullahi Ahmed An-Na'im, Charles Howard Candler Professor of Law at Emory University School of Law, interviewed on 20 October 2010, Coventry.

Books and Articles (in alphabetical order)

Abarqūhī, Shams al-Dīn Ibrāhīm. 1986. *Majma al-Bahrain*. Tehran: Najib Mayel Haravi.

Abel-Smith, Brian, Michael Zander, and Rosalind Brooke Ross. 1973. *Legal Problems and the Citizen; a Study in Three London Boroughs*. London: Heinemann.

Abu-Nimer, Mohammed. 2000. A Framework for Nonviolence and Peacebuilding in Islam. *Journal of Law and Religion* 15 (1/2).

AC Nielsen, and Asia Foundation. 2001. *Survey Report on Citizens' Perceptions of the Indonesian Justice Sector: Preliminary Findings and Recommendations*. Jakarta: Asia Foundation.

Adams, J. Stacy. 1966. Inequity in Social Exchange. In *Advances in Experimental Social Psychology*, Volume 2:267–99. Academic Press. http://www.sciencedirect.com/science/article/pii/S0065260108601082.

Afkhami, Mahnaz. 1994. *Women in Post-Revolutionary Iran: A Feminist Perspective*. In *In the Eye of the Storm: Women in Post-Revolutionary Iran*, ed. Mahnaz Afkhami and Erika Friedl. London: I. B. Tauris.

Afsharnia, Ṭayyab, and Hojat Mobin. 2009. *Judicial Reform and Long Delay*. 1st ed. Tehran: Khursandi.

Ahmadi, Ashraf. 1959. *Law and Justice in the Ancient Persian Empire*. Tehran: Ministry of Culture and Art Publications.

Ahmed, Leila. 1992. *Women and Gender in Islam: Historical Roots of a Modern Debate*. New Haven: Yale University Press

Al-Aamili, Shaikh al-Hur. 1998. *Wasā'il al-Shī'a*. 7th ed. Vol. 18. 20 vols. Qom: Islamic Press.

Ali Ibn 'Abd al-Malik, Muttaqi. 'Kanz al-'ummal'. Ed. H. Razuuq and S. al-Saqqa. Aleppo: Maktabat al-Turath al-Islami, 1969–77.

Ali, Shaheen. 2006. *Conceptualising Islamic law, CEDAW, and Women's Human Rights in Plural Legal Settings: A Comparative Analysis of Application of CEDAW in Bangladesh, India, and Pakistan*. New Delhi: UNIFEM-South Asia Regional Office.

Ali, Shaheen Sardar. 2000. *Equal Before Allah, Unequal Before Man?* Kluwer Law International.

Al-Sharīf al-Radī, Muḥammad. 1974. *Nahjul Balagha*. Tehran: Golshan Print. House.

Alsop, Ruth, Mette Frost Bertelsen, and Jeremy Holand. 2006. *Empowerment in Practice: From Analysis to Implementation*. Washington, DC: World Bank.

Alston, Philip. 1999. *The EU and Human Rights*. Oxford: Oxford University Press.

American Bar Association. Consortium on Legal Services and. 1994. *Legal Needs and Civil Justice: a Survey of Americans: Major Findings of the Comprehensive Legal Needs Study*. Consortium on Legal Services and the Public, American Bar Association.

Amin, Seyed Hassan. 2003. *The History of Law in Iran*. Tehran: Encyclopedia Publications.

Amnesty International. 2010. *Human Rights in Islamic Republic of Iran*. London: Amnesty International.

Anand, Justice A. S. 2004. *Justice for Women: Concerns and Expressions*. Delhi: Universal Law Publishing Co Ltd.

Anderson, Michael. 2003. *Access to Justice and Legal Process Making Legal Institutions Responsive to Poor People in LDCs*. Working Paper. Sussex: Institute of Development Studies.

An-Na'im, A. A. 1990. Islam, Islamic Law and the Dilemma of Cultural Legitimacy for Universal Human Rights. In *Asian Perspectives on Human Rights*, C. E. Welch, Jr. and V. A. Leary, eds. Boulder, CO: Westview.

2008. *Islam and the Secular State: Negotiating the Future of Sharia* Cambridge, MA: Harvard University Press.

Aristotle. 1999. *Nicomachean Ethics*. 2nd ed. Indianapolis, IN: Hackett Publishing.

Asian Development Bank. 2001. *Law and Policy Reform at the Asian Development Bank*. 2000th ed. Manila: Office of the General Counsel Asian Development Bank.

Bagozzi, Richard. 1996. *Principles of Marketing Research*. Cambridge: Blackwell Business.

Barendrecht, Maurits, Peter Kamminga, and Jin Ho Verdonschot. 2008. Priorities for the Justice System: Responding to the Most Urgent Legal Problems of Individuals. *SSRN*.

Bass, Julia, W. A. Bogart, and Frederick Zemans. 2005. *Access to Justice for a New Century: The Way Forward*. Irwin Law, January.

Bassiouni, M. 1982. *The Islamic Criminal Justice System*. London: Oceana Publications.

Batliwala, S. 1994. "The Meaning of Women's Empowerment: New Concepts from Action." In *Population Policies Reconsidered: Health, Empowerment and Rights*, ed. G. Sen, A. Germain and L. C. Chen, pp. 127–38. Boston: Harvard University Press.

Beazer, Margaret, and Josie Gray. 2010. *Access and Justice: Legal Studies for Units 1 and 2*. 10th ed. Melbourne: Oxford University Press.

Becker, Theodore. 1970. *Comparative Judicial Politics: The Political Functionings of Courts*. Chicago: Rand McNally.

Bentzon, Agnete, Anne Hellum, Julie Stewart, Welshman Ncube, and Torben Agersnap. 1998. *Pursuing Grounded Theory in Law: South-North Experiences in Developing Women's Law*. Oslo: Tano Aschehoug.

Berger, Peter, and Richard John Neuhaus. 1996. *To Empower People: from State to Civil Society*. 2nd ed. Washington, DC: American Enterprise Institute.

Bhabha, F. 2007. Institutionalizing Access-to-Justice: Judicial, Legislative and Grassroots Dimensions. *Queens Law Journal* 33, no. 1: 139–78.

Bies, Robert, and Debra L. Shapiro. 1987. "Interactional Fairness Judgments: The Influence of Causal Accounts. *Social Justice Research* 1, no. 2: 199–218.

Blankenburg, Erhard. 1980. *Innovations in the Legal Services*. Cambridge: Oelgeschlager Gunn & Hain.

Bookman, Ann. 1988. *Women and the Politics of Empowerment*. Philadelphia: Temple University Press.

Bridges, Lee. 1998. *Improving Police Station Legal Advice: The Impact of the Accreditation Scheme for Police Station Legal Advisers*. London: Legal Aid Board.

Bridges, Lee, and Alan Paterson. 2007. *Evaluation of the Public Defender Service in England and Wales*. London: The Stationery Office.

Brooker, Penny. 1999. "The 'Juridification' of Alternative Dispute Resolution." *Anglo-American Law Review* 28, no. 1:1–36.

Brown, Steven. 2003. *Empowerment as Subjective Operant*. Washington, DC: World Bank, February 4. http://siteresources.worldbank.org/INTEMPOWERMENT/Resources/486312-1095970750368/529763-1095970803335/brown.pdf.

Buck, Alexy, Nigel Balmer, and Pascoe Pleasence. 2005. Social Exclusion and Civil Law: Experience of Civil Justice Problems among Vulnerable Groups. *Social Policy & Administration* 39, no. 3: 302–22.

Bukhārī, Muḥammad. 1997. *Ṣaḥīḥ al-Bukhārī: the Translation of the Meanings of Sahih al-Bukhari : Arabic-English*. Riyadh: Darussalam.

Bulmer, Martin. 1984. *Sociological Research Methods*. 2nd ed. New Brunswick, NJ: Transaction Books.

Buscaglia, Edgardo. 1996. Introduction to Law and Economics of Development. In *Law and Economics of Development*, 24–29. New Jersey: JAI Press.

Cappelletti, Mauro, and Bryant Garth, eds. 1978. *Access to Justice: A World Survey, vol. 1*. Milan: Sijthoff and Noordhoff – Alphenaandenrijn.

Cappelletti, Mauro, and Bryant Garth, eds. 1979. *Access to Justice: Emerging Issues and Perspectives, vol. 3*. Milan: Sijthoff and Noordhoff – Alphenaandenrijn.

Cappelletti, Mauro, and Bryant Garth. 1981. *Access to Justice and the Welfare State*. Alphen aan den Rijn: Sijthoff.

Cappelletti, Mauro, and John Weisner, eds. 1978 and 1979. *Access to Justice: Promising Institutions, vol. 2*. Milan: Sijthoff and Noordhoff – Alphenaandenrijn.

Carfield, Maggi. 2005. Notes – Enhancing Poor People's Capabilities through the Rule of Law: Creating an Access to Justice Index. *Washington University Law Quarterly* 83, no. 1: 339.

Cass, Michael. 1975. *Legal Needs of the Poor: Research Report*. Canberra: Australian Government Publishing Service.

Cbe, Yash Ghai, and Jill Cottrell. 2009. *Marginalized Communities and Access to Justice*. London: Routledge-Cavendish.

Charn, Jeanne. 2003. Service and Learning: Reflections on Three Decades of the Lawyering Process at Harvard Law School. *Clinical Law Review* 10: 75–93.

Chayes, Abram. 1976. The Role of the Judge in Public Law Litigation. *Harvard Law Review* 89, no. 7 (May 1): 1281–1316.

Clarke, G. and Davies, I. 1992. Mediation – When Is It Not an Appropriate Dispute Resolution Process? *Australian Dispute Resolution Journal* 3:70–8.

Cobb, S. and Rifkin, J. 1991. Practice and Paradox: Deconstructing Neutrality in Mediation. *Law and Society Inquiry* no. 16.

Cohen, Jean. 1998. *Changing Paradigms of Citizenship and the Exclusiveness of the Demos*. Toronto: University of Toronto.

Cohen, Mark A. 2000. Measuring the Costs and Benefits of Crime and Justice. *Criminal Justice* 4: 263–314.

Cohen, S., Barney G. Glaser, and Anselm L. Strauss. 1969. The Discovery of Grounded Theory: Strategies for Qualitative Research. *British Journal of Sociology* 20, no. 2 (June): 227.

Coleman, Jules L. 1992. *Risks and Wrongs*. Cambridge University Press Archive.

Colquitt, J. A., D. E. Conlon, M. J. Wesson, and C. Porter. 2001. Justice at the Millennium: A Meta-Analytic Review of 25 Years of Organizational Justice Research. *Journal of Applied Psychology* 86, no. 3: 425–45.

Commission of Inquiry into Poverty. 1975. *Legal Needs of the Poor* Research Report Law and Poverty Series. Canberra: Australian Government Publishing Service.

Commission on Legal Empowerment of the Poor. 2008. *Making the Law Work for Everyone*. New York: Commission on Legal Empowerment of the Poor.

Cooter, Robert D. 1996. The Theory of Market Modernization of Law. *International Review of Law and Economics* 16, no. 2 (June): 141–72.

Corbin, Juliet M., and Anselm Strauss. 1990. Grounded Theory Research: Procedures, Canons, and Evaluative Criteria. *Qualitative Sociology* 13, no. 1: 3–21.

Coumarelos, Christine. 2006. *Justice Made to Measure: NSW Legal Needs Survey in Disadvantaged Areas*. Sydney: Law and Justice Foundation.

Curran, Barbara, American Bar Association, and American Bar Foundation. 1977. *The Legal Needs of the Public: the Final Report of a National Survey, a Joint Undertaking by the American Bar Association Special Committee to Survey Legal Needs and the American Bar Foundation*. Chicago: American Bar Foundation.

Currie, Albert. 2007. *The Legal Problems of Everyday Life: The Nature, Extent and Consequences of Justiciable Problems Experienced by Canadians*. Ottawa: Department of Justice Canada.

Daicoff, Susan. 2006. Law as a Healing Profession: The Comprehensive Law Movement. *Pepperdine Dispute Resolution Law Journal* 6: 1.

Dakolias, Maria. 2003. *Legal and Judicial Reform: Strategic Directions*. 2nd ed. Washington, DC: World Bank.

Daniel, Elton L. 2001. *The History of Iran*. Westport, CT: Greenwood Publishing.

Daniel, S. S., E. T. Bowe, R. Lallemand, M. N. Yeh, and L. S. James. 1975. Renal Response to Acid Loading in the Developing Lamb Fetus, Intact in Utero. *Journal of Perinatal Medicine* 3, no. 1: 34–43.

Dareini, Ali Akbar. 2010. "Iranian Rejects Politicizing Executions," Associated Press, 1 February 2010. Available online at http://articles.boston.com/2011–06–24/news/29699767_1_esfandiar-rahim-mashaei-hard-line-clerics-iranian-leadership, accessed 18 April 2011.

Darley, John. 2003. The Psychology of Compensatory and Retributive Justice. *Personality and Social Psychology Review* 7, no. 4 (November 1): 324–36.

Darling, L. 2007. Social Cohesion (Asabiyya) and Justice in the Late Medieval Middle East. *Comparative Studies in Society & History* 49: 329–57.

Denzin, Norman. 1994. *Handbook of Qualitative Research*. Thousand Oaks, CA: Sage Publications.

Deutsch, Morton. 1975. Equity, Equality, and Need: What Determines Which Value Will Be Used as the Basis of Distributive Justice? *Journal of Social Issues* 31, no. 3 (July 1): 137–49.

De Vaus, David. 2002. *Surveys in Social Research*. 5th ed. London: Routledge.

Dias, Ayesha. 2009. *Justice for the Poor: Perspectives on Accelerating Access*. New Delhi: Oxford University Press.

Dillman, Don. 2000. *Mail and Internet Surveys: The Tailored Design Method*. 2nd ed. New York: Wiley.

Djankov, Simeon, Rafael La Porta, Laforencio Lopez-de-Silanes, and Andrei Shleifer. 2003. "Courts." *Quarterly Journal of Economics* May: 453–517.

Durant, Will. 1935. *The Story of Civilization, Vol. 1: Our Oriental Heritage*. New York: Simon & Schuster.

Dworkin, Ronald. 1978. *Taking Rights Seriously*. Cambridge, MA: Harvard University Press.

El-Ahdab, A.H. 1998. *Arbitration with the Arab Countries*. 2nd ed. Deventer: Kluwer Law International.

Ebady, Shirin. 2000. History and Documentation of Human Rights in Iran. *Persian Studies Series*, no. 18.

Engle Merry, Sally. 2001. *Changing Rights, Changing Culture, in Culture and Rights: Anthropological Perspectives*, ed. Jane Cowan. Marie-Benedicte Dembour, and Richard Wilson. Cambridge: Cambridge University Press.

2006. Transnational Human Rights and Local Activism: Mapping the Middle. *American Anthropologist* 108: 38–51.

European Commission for the Efficiency of Justice. 2005. *European Judicial Systems: Facts and Figures on the Basis of a Survey Conducted in 40 Councils of Europe Member States*. Strasbourg: Council of Europe Publishing.

Falkmoore, S. 1973. Law and Social Change: The Semi Autonomous Field as an Appropriate Subject of Study. *Law and Society Review* 7: 719–46.

Fazel Lankarani, Mohammad. 2006. *Jame'ul-Masa'el*. Vol. 1. 2 vols. Qom: Mehr.

Feinberg, Joel. 1970. *Doing [and] Deserving: Essays in the Theory of Responsibility*. Princeton, NJ: Princeton University Press.

Ferguson, C. 1999. *Global Social Policy Principles: Human Rights and Social Justice*. London: DFID.

Fishwick, E. 1992. *Back to Basics: Legal Needs in the '90's*. Sydney: Legal Aid Commission of New South Wales.

Fiss, Owen M. 1993. The Limits of Judicial Independence. *University of Miami Inter-American Law Review* 25, no. 1 (October 1): 57–76.

Folger, Robert. 1977. Distributive and Procedural Justice: Combined Impact of Voice and Improvement on Experienced Inequity. *Journal of Personality and Social Psychology* 35, no. 2: 108–19.

Francioni, Francesco. 2007. *Access to Justice as a Human Right*. New York: Oxford University Press.

Friedmann, John. 1992. *Empowerment: The Politics of Alternative Development*. Cambridge: Blackwell.

Gal, S. 1991. Between Speech and Silence: The Problematics of Research on Language and Gender. In *Gender at the Crossroads of Knowledge: Feminist Anthropology in the Postmodern Era*, M. Di Leonardo, ed., pp. 175–203, Berkeley: University of California Press.

Galanter, M. 1981. Justice in Many Rooms: Private Ordering and Indigenous Law. *Journal of Legal Pluralism and Unofficial Law* 19: 1–47.

Galaway, Burt, and Joe Hudson. 1996. *Restorative Justice: International Perspectives*. Amsterdam: Criminal Justice Press.

Genn, Hazel G., and Sarah Beinart. 1999. *Paths to Justice: What People Do and Think about Going to Law*. Oxford: Hart Publishing.

Genn, Hazel G., Alan Paterson, and National Centre for Social Research (Great Britain). 2001. *Paths to Justice Scotland: What People in Scotland Do and Think about Going to Law*. Hart Publishing, October.

Glaser, Barney, and A. L. Strauss. 1967. *The Discovery of Grounded Theory Strategies for Qualitative Research*. Chicago: Aldine.

Glendon, Mary. 1995. A Nation Under Lawyers: How the Crisis in the Legal Profession Is Transforming American Society. *Journal of Legal Education* 45, no. 1: 143.

Golub, Stephen. 2003. *Beyond Rule of Law Orthodoxy: The Legal Empowerment Alternative*. Washington, DC: Carnegie Endowment for International Peace.

Golub, Stephen and Kim McQuay. 2000. Legal Empowerment: Advancing Good Governance and Poverty Reduction. *Law and Policy Reform*. Manila: Asian Development Bank.

Goodale, Mark. 2006. Toward a Critical Anthropology of Human Rights. *Current Anthropology* 47: 485–511.

Gopin, Marc. 2005. *Holy War, Holy Peace: How Religion Can Bring Peace to the Middle East*. New York: Oxford University Press.

Gramatikov, Martin. 2008. A Framework for Measuring the Costs of Paths to Justice. *SSRN*.

Gramatikov, Martin, and Robert B. Porter. 2010. Yes, I Can: Subjective Legal Empowerment. *SSRN*.

Gramatikov, Martin, Maurits Barendrecht, and Jin Ho Verdonschot. 2008. Measuring the Costs and Quality of Paths to Justice: Contours of a Methodology. *SSRN*.

Greenberg, Jerald. 1993. Justice and Organizational Citizenship: A Commentary on the State of the Science. *Employee Responsibilities and Rights Journal* 6, no. 3: 249–56.

Greenberg, Jerald, and Jason Colquitt. 2005. *Handbook of Organizational Justice*. Mahwah, NJ: Lawrence Erlbaum Associates.

Griffiths, John. 1977. The Distribution of Legal Services in the Netherlands Review of De *Weg Naar Het Recht (The Road to Justice)*. *British Journal of Law and Society* 4, no. 2: 260.

Griffiths, J. 1986. What Is Legal Pluralism? *Journal of Legal Pluralism and Unofficial Law* 25: 1–55.

Gromet, Dena, and John M. Darley. 2006. Restoration and Retribution: How Including Retributive Components Affects the Acceptability of Restorative Justice Procedures. *Social Justice Research* 19, no. 4 (December 1): 395–432.

Gumperz, J. 1982. *Discourse Strategies*. New York: Cambridge University Press.

Haeri, Shahla. 1992. Temporary Marriage and State in Iran: An Islamic Discourse on Female Sexuality. *Social Research* 59 (Spring): 201–23.

Halili, Hassan, Kamal. 2006. Employment Dispute Resolution Mechanism from the Islamic Perspective. *Arab Law Quarterly* 20, no. 2: 181–207.

Halliday, Terence, and Lucien Karpik. 1997. *Lawyers and the Rise of Western Political Liberalism: Europe and North America from the Eighteenth to Twentieth Centuries*. Oxford: Oxford University Press.

Hammergren, Linn A. 2007. *Envisioning Reform: Improving Judicial Performance in Latin America*. University Park: Pennsylvania State University Press.

Harding, John. 1982. *Victims and Offenders: Needs and Responsibilities*. London: Bedford Square Press.

Hassan, Kamal. 2006. Employment Dispute Resolution Mechanism from the Islamic Perspective. *Arab Law Quarterly* 20, no. 2 (June 1): 181–207.

Hegtvedt, K., and C. Johnson. 2000. Justice Beyond the Individual: A Future with Legitimation. *Social Psychology Quartely* 63: 298–311.

Held, Colbert C. 2000. *Middle East Patterns: Places, Peoples, and Politics*. Boulder, CO: Westview Press

Heywood, Andrew. 2000. *Key Concepts in Politics*. Basingstoke: Palgrave.

Hirschl, Ran. 2008. The Rise of Constitutional Theocracy. *Harvard International Law Journal Online* 49, no. 72: 73–82.

Hoodfar, Homa. 1999. The Women's Movement in Iran: Women at the Crossroads of Secularization and Islamization. *Women Living Under Muslim Laws, The Women's Movement* no. 1: 13.

Hoodfar, Homa, and Shadi Sadr. 2009. *Can Women Act as Agents of a Democratization of Theocracy in Iran?* Geneva: UNRISD. http://www.gwi-boell.de/downloads/Final_Country_Report_Iran_Oct2009.pdf

Hossain, Sara, Shahdeen Malik, and Bushra Musa. 1997. *Public Interest Litigation in South Asia: Rights in Search of Remedies*. Dhaka: University Press.

Hudson, Joe, Allison Morris, and Gabrielle M. Maxwell. 1996. *Family Group Conferences: Perspectives on Policy & Practice*. Leichard: Federation Press.

Iqbal, Walid. 2001. Courts, Lawyering, and ADR: Glimpses into the Islamic Tradition. *Fordham Urban Law Journal* 28: 1035.

Irwin, Robert. 2002. The Privatization of 'Justice' under the Circassian Mamluks, *Mamluk Studies Review* 6 : 63–70.

Izutsu, Toshihiko. 1966. *Ethico-Religious Concepts in the Qur'ān*. Montreal: McGill University Press.

Jafari-Langroudi, Mohammad Jafar. 1997. *Encyclopedias of Civil and Commercial Law*. 6th ed. Tehran: Amīr Kabīr.

Johnsen, Jon T. 1999. Legal Needs Studies in a Market Context. In *Transformation of Legal Aid*. Oxford: Oxford University Press.

Johnson, Earl. 1978. *Justice and Reform: The Formative Years of the American Legal Services Program*. New Brunswick, NJ: Transaction Publishers.

Kabeer, Naila. 1999. Resources, Agency, Achievements: Reflections on the Measurement of Women's Empowerment. *Development and Change* 30, no. 3 (July 1): 435.

2001. "Reflections on the Measurement of Women's Empowerment." In *Discussing Women's Empowerment – Theory and Practice*. Sida Studies No. 3. Stockholm: Novum Grafiska AB.

Kamel, Cf. Taymour. 1982. The Principle of Legality and Its Application in Islamic Criminal Justice. In *The Islamic Criminal Justice System*,

Mahmoud Cherif Bassiouni, ed., pp. 149–69. London/Rome/New York: Oceana Publications.

Kamali, M. H. 1991. *Principles of Islamic Jurisprudence*. Cambridge: Islamic Texts Society.

Kandiyoti, Deniz. 1991. *Women, Islam and the State*. London: Macmillan.

Kar, Mehranguiz. 1999. *Elimination of Gender Discrimination: A Comparison of the Convention On Elimination of All Forms of Discrimination Against Women (CEDAW) and Iran's Contemporary Laws*, Tehran: Qatreh.

2000. *Violence against Women in Iran*. Tehran: Roshangaran.

2001. *Women's Participation in Politics: Obstacles and Possibilities*. Tehran: Roshangaran.

2001. Women's Strategies in Iran from the 1979 Revolution to 1999. In *Globalization, Gender and Religion: The Politics of Women's Rights in Catholic and Muslim Contexts*, ed. Jane Bayes and Nayereh Tohidi. New York: Palgrave.

Katouzian, Homa. 1997. Arbitrary Rule: A Comparative Theory of State, Politics and Society in Iran. *British Journal of Middle Eastern Studies* 24, no. 1 (May 1): 49–73.

Kaushik, P. D. 2007. *Women Rights: Access to Justice*. New Delhi: Bookwell Publications.

Khadduri, Majid. 1946. Human Rights in Islam. *Annals of the American Academy of Political and Social Science* 243: 77–81.

1984. *Islamic Conception of Justice*. Baltimore: John's Hopkins University Press.

Khalid, M. I. 1976. Wali al-Mazalim or Muslim Ombudsman. *Journal of Islamic and Comparative Law* 6: 1–9.

Khomeini, Ruhollah Musavi. 2001. *Tahrirul-Wasilah*. Vol. 2. 4 vols. Imam Khomeini Press.

Kian-Thiebaut, Azadeh. 2002. Women and the Making of Civil Society. *In Twenty Years of Islamic Revolution: Political and Social Transition in Iran since 1979*, ed. Eric Hooglund. Syracuse, NY: Syracuse University Press.

Klaming, Laura, and Ivo Giesen. 2008. Access to Justice: The Quality of the Procedure. *SSRN*.

Konow, James. 2003. Which Is the Fairest One of All? A Positive Analysis of Justice Theories. *Journal of Economic Literature* 41, no. 4: 1188.

Krause, S. 2000. The Spirit of Separate Powers in Montesquieu. *Review of Politics* 62: 231–65.

Krishnan, Jayanth K. and Galanter, Marc. 2004. Bread for the Poor: Access to Justice and the Rights of the Needy in India. *Hastings Law Journal* 55, no.4: 789–834.

Larkins, Christopher M. 1996. Judicial Independence and Democratization: A Theoretical and Conceptual Analysis. *American Journal of Comparative Law* 44, no. 4 (October 1): 605–26.

Latimer, Jeff. 2001. *The Effectiveness of Restorative Justice Practices: A Meta-Analysis*. Toronto: Department of Justice Canada.

Law Reform Commission. 1994. *Equality before the Law: Justice for Women*. Sydney: Law Reform Commission.

Legal Services Commission. 2005. *Independent Peer Review*. London: The Legal Services Commission, November. http://www.legalservices.gov.uk/docs/civil_contracting/Independent_Peer_Review_Process1105.pdf.

Leventhal, G. S., and J. Gergen Kenneth. 1980. What Should be Done with Equity Theory? New Approaches to the Study of Fairness in Social Relationships. In *Social Exchange: Advances in Theory and Research*, 27–55. New York: Plenum Press.

Lind, E. 1990. In the Eye of the Beholder: Tort Litigants' Evaluations of Their Experiences in the Civil Justice System. *Law and Society Review* 24, no. 4: 953.

Lind, Edgar Allan, and Tom R. Tyler. 1988. *The Social Psychology of Procedural Justice*. New York: Springer.

Lundy, P. 2008. Whose Justice? Rethinking Transitional Justice from the Bottom Up. *Journal of Law and Society* 35, no. 2 (June 1): 265–92.

Majlesi, Muhammad Baqir. 2000. *Bahar – ul- Anvar*. Vol. 76. 110 vols. Chicago: Open School.

Malhotra, Anju, Ruth Ruth Schuler, and Carol Boender. 2002. *Measuring Women's Empowerment as a Variable in International Development*. Working Paper. Washington, DC: World Bank.

Markovsky, Barry, and Karen Hegtvedt. 1995. Justice and Injustice. *Sociological Perspectives on Social Psychology* (January 1): 257–80.

Marshall, Thomas. 1950. *Citizenship and Social Class and Other Essays*. Cambridge: Cambridge University Press.

Marshall, Tony F. 1985. *Alternatives to Criminal Courts: the Potential for Non-Judicial Dispute Settlement*. Brookfield: Gower Publishing.

Maru, Vivek. 2009. *Access to Justice and Legal Empowerment: A Review of World Bank Practice*. Washington, DC: World Bank.

Maxwell, G., C. Smith, P. J. Shepherd, and A. Morris. 1999. *Meeting Legal Service Needs*. New Zealand: Institute of Criminology, Victoria University of Wellington.

McClymont, Mary E., and Stephen Golub. 2000. *Many Roads to Justice: The Law-Related Work of Ford Foundation Grantees around the World*. Ford Foundation.

McManis, Charles R. 1981. "The History of First Century American Legal Education: A Revisionist Perspective." *Washington University Law Quarterly* 59: 597–625.

Meene, Ineke van de, and Benjamin van Rooij. 2008. *Access to Justice and Legal Empowerment: Making the Poor Central in Legal Development Co-operation*. Amsterdam: Leiden University Press.

Menkel-Meadow, Carrie. 2007. Restorative Justice: What Is It and Does It Work? *Annual Review of Law and Social Science* 3, no. 1 (December): 161–87.

Messick, Richard. 1999. Judicial Reform and Economic Development: A Survey of the Issues. *World Bank Research Observer*.

Michelson, Ethan. 2007. Climbing the Dispute Pagoda: Grievances and Appeals to the Official Justice System in Rural China. *American Sociological Review* 72: 459–85.

Miller, David. 1979. *Social Justice*. Oxford: Clarendon Press.

Miller, Geoffrey. 1998. Class Actions. in *New Palgrave Dictionary of Economics and the Law*, Peter Newman, ed., pp. 257–262. London: Macmillan Press.

2002. Commentary: On the Costs of Civil Justice. *Texas Law Review* 80, no. 7: 2115.

Mir-Hosseini, Ziba. 1996. *Women and Politics in Post-Khomeini Iran: Divorce, Veiling and Emerging Feminist Voices*. In *Women and Politics in the Third World*, ed. H. Afshar, pp. 149–69. London: Routledge.

2000. *Marriage on Trial: A Comparative Study of Islamic Family Law in Iran and Morocco*. London, I. B. Tauris.

Moazami, Shahla. 2007. *Access to Justice for Disadvantaged Groups: The Case of Women in Iran*. UNDP. http://regionalcentrebangkok.undp.or.th/practices/governance/a2j/docs/CaseStudy-07-Iran.pdf.

Mojab, Shahrzad, and A. Hojabri, eds. 2000. *Women of Iran: A Subject Bibliography*. Cambridge, MA: Iranian Women's Studies Foundation.

Moore, Joanne, and M. Cherif Bassiouni. 1999. The Sharia Islamic Law: What Muslims in the United States Have in Common? In *Immigrants in Courts*. Seattle: University of Washington Press.

Moorhead, Richard. 1998. Legal Aid in the Eye of a Storm: Rationing, Contracting, and a New Institutionalism. *Journal of Law and Society* 25, no. 3: 365–87.

2003. Access to Justice after Universalism: Introduction. *Journal of Law and Society* 30, no. 1 (March 1): 1–10.

Moorhead, R., and Pascoe Pleasence, P. 2003. *After Universalism: Re-Engineering Access to Justice*. Oxford: Blackwell.

Morgen, Sandra, and Ann Bookman. 1988. *Women and the Politics of Empowerment*. Philadelphia: Temple University Press.

Morris, Pauline, and Richard White. 1973. *Social Needs and Legal Action*. Law in Society. London: Robertson.

Muralidhar, S. 2004a. *Law, Poverty and Legal Aid: Access to Criminal Justice*. New Delhi: LexisNexis Butterworth.

2004b. *Law, Poverty and Legal Aid: Access to Criminal Justice*. New Delhi: LexisNexis Butterworth.

Nadjafi, Ali Hossein. 2007. *Victimology*. Tehran: Shahid Beheshti University.

Naffine, N. 2002. In Praise of Legal Feminism. *Journal of the Society of Public Teachers of Law* 22: 71–101.

Na'īm, 'Abd. 2008. *Islam and the Secular State: Negotiating the Future of Shari'a*. Cambridge, MA: Harvard University Press.

Namāzī Shāhrūdī, 'Alī. 1997. *Mustadrak Safīnat al-biḥār*. Qum: Mu'assasat al-Nashr al-Islāmī al-tābi'ah li-Jamā'at al-Mudarrisīn bi-Qum al-Musharrafah.

Narayan, Deepa. 2002. *Empowerment and Poverty Reduction a Sourcebook*. Washington, DC: World Bank.

Narayan, Deepa, Robert Chambers, Meera K. Shah, and Patti Petesch. 2000. *Voices of the Poor: Crying Out for Change*. World Bank Series. Oxford: Oxford University Press.

Nasr, Seyyed Hossein. 1999. *Religion and the Order of Nature*. New York and Oxford: Oxford University Press.

Nicholson, J. 1993. Judicial Independence and Accountability: Can They Co-Exist? *Australian Law Journal* 67: 404–5.

North, Douglass C. 1981. *Structure and Change in Economic History*. New York: W. W. Norton.

Oakley, Ann. 2000. *Experiments in Knowing: Gender and Method in the Social Sciences*. New York: New Press.

Oxaal, Zoë and with Sally Baden. 1997. *Gender and Empowerment: Definitions, Approaches and Implications for Policy*. Brighton: Institute of Development Studies.

Paidar, Parvin. 1995. *Women and the Political Process in Twentieth-Century Iran*. Cambridge: Cambridge University Press.

Palacio, Ana. 2006. Legal Empowerment of the Poor: An Action Agenda for the World Bank. Washington, DC: World Bank. http://rru.worldbank.org/FPDForum/documents/2006/background/legal_empowerment_of_poor.pdf.

Parker, Christine. 1999. *Just Lawyers: Regulation and Access to Justice*. Oxford: Oxford University Press.

Plato. Allan David Bloom, ed. 1991. *The Republic of Plato*. New York: Basic Books.

Pleasence, Pascoe, Great Britain: Legal Services Commission, Nigel Balmer, Legal Services Research Centre, and Alexy Buck. 2004. *Causes of Action: Civil Law and Social Justice*. Norwich: The Stationery Office, March.

Posner, Richard A. 1993. *The Problems of Jurisprudence*. Cambridge, MA: Harvard University Press.

Prillaman, William. 2000. *The Judiciary and Democratic Decay in Latin America: Declining Confidence in the Rule of Law*. Westport, CT: Praeger.

Ranis, Gustav, Frances Stewart, and Emma Samman. 2005. *Human Development: Beyond the HDI*. New Haven, CT: Economic Growth Center of Yale University.

Ravandi, Murteza. 1989. *The Development of Law and Justice in Iran*. Tehran: Cheshme Publications.

Rawls, John. 1971. *A Theory of Justice*. Cambridge, MA: Harvard University Press.

1993. *Political Liberalism*. New York: Columbia University Press.

Regan, Francis. 1999. *The Transformation of Legal Aid: Comparative and Historical Studies*. Oxford: Oxford University Press.

Rhode, Deborah L. 2004. *Access to Justice*. Oxford: Oxford University Press.

Rosen, Lawrence. 2000. *The Justice of Islam: Comparative Perspectives on Islamic Law and Society*. Oxford: Oxford University Press.

Rosenn, Keith S. 1987. The Protection of Judicial Independence in Latin America. *University of Miami Inter-American Law Review* 19, no. 1 (October 1): 1–35.

Rottman, D. B., and A. J. Tomkins. 1999. Public Trust and Confidence in the Courts: What Public Opinion Surveys Mean to Judges. *Court Review* (Fall): 24–31.

Rowlands, Jo. 1995. Empowerment Examined. *Development in Practice* 5, no. 2 (May 1): 101–7.

Rush Social Research Agency. 1996. *Legal Assistance Needs Phase I: Estimation of a Basic Needs-Based Planning Model*. Barton: Legal Aid and Family Services Division.

1999. *Legal Assistance Needs Project Phase Two: Summary Report*. Barton: Family Law and Legal Assistance Division.

Russell, Peter, and David M. O'Brien, eds. 2001. *Judicial Independence in the Age of Democracy: Critical Perspectives From Around the World*. Charlottesville: University Press of Virginia.

Saaidi, Mansour, and Mina Behrooz. 2003. *Judicial Reform*. 1st ed. Tehran: Ministry of Justice.

Safi Golpaygani, Lotfollah. 1997. *Jame'ul-Ahkam*. Vol. 2. 2 vols. Qom: Hazrat Masomeh Press.

Sarantakos, S. 1993. *Social Research*. Basingstoke: Macmillan.

Savory, Roger. 1974. The Safavid State and Polity. *Iranian Studies* 7, no. 1/2 (January 1): 179–212.

Schetzer, Louis. 2003. *Access to Justice and Legal Needs: A Project to Identify Legal Needs, Pathways and Barriers for Disadvantaged People in NSW*. Sydney: Law and Justice Foundation of New South Wales.

Schneegans, Susan. 2010. *UNESCO Science Report: The Current Status of Science Around the World*. Science Report Series. Paris: UNESCO.

Sdrzadh Afshar, Mohsen. 1993. *Civil and Commercial Proceedings*. Tehran: Jihad University.

Seidman, Robert. 1978. *The State, Law, and Development*. London: Croom Helm.

Sen, Gita, and Adrienne Germain. 1994. *Population Policies Reconsidered: Health, Empowerment, and Rights*. Boston: Harvard University Press.

Sherif, Mohamed Ahmed. 1975. *Ghazali's Theory of Virtue*. New York: State University of New York Press.

Sherr, Avrom, Richard Moorhead, and Alan Paterson. 1994. *Lawyers, the Quality Agenda: Assessing and Developing Competence and Quality in Legal Aid*. London: H.M.S.O.

Silver, Charles. 2002. Does Civil Justice Cost Too Much? *Texas Law Review* 80, no. 7: 2073.

Smirnov, Theories. 1996. Understanding Justice in an Islamic Context: Some Points of Contrast with Western *Philosophy. East & West* 46, no. 3: 337.

Smith, M. G. 1969. Some Developments in the Analytic Framework of Pluralism. In *Pluralism in Africa*, ed. L. Kuper and M. G. Smith., pp. 415–58. Berkeley: University of California Press.

Solomon, Barbara. 1976. *Black Empowerment: Social Work in Oppressed Communities*. New York: Columbia University Press.

Starr, June. 1992. *Law as Metaphor: From Islamic Courts to Palace of Justice*. Albany: State University of New York Press.

Storskrubb, Eva, and Jacques Ziller. Access to Justice in European Comparative Law. Contribution to Book. http://cadmus.eui.eu/handle/1814/7782.

Strickland, Ruth Ann. 2004. *Restorative Justice*. New York: Peter Lang, May.

Strauss, A. and, J. Corbin. 1994. Grounded Theory Methodology. In *Handbook of Qualitative Research*, N. K. Denzin and Y. S. Lincoln, eds., pp. 217–285. Thousand Oaks, CA: Sage.

Sudarshan, Ramaswamy. 2003. Rule of Law and Access to Justice: Perspectives from UNDP Experience. Paper presented at the European Commission Expert Seminal on Rule of Law and the Administration of Justice as part of Good Governance, Brussels, 3–4 July.

Sweeney, Paul D., and Dean B. McFarlin. 1997. Process and Outcome: Gender Differences in the Assessment of Justice. *Journal of Organizational Behavior* 18, no. 1 (January): 83–98.

Task Force on Civil Equal Justice Funding. 2003. *Final Report and Recommendations of the Task Force on Civil Equal Justice Funding*. Washington: Washington State Supreme Court, September.

Tata, Jasmine, and Lynn Bowes-Sperry. 1996. Emphasis on Distributive, Procedural, and Interactional Justice: Differential Perceptions of Men and Women. *Psychological Reports* 79: 1327–30.

Teehankee, Julio C. 2003. Background Paper on Access to Justice Indicators in the Asia-Pacific Region. La Salle Institute of Governance With the Support of the United Nations Development Program. http://regionalcentrebangkok.undp.or.th/practices/governance/a2j/docs/AccesstoJusticeIndicators.pdf.

Thibaut, John. 1975. *Procedural Justice: A Psychological Analysis*. New York: Lawrence Erlbaum Associates.

Transparency International. 2007. *Global Corruption Report: 2007 Corruption in Judicial Systems*. Leiden: Cambridge University Press.

Törnblom, Kjell, and R. Vermunt. 2007. Towards an Integration of Distributive Justice, Procedural Justice, and Social Resource Theories. *Social Justice Research* 20, no. 3 (September 1): 312–35.

Trubek, David M., and Marc Galanter. 1974. Scholars in Self-Estrangement: Some Reflections on the Crisis in Law and Development Studies in the United States. *Wisconsin Law Review* 1974: 1062.

Trubek, David M., and Alvaro Santos. 2006. *The New Law and Economic Development: A Critical Appraisal*. New York: Cambridge University Press.

Tull, Donald, and Dell Hawkins. 1987. *Marketing Research: Measurement and Method: A Text with Cases*. New York: Macmillan.

Turabi, Hasan. 1980. *Tajdid Usul al-Fiqh al-Islami*. Khartum: Dar al-Fikr.

Tyler, T. 1996. The Relationship of the Outcome and Procedural Fairness: How Does Knowing the Outcome Influence Judgments About the Procedure? *Social Justice Research* 9, no. 4: 311–26.

Tyler, Thomas. 1987. *What Is Procedural Justice?: Criteria Used by Citizens to Assess the Fairness of Legal Procedures*. Evanston: Kellogg Graduate School of Management.

Tyler, Tom. 2006a. Restorative Justice and Procedural Justice: Dealing with Rule Breaking. *Journal of Social Issues* 62, no. 2 (June 1): 307–26.

Tyler, Tom R. 2006b. *Why People Obey the Law*. Oxford: Princeton University Press.

Umbreit, Mark S. 1985. *Crime and Reconciliation: Creative Options for Victims and Offenders*. Nashville, TN: Abingdon Press.

Upham, F. 2002. *Mythmaking in the Rule of Law Orthodoxy*. Working Paper. Rule of Law Series. Washington: Carnegie Endowment for International Peace.

Vakil, Sanam. 2011. *Women and Politics in the Islamic Republic of Iran: Action and Reaction*. New York: Continuum.

Vacovec, Kenneth, and Massachusetts Legal Needs Survey Advisory Committee. 2003. *Policy Implications of the Massachusetts Legal Needs Survey*. Boston: Massachusetts Legal Needs Survey Advisory Committee.

Valkonen, I. 1975. Report from the National Representatives of the Scandinavian Nurses' Federation's Meeting in Iceland. *Sairaanhoitaja. Sjuksköterskan* 50, no. 19 (October 7): 16–20.

Van den Bos, K. 2005. What Is Responsible for the Fair Process Effect? In *Handbook of Organizational Justice*, J. Greenberg and J. A. Colquitt, eds., pp. 273–300. Mahwah, NJ: Erlbaum.

Van den Bos, Kees, and Joost Miedema. 2000. Toward Understanding Why Fairness Matters: The Influence of Mortality Salience on Reactions to Procedural Fairness. *Journal of Personality and Social Psychology* 79, no. 3: 355–66.

Van den Bos, Kees, Henk A. M. Wilke, and E. Allan Lind. 1998. When Do We Need Procedural Fairness? The Role of Trust in Authority. *Journal of Personality and Social Psychology* 75, no. 6: 1449–58.

Verdonschot, Jin Ho, Maurits Barendrecht, Laura Klaming, and Peter Kamminga. 2008. *Measuring Access to Justice: The Quality of Outcomes*. SSRN.

Wadud, Amina. 1995. Towards a Qur'anic Hermeneutics of Social Justice: Race, Class and Gender. *Journal of Law and Religion* 12, no. 1 (January 1): 37–50.

Walzer, Michael. 1983. *Spheres of Justice: A Defense of Pluralism and Equality*. New York: Basic Books.

Weinrib, Ernest Joseph. 1995. *The Idea of Private Law*. Cambridge, MA: Harvard University Press.

Wenzel, Michael. 2006. A Letter from the Tax Office: Compliance Effects of Informational and Interpersonal Justice. *Social Justice Research* 19, no. 3 (September 1): 345–64.

Wiggins, Mark, and Catherine Stevens. 1999. *Aviation Social Science: Research Methods in Practice*. Aldershot: Ashgate.

Williams, P. 1994. The Cost of Civil Litigation: An Empirical Study. *International Review of Law and Economics* 14, no. 1: 73–86.

Wilmot, A. 2005. Designing Sampling Strategies for Qualitative Social Research: With Particular Reference to the Office for National Statistics' Qualitative Respondent Register. *Survey Methodology Bulletin Office for National Statistics*, no. 56: 53–65.

Women and Children Legal Research Foundation. 2008. *Women's Access to Justice, Problems and Challenges*. Kabul: Women and Children Legal Research Foundation, July 21. http://www.wclrf.org/English/eng_pages/Researches/Women_a_t_Justice/WATJ.pdf.

Woolf, Harry. 1996. *Access to Justice: Final Report to the Lord Chancellor on the Civil Justice System in England and Wales*. London: HMSO.

World Bank. 2003. *Legal and Judicial Reform: Strategic Directions*. Washington, DC: World Bank.

Wright, Martin. 1996. *Justice for Victims and Offenders: A Restorative Response to Crime*. Winchester: Waterside Press.

Yrigoyen Fajardo, Raquel. 2005. *Pathways to Justice: Access to Justice with a Focus on Poor, Women and Indigenous Peoples*. Phnom Penh: Ministry of Justice Cambodia.

Zander, M. 1978. *Legal Service for the Community*. London: Temple Smith.

Zehr, Howard. 1990. *Changing Lenses: A New Focus for Crime and Justice*. Scottsdale: Herald Press.

Zeitune, José. 2004. International Principles on the Independence and Accountability of Judges, Lawyers and Prosecutors: A Practitioners' Guide. International Commission of Jurists.

Zerang, M. 2002. *Development of the Legal System in Iran*. Tehran: Islamic Revolution Documentation Center.

Index